web
developer's guide to
multimedia
& video

Nels Johnson

 CORIOLIS GROUP BOOKS

PUBLISHER	**KEITH WEISKAMP**
PROJECT EDITOR	**TONI ZUCCARINI**
COVER ARTIST	**GARY SMITH**
COVER DESIGN	**ANTHONY STOCK**
INTERIOR DESIGN	**MICHELLE STROUP**
LAYOUT PRODUCTION	**ROB MAUHAR**
PROOFREADER	**SHELLY CROSSEN**
INDEXER	**LAURA LAWRIE**

The Coriolis Group, Inc.

7339 E. Acoma Drive, Suite 7

Scottsdale, AZ 85260

Phone: (602) 483-0192

Fax: (602) 483-0193

Web address: http://www.coriolis.com

ISBN 1-883577-96-9 : $39.99

Printed in the United States of America

10 9 8 7 6 5 4 3 2 1

To my parents.

Acknowledgments

The following people contributed to the success of this book: Carl Johnson, Jody Banks, Frank Trozzo, Christine Perey, Holger Petersen, Dixie Clow, Jeff Tiedrich, Tim Byars, Keith Cooley, Gary Clayton, JoAnn Uhelszki, and Rollo's Kitchen.

Extra special thanks to Cathie Nelson, Fred Gault, Galan Bridgman, John Barrows, Tim Tully, Keith Weiskamp, Toni Zuccarini, and Life in a Blender.

Contents

Introduction

Web Developer's Guide to Multimedia and Video is intended to be just that—a guide. If you want to create high quality multimedia files and publish them via the World Wide Web, this book will show you how to do it. Simply put, the information presented within is designed to help you deliver animation, audio, and desktop video from a Web site with as little trouble as possible.

You do not need to be a software developer or a professional video technician to benefit from this book, but a background in PC-based multimedia will certainly help. Also, some experience with HTML or a Web page creation tool (such as Microsoft's Internet Assistant) is recommended, but not required. If you are building a site using any type of multimedia, this book will be a valuable resource.

The main goal of *Web Developer's Guide to Multimedia and Video* is to give you the bigger picture when it comes to publishing and playing media files on the Web. Sure, you can construct a Web site, capture some multimedia clips, and then include them on your home page for visitors to download or enjoy in real time. The hard part is performing either one of these particular tasks in relation to the other—a skill which is essential for professional site management. It's this integration of skills that marks a true multimedia Web designer.

For instance, most Web servers need additional software and special configuration before they can stream video and audio to users in real time. Conversely, any multimedia file offered on a Web site for downloading should be specially created for that purpose. No one wants to spend time and money downloading bloated movie files they only play once. Nor do they want to click on a streaming movie and find it unavailable or watch it play in fits and starts.

To clarify and confront these issues, this book presents step-by-step examples of how to capture and compress Web-based media, and how to configure Web servers to play those media—all based on the experiences of people currently maintaining successful, media-rich Web presences.

While the bulk of the book is devoted to working with the current tools available for creating Web media assets, and with the server software that lets you dispatch those assets to your audience, there is also an overview section (Chapters 1 through 3). This section provides an assessment of the current climate for multimedia on the Web, with an understanding of what's out there now and what may be just around the corner.

Chapters 4 through 9 get right into making movies, audio clips, and other types of Web-based multimedia—such as MIDI and mod files. Editing programs are discussed, as are video and audio capture hardware. Cross-platform issues (Mac vs. Windows) are addressed in detail. You'll learn what's essential for creating and using multimedia, and what the professionals are using.

Chapters 10 through 15 cover the authoring tools and programming languages that put media files to work, including HTML, CGI, and Java. Finally, Chapters 16 and 17 take you through the process of setting up a Web media production studio and building a World Wide Web server.

At the end of the book you'll find two interviews with prominent Web designers. Appendix A contains an interview with the proprietor of the Blue Wolf Network's Browseteria site (located at *http://www.bluewolfnet.com*), John Barrows. Mr. Barrows candidly discusses the publishing and management issues inherent in running such a media-rich Web site—one of the first of its kind.

Appendix B features an equally insightful interview with Tim Tully, Technical Editor of *NewMedia* magazine and digital media producer at Hyperstand—*NewMedia's* online counterpart (located at *http://www.hyperstand.com*). This interview concerns itself with the technical aspects of running a multimedia site, including tips and ideas for improving performance.

The emphasis throughout *Web Developer's Guide to Multimedia and Video* is on so-called *streaming* technology, but making high-quality clips just for downloading also gets plenty of attention. In effect, all the multimedia bases are covered, so you can learn how to create and present whatever types of multimedia are necessary to fit your site's needs.

If you are excited about publishing QuickTime and AVI movies (as well as sound and MIDI files) on your Web site, you will find this book valuable. If you want to push the envelope even more by streaming your movies and audio clips in real time, this book will be even more helpful. This book will show you how to create the multimedia tricks you've always wanted to use on your site, so your Web site can be multimedia-rich and user friendly.

Chapter **1**

The Current Climate

It's an interesting time for the Internet, and for PC-based multimedia. Two years ago you could hear the wind whistle through the World Wide Web. On the multimedia side, publishers were perfecting the art of quarter-screen desktop video and worrying about how fast CD-ROMs would spin by Christmas. Neither development area had much in common with the other on a commercial basis, although future intersections were often discussed.

Things are different now. Consumer markets are perceived as primed for *media on demand*—the combination of Web technology and PC-based multimedia. To satisfy these perceived appetites, new technologies have arisen—several of which have finally turned into shipping products. This book is about using such products, and making sense of the underlying technology.

Some industry observers believe the marriage of multimedia and the Web is a shotgun wedding. No one doubts anymore that the digital online revolution is inevitable, but persistent rumors abound regarding imminent Web

Figure 1.1

A media-rich Web site.

brownouts (as opposed to daily slowdowns) due to bandwidth-hogging by unregulated multimedia streams (we'll get into streaming in the next few chapters).

Despite these grim warnings, no one seems particularly inclined to practice bandwidth environmentalism. Software developers, hardware manufacturers, and Web-based publishers are embracing the new technologies wholeheartedly. Beyond normal blind ambition and naked greed, the thought seems to be let it burn.

In other words, if the Web sags (or even snaps) under the load, so be it. A bigger, more powerful Web—or maybe even a revamped Internet itself—will be built, however slowly, to take its place. Sure, it may be a royal pain for everyone, but there's just too much money and power involved to think the Web will stay busted for long (assuming it breaks down in the first place).

If you buy that argument, you'll probably like the one that says your investment in developing multimedia assets for the Web now will remain solid in the future. The key to

Worried about security issues? Well, so is everybody. But that's not going to stop the inevitable migration of commerce to the Web. It may not even slow it down very much.

Figure 1.2
The players club.

this strategy is the fact that (generally speaking) it's the hardware that's going to change, not the software.

Companies like Microsoft and Apple, who established the file formats and wrote the software engines that play most of today's multimedia clips, do not want to repeat those tasks just because someone else's communications network can't bear the load. In other words, even if the Web does get a major hardware overhaul, we may still find lots of QuickTime and AVI movies when we go Net surfing.

This book does not predict the future of Web-based multimedia, much less the fate of the Web itself. Instead, it presents field-tested strategies for getting good performance from the tools now available for creating Web-based media and deploying those files on Web sites. As with most software standards, the more files in circulation that support them, the longer it takes for those standards to be replaced.

Traditional Web-Based Media

Let's begin by looking at some traditional types of multimedia files that are currently being offered on the Web, then move on to the newer, more exotic varieties. This is basically just a roll call, but it always helps to identify the existing players in any competitive arena.

A good way to differentiate traditional multimedia files (like the ones that follow) from the newer forms is to remember that once those files are successfully downloaded, it doesn't really matter how you obtained them. A movie sucked in off the Web will play just as well (or poorly) as the same movie copied over to your system from a CD-ROM or a LAN.

QuickTime

QuickTime is Apple's mature and highly regarded engine for playing multimedia files in general and video in particular. It is essentially time-based—as opposed to frame-based (like Microsoft's Video for Windows engine).

A single still image, for instance, can be a QuickTime movie, as can a so called *sound-only* clip, each of which occupies a separate *track* in a movie. On the other hand, you can make a QuickTime clip with all kinds of tracks, each of which may be played at the player program's discretion. Good examples of multiple tracks are separate audio tracks for different languages, MIDI tracks for controlling digital musical gear, and text tracks for displaying text in the video window.

Being time-based, QuickTime recognizes that discrete events (such as MIDI notes or a video frame that doesn't change for a few frames) can have variable time lengths.

Note: While QuickTime cannot currently be streamed over the Web on demand, Apple has made some inroads in adapting it for the Net in general. Chapter 5 has all the details.

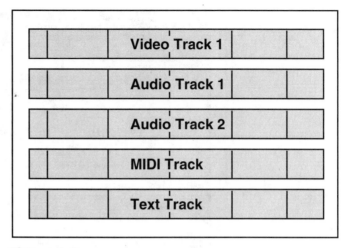

Figure 1.3
QuickTime movie tracks.

This allows for storing just one such note frame along with a value denoting its duration—unlike Video for Windows, which stores as many whole frames as necessary to render the unchanging event over a given time period.

As of this writing, the most recent versions of QuickTime are 2.5 for the Mac and 2.1 for Windows. The Windows version is still essentially a playback-only solution, although you can save into the QuickTime format from applications like Premiere for Windows. Apple keeps the most recent versions of each product posted on its Web site: *http://www.quicktime.apple.com.*

One of the keys to working successfully with QuickTime is understanding when to use a certain compressor, or *codec.* The original QuickTime codecs were Raw, Animation, Graphics, JPEG, Apple Video (a.k.a. Road Pizza), and, slightly later, Cinepak. These core compressors are still part of the Mac QuickTime extension, and are supported by QuickTime for Windows.

Other third-party codecs, such as Intel's Indeo for the Mac, sometimes ship with Macintosh systems, but there

All of the core Mac QuickTime codecs were ported to QuickTime for Windows in the original version. However, the latest Mac QuickTime init may not be completely symmetrical with the latest Windows QT libraries.

Figure 1.4

The QuickTime WebMasters' site.

are few standard practices in this regard. At the high end of the QuickTime customer spectrum, where full-screen productions are edited and output back to videotape, new custom codecs are common, particularly ones that preserve image quality at all costs.

In the multimedia world, however, it's safe to say that things really haven't changed much (in terms of new codecs) since the early days of QuickTime. Here's a rundown of the workhorse QuickTime codecs.

RAW

One good use for None is transporting raw Mac movies to the Windows environment, where they can be loaded and then compressed with another codec by Premiere 4.2.

Also known as None, this is less a standard compressor than an uncompressed encoding scheme. In other words, no serious compression is applied when you save (or capture) a QuickTime movie in this format. In fact, you may be effectively *un*compressing a movie if you do this, with no gain in data richness.

ANIMATION (RLE)

The Animation codec was developed to compress and play QuickTime animated movies. Since Run Length

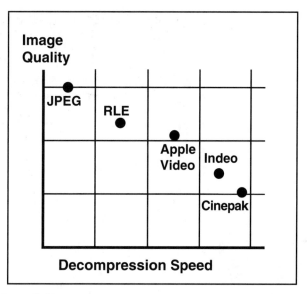

Figure 1.5

Codec efficiency.

Encoding (RLE) is the compression algorithm, this is not a good choice for compressing real video clips, although it does do well for sequences with lots of single-color planes (like cartoons). Given the resurgence of animation on the Web, perhaps this codec will get renewed attention.

GRAPHICS (SMC)

The Graphics compressor is similar to the Animation codec, although the former usually wins in both rendering speed and compressed file size. The Graphics codec is commonly used for so-called computer-graphics sequences, where the images have been created by rendering software as opposed to by hand.

JPEG

Based on the ANSI standard (Document 10918-1), the JPEG codec is mainly used for archiving QuickTime movies. You can play a JPEG movie with MoviePlayer, but performance will likely be unacceptable—unless you have special hardware in your system, in which case the movie will probably look great.

Most high-end video capture cards use some type of so-called motion JPEG (MJPEG) compressor to encode and play back raw capture files. Since these cards are often used in systems that output to videotape, high image quality is crucial.

VIDEO (ROAD PIZZA)

This was the original QuickTime compressor, and the codec of choice for all the 160 × 120 movies that circulated in the early days of multimedia. Unlike movies encoded with Cinepak, Video-encoded movies take as long to compress as they do to decompress, although their file sizes are usually larger than otherwise similar Cinepak movies. There are still times when the Video codec is a viable or even preferable alternative, but Cinepak has pretty much stolen the show at this point.

CINEPAK

This codec was created for the specific purpose of compressing movies for speedy decompression and playback from CD-ROM. The trade-off is that Cinepak movies take a

A Video-encoded movie.

Most movies compressed with the Video codec do not exceed the 160 × 120 frame. Cinepak clips can have much bigger frames.

Figure 1.6
A 320 × 240 Cinepak frame.

relatively long time to compress (as opposed to, say, Video). This is less of an issue now that PCs are much more powerful than they were two or three years ago.

Cinepak may rule the software-only decompressors category for the foreseeable future in the kingdom of non-streaming codecs. It's free, it's fast, it's cross-platform (covered in later chapters), and everybody uses it. What more can you want from a codec (apart from streaming)?

INDEO

By the time you read this, the Mac version of Indeo Video Interactive may be available (see the description of IVI in the Video for Windows codec section later in this chapter).

Indeo on the Mac hasn't caught on like it has on the PC, despite Intel's marketing efforts, but it is a worthy adversary of Cinepak on both platforms. The general wisdom is to use Cinepak if you want your movies a little smoother, and Indeo if you want slightly better resolution—especially on slower computers.

The best place to go for the latest version of Indeo is Intel's Web site (*http://www.intel.com*), since new releases don't necessarily track new versions of QuickTime itself. Intel also has quite a body of literature concerning cross-platform development with Indeo on their site.

TrueMotion-S

Somewhere behind Indeo in the third party codec pantheon is TrueMotion-S from Horizons Technology. Performance of the product has improved over the last year or two, but you still have to pay a license fee of some type to make full use of the software. For complete information, go and visit their Web site at *http://www.horizons.com*, shown in Figure 1.7.

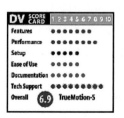

The bottom line here is that QuickTime is a complex enough technology to be different things to different people. Software developers usually exploit it as a powerful toolkit for playing time-based media from within their applications.

Figure 1.7

Horizons Technology's Web site.

For users, especially graphics professionals, QuickTime provides a standard way of dealing with almost all multimedia data, including audio, video, and still images. This facility has even greater value on the Mac, where QuickTime ships standard with the operating system (which is optimized for working with QuickTime).

Video for Windows (AVI)

When it came out of the gate late in 1992, Video for Windows was Microsoft's direct response to the 1.0 release of Apple's QuickTime for Windows (developed by the San Francisco Canyon Company, under contract to Apple). Back then, VfW was a relatively poor performer compared to QuickTime, although now both are mature enough to perform equally well (despite knee-jerk protests from Mac purists).

Technically speaking, an AVI file is a type of RIFF (Resource Interchange File Format) file—a Microsoft standard. Other types of RIFF files include WAV audio files and standard Windows bitmaps. You can get more information on this subject from two books: *Windows Multimedia Programmer's Guide* and *The Video for Windows Development Kit Programmer's Guide.*

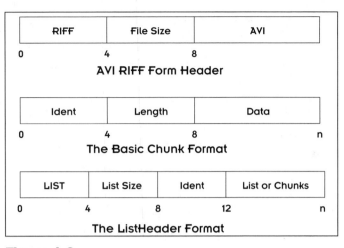

Figure 1.8

The RIFF file format.

As of this writing, the most recent version of Video for Windows is 1.1e, although that version is specifically targeted to work with Windows 3.1. Windows 95 and NT have their own version of VfW built in. In other words, in those environments, AVI movies just play—assuming you have installed the operating systems correctly (especially the multimedia components).

Warning: Do not install VfW 1.1e into a Windows 95 environment under any circumstances!

Granted, Video for Windows employs a much less elegant design than QuickTime, but its ambitions are much more modest. All VfW wants to do is play video frames and audio chunks, which it does very well. There is no sophisticated track management, and no sense of frame duration (as in QuickTime).

As with QuickTime, the key to success with Video for Windows is knowing the correct codec for each situation. The original VfW compressors were RLE, Video 1, and Indeo (Cinepak came later). There was also a raw codec (similar to Apple None) named YUV9. All of the VfW codecs are implemented as standalone DLLs, as opposed to being folded into one big file like the Mac QuickTime init. Same goes for the QuickTime for Windows codecs.

If you use a professional-grade video capture board under Windows (like the Targa or DPS Perception), you have probably installed a special, proprietary VfW codec for that particular card. Video for Windows will treat the proprietary codec just like any other VfW compressor that registers itself correctly.

In Windows, as in the Mac multimedia world, things really haven't changed much in terms of new codecs since the early days of Video for Windows (except for overall better performance). Here's the who's who of standard VfW compressors.

INDEO

Intel's Indeo Video codec has been through numerous changes since its inception. The latest version (4.1, also known as Indeo Video Interactive or IVI) has been rewritten from scratch. It is based on an advanced hybrid wavelet algorithm and is a formidable piece of software engineering.

As with many types of newer multimedia software, IVI's full potential is realized only on high-end PCs, such as Pentiums and Power Macs. On 486s and below, you should probably stick with Indeo Video version 3.2. If you are already working with Indeo but have not looked at IVI yet, you'll be impressed with the new features it offers.

Figure 1.9
An Indeo Video Interactive frame.

CINEPAK

Cinepak under Windows works just like its Mac counterpart. If you convert a Mac Cinepak movie to a VfW Cinepak movie with one of the tools described in Chapter 15, the encoded data stream will remain the same.

Is Cinepak better than Indeo? Certainly the former has a bigger market share, but it depends on what you want from it. Again, one rule of thumb many people use is to go with Cinepak for greater playback smoothness, but Indeo for better image resolution (on fast machines).

As noted in the section on Mac codecs, TrueMotion-S from Horizons Technology is also available as a Video for Windows compressor.

VIDEO 1

Originally developed by Media Vision, Video 1 was acquired by Microsoft as the original video compressor for VfW. It has pretty much seen its day, although occasionally it finds some special uses, especially when 8-bit encoding is required. However, Cinepak is usually better than Video 1 for encoding any video footage.

RLE

This codec can be very useful for making movies from screen captures. Similar to the Animation compressor on the QuickTime side, RLE is lossless (no data is discarded

Figure 1.10
An RLE screen capture.

at compression time) by design, although it only supports 4-bit and 8-bit pixel depths (unlike the QuickTime version).

JPEG

Although Microsoft announced a standard .DIB (Device Independent Bitmap) extension for storing JPEG-format still images and motion sequences, there is no JPEG codec per se for Video for Windows as of this writing. As noted earlier, most high-end capture cards come with their own MJPEG codecs, which are generally proprietary and incompatible with each other.

MPEG

There is a lot of hype about MPEG, and a lot of it does not translate into viewer satisfaction—mainly because few MPEG files posted on the Web have audio tracks. On the plus side, MPEG files tend to be relatively small and there is a good selection of player programs available for Windows, the Mac, and even unix.

Again, don't expect great (or any) audio performance from software-only MPEG players. Sure, it's gratifying to see video sequences that you can download from the Web without a lot of trouble, but for the time being this is not so much solid entertainment as sheer novelty.

MPEG is an acronym for the Motion Picture Experts Group, which has defined several MPEG standards for storing sound and video. The first such standard, MPEG 1 (or just MPEG), assumes that the video is stored on CD-ROM.

MPEG 2 video is generally targeted for the broadcast and movie theater markets, and is just now being put into practice. The next incarnation, MPEG 3, was originally aimed at the HDTV world but was dropped when MPEG 2 was found to fill this role as well. MPEG 4, still in development, is planned to take advantage of fiber optics networks.

Back in the real world, most Web surfers must content themselves with MPEG 1 video clips. For Windows 95 users, a good MPEG viewer is VMPEG Lite by Stefan

Figure 1.11

An MPEG video frame.

Eckhart, available at the FTP address *ftp://ftp.netcom.com/ cf/cfogg/vmpeg/vmpeg17.exe*. A popular MPEG player for the Mac is Sparkle by Maynard Handley, available at *http:// wuarchive.wustl.edu/system/mac/info-mac/gst/mov/ sparkle-25.hqx*.

Software-only MPEG—as a serious competitor to Cinepak and Indeo—remains a moving target to this day. Hardware-assisted MPEG products, such as CD-ROM games that require the RealMagic card, have come and gone, and even those had problems. Microsoft is reported to be working on a solid standard, but as of this writing it hasn't hit the market.

Streaming Web-Based Media

Now let's talk about the new technologies—specifically the ones that are currently shipping. It's understood that all these new solutions are limited by bandwidth in general and hardware (such as modems and routers) specifically.

What follows here is an overview; detailed instructions for using most of these products can be found in later chapters.

Streaming Audio

We'll start with sound, which is much easier to deliver than video. The first streaming audio product to find a big market on the Web was RealAudio from Progressive Networks, which now supports both 14.4 kbps and 28.8 kbps rates. Most people feel that 14.4 is acceptable for speech, while 28.8 is much better for music.

If you want to serve RealAudio streams from your Web site, you'll have to get the retail server software from Progressive Networks (*http://www.realaudio.com*). Both Windows and Mac solutions are available, and player software for both platforms is free. As you'll see in the chapter devoted to RealAudio, Progressive Networks is aggressively on the move to retain its market share.

StreamWorks, from Xing Technology, is RealAudio's chief competitor (in market, if not technical, terms), but is more high-end. Server software is required, but currently there is no such software for the Mac. StreamWorks begins to shine with fast Internet connections like 56 kbps (for 32 kHz mono audio) and 128 kbps (CD-quality, 44.1

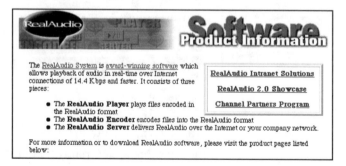

Figure 1.12

The RealAudio Web page.

Figure 1.13

Xing's Web site.

KHz audio). You can sample their various wares at *http://www.xingtech.com*, shown in Figure 1.13.

Streaming Video

On the Windows side, the product getting the most attention, as of this writing, is VDOLive, from VDOnet (*http://www.vdolive.com*). As with RealAudio, retail server software is required, while the player software that works with your HTML browser is free at VDOnet's Web site. By the time you read this, a Mac version of the viewer should be shipping.

Technically speaking, VDOLive is scaleable and uses a sophisticated, proprietary communications protocol. Scaleability permits a powerful PC (with a high-bandwidth Web connection) to deliver proportionately higher-quality video, while sustaining a minimum quality level for low-end machines. Although it is not enabling technology per se (i.e., free), VDOnet has marketed their product aggressively and has been quite responsive to its customers.

Shockwave

Currently implemented as a Netscape plug-in, Macromedia's Shockwave provides a way to play Director movies in your Web browser—including audio (get the plug-in at

Other streaming video solutions are also shipping (including one from Xing Technology, noted above) but VDOLive is the current star. References to competing technologies are scattered throughout this book, and later, we'll take a look at some of the upcoming video streaming products.

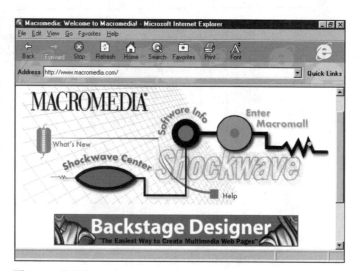

Figure 1.14

The Shockwave home page.

http://www.macromedia.com, shown in Figure 1.14). One problem is, even though Director files tend to be smaller than QuickTime and AVI video files, they can still take up hundreds of kilobytes.

However, Shockwave does currently provide a free way to approximate Web video on demand. It is free for the downloading, and no server-side software or special handling is required, save for some minimal configuration details. If you want animated banners and logos, Shockwave will do the job nicely.

VRML

Probably the most exciting aspect of VRML is the user's ability to navigate through a so-called VRML world. Even today's most complex worlds take up much less than a megabyte of storag—just right for relatively quick downloading.

Because this is a book on Web-based *multimedia* (and video in particular) it can't go into much detail on VRML (Virtual Reality Modeling Language), even though VRML is an exciting technology and part of the future of the Web. The short story is that VRML is a compact, 3D, Web data type that can be transmitted to Web browsers much faster than video and animation.

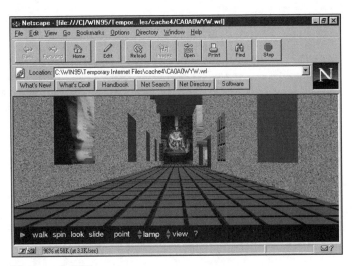

Figure 1.15

A VRML-based site.

Java

Quite apart from the realm of sampled video and audio multimedia files is Sun Microsystems' Java. Like C++, Java is a so-called *platform-independent* programming language. Developers who use it work with scripts, which are compiled into Java applets. Such applets can be placed directly into HTML documents.

Because a Java applet is essentially an executable program, it can animate graphics sequences, render primitive animations from scratch, and perform all kinds of interactive maneuvers. Chapter 12 contains a section on Java programming basics.

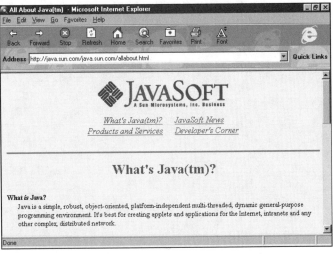

Figure 1.16

The Java home page.

When a user surfs to a Web page that contains a Java applet, the applet is downloaded behind the scenes to the user's local machine to do whatever work is required of it (assuming the user's browser is Java-enabled). Since Java is designed as an open standard, you can produce both development and run-time solutions for it.

As of this writing, the products covered in this chapter comprise the bulk of the Web-based multimedia solutions that developers are now using to enhance their Web sites. Again, while the flashiest effects can come from media that start playing immediately, the value of downloadable assets should never be overlooked. Hopefully, the chapters that follow will help you to embellish your site (or enjoy someone else's site) using both types of media.

What the near future holds for Web media developers (and what it doesn't).

Key Topics:

- **ISDN, xDSL, and cable modems**

- **The intranet**

- **The changing role of the video server**

What's Ahead

In Chapter 1 we talked about the current climate for Web media development, mainly from a software perspective. The point was to show that there are some powerful tools and enabling technologies available for multimedia developers, and some equally formidable Web products for exploiting the results of working with those tools.

So why are many people still dissatisfied after spending part of their precious TV time skimming around the Net, perhaps even visiting a few media-rich sites? The answer is, simply, hardware bandwidth restrictions. BIG bandwidth restrictions, when you think about what people really want. Ever try to Hoover a triple-thick shake through a plastic cocktail straw?

It's safe to say (as of this writing) that most log-on users have not yet experienced the Web at modem speeds greater than 28.8 Kbps. Okay, maybe at work your computer is part of a LAN connected to a T1 line. Then again, if there are a number of coworkers online simultaneously, your effective throughput may even be *below* 28.8. Welcome to the modern office.

21

Nobody doubts that things will get better in the long run. The overwhelming question is *when*. Some related issues are:

Some people seriously believe the Web is going to be totally overloaded by Fall 1996, and that the peak period slowdowns we experience now are just tremors foreshadowing the big meltdown to come.

- Will we use the coming better service to be more productive or will we just squander it? Your answer may well depend on how you feel about human nature in general.

- Will our appetites always exceed the currently available bandwidth? Most people seem to have reached their tolerance for television, but that's probably not a fair comparison.

- To what extent will users and developers have to upgrade their systems to enjoy new bandwidth breakthroughs?

- How much is all of this really going to cost?

No one knows the *specific* answers to these questions. They may pretend to, but they don't. Also (as with most new technology), fast answers that seem obvious have a funny way of turning out nearly opposite from the actual results.

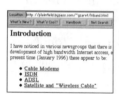

Check out *http:// plainfield.bypass .com/~gzaret/ hiband.html.*

As a Web media developer, you need to be aware of the emerging hardware solutions that will carry your digitized

High-Speed Internet Access Technologies						
Access Method	Leading Players	Data rate to end user	Data rate from end user	Pros	Cons	Timetable
Cable Modems	Time-Warner, AT&T/HP, Sun/Motorola	10-30Mbps	700kbps to 30Mbps	Speed, cable company installs	Must wait for cable company to upgrade service	1996-1997
ISDN	Telcos and comm vendors	64 to 128kbps	64 to 128kbps	Products now available	Hard to install	Now
ADSL	Telephone companies	Up to 6Mbps	640kpbs	Uses existing telephone wire	Lack of standards, late to market	Mid-1997

Figure 2.1

A good bookmark for newer technology.

content across the Internet to the user. The sections that immediately follow will cover the most prominent of these new transmission standards.

Later in this chapter, we'll look at the so-called intranet (as opposed to the Internet), and the opportunities it may present for Web media developers. Finally, we'll discuss the changing role of the video server, and the implications of those changes.

Transmission Standards

ISDN

Practically speaking, the next step up in speed from 28.8 kbps is ISDN (Integrated Services Digital Network). While ISDN can deliver up to a four-fold increase in performance over 28.8 (depending on the package you sign up for), many experts feel it is already a dated technology. Of course, this won't stop the mass market from embracing it well into the future.

Right now you can get dial-up ISDN service for under $30 per month in many metropolitan areas (installation fees are usually not included). Per minute charges, if assessed, can be substantial. In fact, some phone companies (like Pacific Bell, shown in Figure 2.2) are trying to get permission to increase such charges.

If you want to run a Web server with just an ISDN connection *and* stream multimedia assets to more than a couple of users simultaneously, good luck. You can almost get by with ISDN if you just offer text and graphics, but even adding one RealAudio track will cause general performance problems if you try to compete with other sites with better than ISDN access.

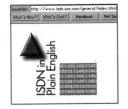

In some areas, you can now get dial-up ISDN Internet access on a per-call basis— assuming you have an ISDN line. Check with your ISP for details.

Figure 2.2

The Pacific Bell site.

This is not to say you can't run a multimedia Web site on ISDN, just that it may be a bad idea outside of a private or testing type of site. Also, be aware that staying online continuously, even with lowly ISDN service, is not for the faint of wallet. This may change in the near future, however, as providers get more competitive.

Finally, it is worth noting that paying for an ISDN line does not guarantee high-quality ISDN Internet access. In other words, you still have to find an ISP (Internet Service Provider) who will give good service on your ISDN connection.

Once the big players like AT&T get their high bandwidth Internet access sorted out, ISDN's star may rise again. As of this writing, a lot of ISDN Internet access is handled by smaller ISPs who offer various levels of quality in the service department.

T1 Lines

Like ISDN, T1 lines are already a fact of life, but not everybody has one, mostly due to expense but also because of installation logistics. Wiring a small office for

T1 service, particularly if you are not downtown, is still cost-prohibitive—especially if it does not contribute to your core business.

If you work for a big corporation, in an industry that needs a T1 line (like publishing, communications, or software development), you may have *fractional* T1 service, whereby you share your T1 access with others via a LAN, as shown in Figure 2.3. As noted, too much sharing will degrade performance for all current users.

Apples to apples, a standard T1 line delivers bandwidth equal to somewhere around 12 ISDN lines. (You could say this works out to roughly 50 28.8 lines, but the math starts to get fuzzy here.) A better way to quantify T1 performance is to peg it at slightly over 1.5 Mbps (note megabytes rather than kilobytes per second).

Prices for T1 service can run from $500 to over $1,500 per month, depending on location. Also, you'll probably have to shell out for some additional equipment, such as a router, which can easily total over $3,000 right up front.

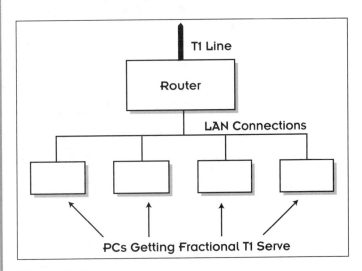

Figure 2.3
Shared T1 service.

If you've ever floored a Jaguar XJ6 on an open highway after driving a VW Rabbit, you'll understand why some people don't flinch even at these prices.

Cable Modems

Cable modems are indeed new technology, even though the hype is at fever pitch and growing. According to most analysts, consumers won't find them generally available until the first half of 1997—even though trials have already commenced in test sites around the country.

The bottom line: from 10 to 40 Mbps at what ISDN costs now (under $30 per month), assuming you believe the hype. The new cabling scheme that makes this all possible is known as Hybrid Fiber Coax (HFC). Remember that generic T1 lines can do around 1.5 Mbps.

Note: HFC actually evolved from the television industry model, which is based on a one to many broadcast principle. This is quite different than the many to many Web model.

The cable modem itself will allegedly do for data received via an HFC line what your Supra FAX Modem 288 does for incoming data from a standard telephone line (at least as far as your computer is concerned). Pricing on all this new hardware has not been finalized.

Here's the catch: Data flow in the cable modem world is nonsymmetrical. In other words, while loads of data will

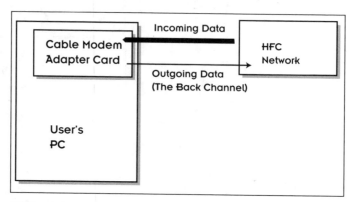

Figure 2.4

Asymmetrical data flow.

To get the complete story on the progress of the cable modem industry, don't forget to do Yahoo and Alta Vista searches (or whatever your favorite search tool happens to be).

come barreling in, data outflow (the so-called *back channel*) will be much slower—probably at around ISDN rates. This is great for users, but business as usual for Web media servers looking for a break.

Here's another catch: the up to 40 Mbps data rate mentioned above may be slightly misrepresented by the hype masters. While this is indeed awe-inspiring bandwidth, you could have to *share* it with hundreds of other cable subscribers, each of whom gets a slice.

Let's try some rough math, even if it is fuzzy. We'll say a T1 line at 1.5 Mbps equals fifty 28.8 lines. If a cable modem equals 26 T1 lines (40 divided by 1.5), then a cable modem should provide the aggregate bandwidth necessary for 1,300 (50 × 26) 28.8 connections. Figure 2.5 illustrates these calculations.

This could mean that if you're browsing the Web with a cable modem, but a thousand other subscribers to your cable company are online at the same time, you'll be no better off than you are with your 28.8 kbps modem right now.

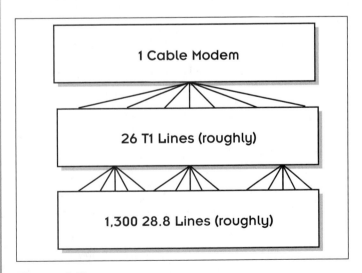

Figure 2.5
Bandwidth trickle-down.

Furthermore, since cable modems are supposed to blaze through current bottlenecks, there had better be no more than 26 other people sharing the pipe if you want T1 quality service. When you apply the above formula to the cable modem back channel, things start to look even grimmer—especially for Web media producers.

Of course, this is a gross simplification of the actual mechanics, but the basic principles remain. So are cable modems are a bust? Not by a long shot. Look who's playing: AT&T, Hewlett-Packard, IBM, Intel, Motorola, Scientific-Atlanta, and Zenith, among others. Perhaps by the time you can buy one at CompUSA (or from Viacom) we'll be doing the math differently.

xDSL

For late-breaking xDSL news, check out the ADSL forum at http://www.ads .com/adsl/home_page .html. Also worth monitoring is Dan Kegel's ADSL Page at http://www.isdn .ocn/dank/isdn/ adsl.html.

This acronym is still in flux—some people still say ADSL—but the last three letters stand for Digital Subscriber Line (the A stands for asymmetric). Like the cable modem, DSL promises faster, cheaper Internet service, at least for dial-up users. The numbers in play as of this writing suggest performance gains in the range of 1000 to 2000 percent (10 to 20 times better than current access standards).

The best way to think of xDSL may be as ISDN on steroids. Such increased performance is mainly due to improvements in hardware and software since the time when ISDN was conceived. For example, data compression algorithms are now much more sophisticated than they were ten years ago, as are digital signal processing strategies.

If you factor in advancements in IC (integrated circuit) technology and the ever more dense silicon going into compact electronics devices, you can begin to see how xDSL makes sense. From this perspective, ISDN really is an outmoded standard (even though consumer markets are just catching up with it).

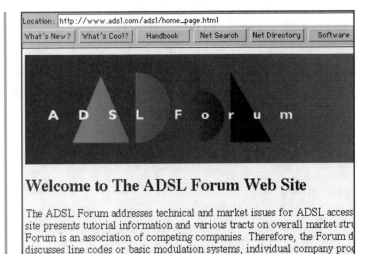

Figure 2.6

The ADSL home page.

It's no wonder that phone companies are excited about xDSL. Cable modem deployment will probably be controlled by cable companies, who are fast becoming the phone companies' sworn enemies. If things go as planned, xDSL service will be delivered over existing twisted-pair phone lines—as opposed to yet-to-be-installed networks like the HFC matrices which cable modems depend on.

Current reports concerning xDSL transfer rates cite anywhere from 6 to 8 Mbps (over regular household phone lines). The bad news is that, as with cable modems, the back channel throughput is significantly slower—perhaps only 15 percent as fast as the data stream coming *from* the server.

The way things are going, general availability of xDSL could be up to a year away, which roughly parallels the cable modem roll-out schedule. And there's a bit of a marketing dilemma: just as ISDN should be catching on in spades, the xDSL marketing teams will want to hog the spotlight. It will be interesting to see how this plays out, both on its own terms and in relation to cable modem marketing.

The MBone

This is a term that radical Webheads like to whisper conspiratorially, but it doesn't have that much meaning yet for the mass consumer markets. Abstractly speaking, the MBone is a portion of the Internet backbone that is reserved for video. In effect, it is a digital television channel.

If you've heard the buzzword video dial tone, you are getting close to MBone land. Although Web media developers probably won't be creating content specifically for MBone channels any time soon, the MBone model may trickle down to the desktop faster than current desktop models trickle up.

Regular MBone users, however, form a rather select club. The basic price of admission is a dedicated T1 line, and the ante goes up from there. This is a legitimate part of the Internet, as indicated by the number of publicized MBone multicasts (mostly musical performances by high-tech musicians), but it is less of a product than an evolving standard.

Brave New Software

Before we get into the intranet, let's talk about coming advances in software (since all we've covered so far in the chapter is hardware). We can break this down into the two standard categories: system software and applications software.

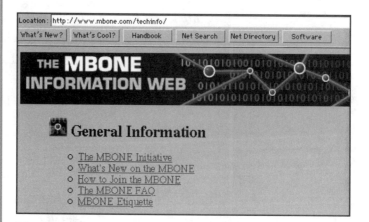

Figure 2.7

The shape of the MBone.

Without its own OS, Java running on Intel-based machines will always be a hostage to Windows, so it's not hard to understand why this big push is happening now. The reality check is that it takes years for mission-critical operating systems to mature.

Cool new applications will certainly help drive Web markets, but the real advances in performance will be the result of breakthroughs in operating systems—specifically network operating systems such as Windows NT.

This is a very loaded discussion area, but it's hard to ignore some basic facts. Hate it as you might, Windows now owns the desktop—especially the corporate desktop. Once users with Windows 95 and NT Pentiums get used to browsing Web sites powered by NT Server 4.0 with BackOffice and the IIS Web Server (covered in Chapter 17), they may choose not to look back.

The only real hope for people who still choose to resist Microsoft technology may be Java, but it's a big gamble. The extent to which Java is being promoted suggests that Sun is betting its future on the product. There has been a lot of excitement at recent Java developer conferences about the proposed Java operating system, and Sun is trying to lure as many talented engineers as possible to work on it or develop Java applications to run on it.

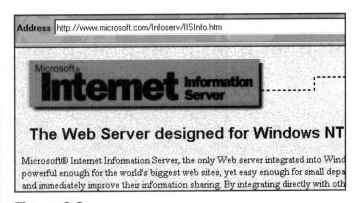

Figure 2.8
Microsoft's Internet Information Server.

The Intranet

Who says you can only produce Web media for the *World Wide* Web? Furthermore, why should you have to keep waiting for Internet technology to mature to the point where average users can enjoy the Web-based media assets (streaming and otherwise) that you can produce today?

As you may be aware, many large corporations (and smaller companies that can afford it) are building internal PC networks based on TCP/IP connections—as opposed to upgrading their existing LAN software.

Just as Internet computers are connected to the Web with modems and phone lines, intranet machines are connected via network cards and (more often than not) Ethernet cables.

These private TCP/IP networks, collectively known as the *intranet*, behave almost exactly like the external Internet when it comes to email, user-to-user file transfers, and (most important for readers of this book) media files. A big difference is that the intranet has bandwidth to spare and a genuine need for desktop video applications.

Even small companies can create cool intranet sites for a minimal investment, usually under $1,000 for each machine. If this all seems like the bush leagues compared to the wild and woolly Internet at large, it's not. Lots of

Figure 2.9

Intranet connections.

talented Web developers are making good money working on intranet contracts, and for good reason: It's not easy to do it right.

Here are some products currently available for making a company's computer network part of the intranet.

SuiteSpot

SuiteSpot is the Netscape intranet management solution. Included in the package are email and news modules, as well as a Yahoo-like directory and general site management services. SuiteSpot runs on Unix and Windows NT, and includes built-in support for Java, VRML, Shockwave, and various brands of databases (such as Oracle and Sybase).

Since Netscape has always been ahead of the curve in introducing new media-centric features to its browsers, it makes sense to have SuiteSpot as your intranet server if you hope to fully exploit these features. Complete information on SuiteSpot is available at the Netscape Web site, *http://www.netscape.com.*

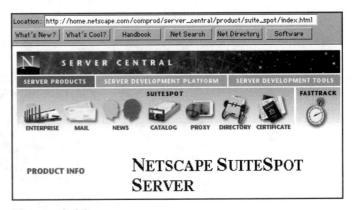

Figure 2.10
Netscape's SuiteSpot.

Oracle Universal Server

Oracle's Universal Server feels like a heavier product than Suite Spot in the way that it's marketed, but both provide the same essential services for the machines on their respective intranets. Of special note to Web media developers should be the Oracle Video Option component.

Originally targeted for Windows NT, Sunsoft Solaris, and HP/UX (to run on HP9000 systems), this scalable product reportedly leverages Oracle's database technology to organize video for efficient delivery across multiple types of networks. Naturally, lots more (and more timely) information may be obtained at *http://www.oracle.com*.

Starlight StarWorks

When this chapter was written, Starlight Networks was reportedly readying an NT-based video server solution for the intranet, scheduled to ship in Fall 1996. Starlight's current high-end networked video product, StarWorks, runs on various flavors of Unix. Starlight's Web site, *http://www.starlight.com*, has all the current details.

Figure 2.11
The Oracle Universal Server.

Remember that this list of products is only meant to suggest what's really out there. Also, because corporate intranets are essentially private domains, there is a lot of room for customization—and products that lend themselves to customization.

Figure 2.12
Starlight Networks' StarWorks.

Microsoft Media Server

Finally, there is the Microsoft solution—at least in theory. When it was called Tiger, the available specs said the product was scalable, NT-specific, and ran on clustered high-end PCs that functioned as a composite virtual server, with media data striped across both hard drives and the PCs themselves—quite an ambitious design.

The word now seems to be that the high performance part of the product is still called Tiger, but is targeted specifically for hotel video systems and the (admittedly fuzzier) home markets. The intranet part of the Microsoft Media Server is reportedly code-named Bengal.

On the other hand, unofficial information on Tiger seems plentiful.

For whatever reason, official information on all aspects of this product are scarce. See for yourself by doing a search at the Microsoft Web site using any of the above key words (Tiger, Bengal, Media Server). Who knows, perhaps by the time this books is published Bengal will be tearing up the intranet landscape.

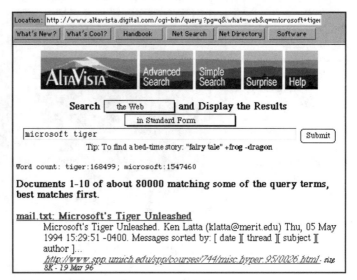

Location: http://www.altavista.digital.com/cgi-bin/query?pg=q&what=web&q=microsoft+tiger

What's New? | What's Cool? | Handbook | Net Search | Net Directory | Software

AltaVista | Advanced Search | Simple Search | Surprise | Help

Search [the Web] and **Display the Results**
[in Standard Form]

microsoft tiger [Submit]

Tip: To find a bed-time story: "fairy tale" +frog -dragon

Word count: tiger:168499; microsoft:1547460

Documents 1-10 of about 80000 matching some of the query terms, best matches first.

mail.txt: Microsoft's Tiger Unleashed
Microsoft's Tiger Unleashed. Ken Latta (klatta@merit.edu) Thu, 05 May 1994 15:29:51 -0400. Messages sorted by: [date][thread][subject][author]...
_http://www.spp.umich.edu/spp/courses/744/misc.hyper_95/0026.html_ - size 8K - 19 May 96

Figure 2.13

Will the Tiger burn bright?

The Changing Nature of the Video Server

One of the few things that Web media developers *can* be certain of is that the definition of the video server will change. In fact, it is changing right now. So let's just pose the question: What is a video server?

After all, VDOLive movies stream from server hardware running VDOnet's proprietary server software. Elsewhere in cyberspace (which includes the intranet), Oracle Universal Servers deliver media assets over corporate intranets, as do Microsoft Media Servers.

If you define a video server by the functions it performs, you can argue that the basic requirement for a video server—aside from being visible to network users—is that it provides video on demand (or in this case, desktop video on demand).

To really get into these issues, make a point to visit the Apple site (http://quicktime.apple.com) and read about their vision of video on demand (even if you don't use a Mac).

What this means is that a video clip requested by a user must start playing immediately— from the beginning. Some streaming products, like Apple's QuickTime TV, just let you tune into movie streams already in progress.

Now comes the crucial question: How important is quality? This is where any definition of a video server starts to blur. Obviously, there is a substantial quality gap between VDO movies served on the Web and, say, video streamed on a LAN by the Microsoft or Oracle products.

Still, each solution qualifies as a video server, despite the limitations of their respective environments. The grid shown in Figure 2.14 provides a sharper focus on this point.

Sun First to Introduce Industry's Most Scalable, Affordable Video Servers for the Enterprise

MOUNTAIN VIEW, Calif. - October 18, 1995 - Sun Microsystems Computer Company today unveiled the first complete line of video servers targeted at the enterprise, offering the industry's best scalability and affordability and designed specifically for network-based interactive video. The Sun(TM) MediaCenter(TM) 5, 20 and 1000E build on Sun's server, networking, and client/server expertise and feature unique software that now allow companies to manage, distribute and integrate video as a common data type into existing corporate networks.

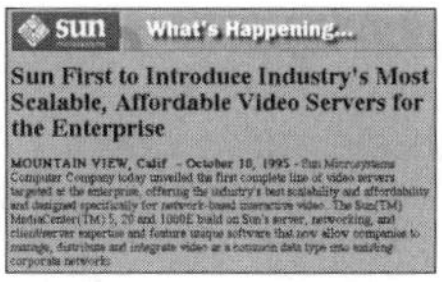

Strictly speaking, Web video on demand already exists, thanks to VDOLive. This means that a PC running VDO Server software is already a bona fide video server. It may seem obvious, there are has implications for people struggling to impose some type of order on all this new technology.

	High Quality Video	Low Quality Video
Internet	Microsoft Media Server? Oracle Universal Server? Others? When?	VDOLive Xing Others?
Intranet (LANs)	Starlight Networks Microsoft Media Server? Oracle Universal Server?	Who cares?

Figure 2.14

Ranking video servers.

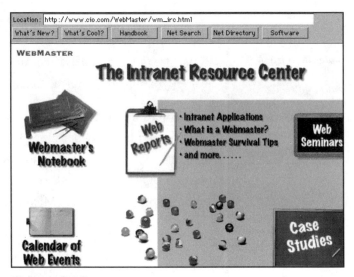

Figure 2.15

Cruising the *intra*net.

The last question (for now) raised by the above arguments is: When is that darn quality going to improve? If you remember, we posed the same question at the beginning of this chapter, but from a different point of view. One answer here is that it already has—on the intranet. In a big enough corporation, depending on the type of video content you are looking for, you might forget that you're not on the Internet.

A year or so ago, a video server was easier to define—essentially because it was a province of the Local Area Network. As that older definition starts to fragment, it probably means that the underlying hardware and software are indeed improving, which should lead to advances in quality across the board.

Chapter **3**

The Impact of Web-Based Media

This chapter may be the least geeky in the book. Instead of addressing technical issues, it focuses on the extent to which multimedia assets have already proliferated on the Web—as well as the consequences and implications of this ongoing proliferation.

In this chapter, I'll be pointing to, commenting on, and providing screen shots from some particularly media-rich sites. Because showing is usually better than telling, I recommend that you take the time to actually visit these locations yourself.

So far, Web sites with compelling multimedia assets tend to be run by computer, entertainment, broadcasting, and publishing companies. What's more interesting, however, is that Web media proliferation is affecting these companies in other areas than just their ad hoc Web sites.

In other words, the media files you play or download at those sites are no longer just teasers for retail products (like movies, records, and books). This may seem obvious at first, but it's worth remembering when you are completely immersed in a site that is well designed and media-rich.

What's now starting to happen is entertainment, broadcasting, and publishing that *originates* on the Web. This wouldn't be possible if Web-based media were universally judged not-ready-for-prime-time. Internet publishing projects couldn't stay in business without audiences, and some of them are going extremely strong (based on reported hit counts).

Our survey will cover sites that offer multimedia files essentially as trailers, and also those that publish original works on the Web. At the end of this chapter, we'll discuss some basic copyright issues. Later in this book, in Appendix A, I'll feature a particularly ambitious venture, The Blue Wolf Network, which uses almost all the Web media types currently available.

Since most companies who make Web-related software are working overtime to keep their product lines competitive, the examples in this chapter may be slightly dated by the time you read this. But you should still check out the Web sites to see if they now offer even better examples.

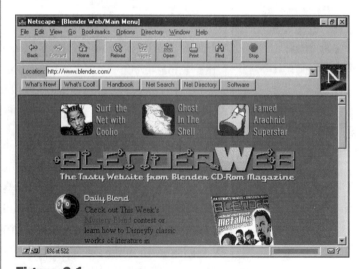

Figure 3.1
The Blender Web site.

Computer Industry Sites

Sure it's inbred, but the impact of Web media may be most felt in the ranks of the personal computer industry itself. Even if publishing and broadcasting give way to wholesale information retrieval as a means of making serious money on the Web, the glory of providing the underlying technology for Web media playback will burn brightly for a while longer.

And why not exploit that new technology as soon as it's presentable? Microsoft, Sun, Apple, and Netscape (among others) certainly rise to the occasion in this department—even in product areas that are not specifically Web-oriented. Let's look at some examples.

Cinemania

Remember to use the View Source feature of your browser to see how the HTML programming for pages like these was done. In this case, once you have the source document open, you can search for the word MARQUEE.

The address of this page is *http://www.msn.com/Cinemania/Reviews/ReviewsHome.htm.* Some of its multimedia characteristics are:

1. Animated GIF in the letter A of Striptease

2. Marquee (animated text) of *Also New This Week*

3. An underlying image map

Unfortunately (depending on your taste), there is no AVI movie available for this review, although many entries at the Cinemania site do have references to downloadable clips. The *Eraser* (with Arnold Schwarzenegger) review, for example, contains a 15-second, 160 × 120 clip, weighing in at slightly under 800 K.

A clip from the film Eraser.

Intel

The illustration in Figure 3.3 was taken from the site at *http://its.intel-inside.com/intro.html.* It's the first page of an online puzzle whose multimedia attributes include:

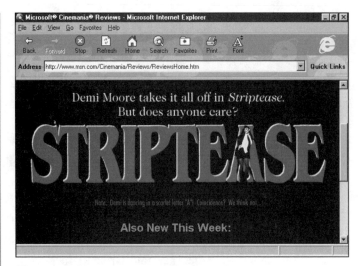

Figure 3.2

A Microsoft *Cinemania* Web page.

1. AVI movies

2. Java applets

3. VRML objects

4. WAV audio files

5. A proprietary animation engine

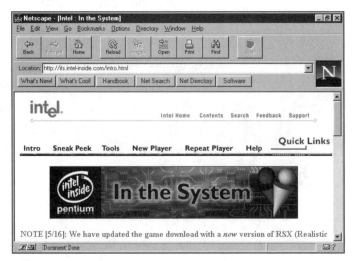

Figure 3.3

Intel's In the System.

Apple

One of Apple's media-enriched Web ventures is the *Mission: Impossible* tie-in page at *http://www.mission.apple.com*, shown in Figure 3.4.

Some of the technologies employed at this Apple site are:

1. QuickTime

2. RealAudio

3. Shockwave

4. Sophisticated HTML conventions

Progressive Networks

Not as broad in scope as the Microsoft, Intel, and Apple sites—but equally ambitious—is Progressive Networks' Timecast program for special audio events. Past Webcasts include online previews of new works by major recording artists (see Figure 3.5). Progressive Networks is the developer of RealAudio, one of the leading streaming audio solutions.

Figure 3.4
Apple's Mission:Impossible tie-in.

Figure 3.5

A Timecast presentation.

Movie Industry Sites

No doubt about it, movie industry Web pages will be heavily
weighted with QuickTime and AVI clips, as opposed to other
types of multimedia, although sometimes you may be
pleasantly surprised. Let's start by surfing to Paramount,
whose *Mission: Impossible* site (shown in Figure 3.6, and
not to be confused with Apple's *Mission:Impossible* tie-in)

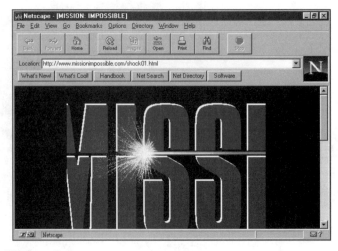

Figure 3.6

Paramount's *Mission: Impossible* page.

has a couple of nicely done Shockwave movies. The URL is *http://www.missionimpossible.com/shock01.html*.

Another media-rich movie site is the one maintained by Sony Pictures, at *http://www.spe.sony.com/Pictures/ SonyMovies/index.html*.

A fair amount of work went into the Sony site, and it shows. If you browse the other areas of the installation, you'll find more sophisticated uses of Web-based media.

The Web media technologies featured at the Sony Pictures site consist of the following:

1. Shockwave movies

2. QuickTime clips

3. AVI clips

4. WAV, AIFF, and AU audio clips, including full length songs by major recording artists

5. Animated GIFs

6. Java

The Sony movie pages also have a number of clever games and contests which combine many of the multimedia elements listed above.

Figure 3.7
Sony Pictures' home page.

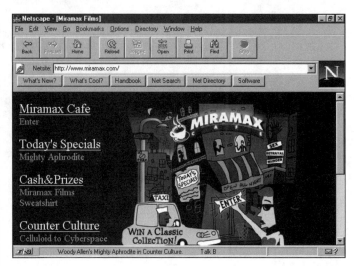

Figure 3.8

The Miramax home page.

Let's press on to Miramax (*http://www.miramax.com*), shown in Figure 3.8. Not as chock full of clever animations and audio clips as the Sony presence, these pages are nevertheless rich in downloadable QuickTime movies (17 of them are from *Pulp Fiction* alone).

Broadcast Industry Sites

It's hard to predict what you'll find at the sites run by the big players, but several of the top networks have already invested in streaming video and audio solutions from VDOnet, Xing, and Progressive Networks. While such solutions will only become mission critical over time, the clock does seem to be ticking.

Exploring the corridors of the NBC Web site (at *http://www.nbc.com*, shown in Figure 3.9) yielded the following nuggets, as of this writing:

1. Animated GIFs (of athletes in the NBC Sports section)

2. Java scripts (for text crawls)

Another broadcaster site worth browsing: http://www.kpix .com/video

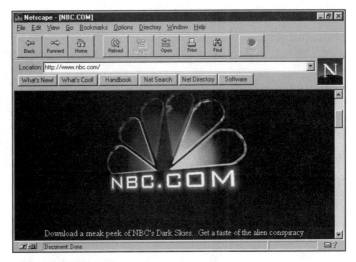

Figure 3.9
The home page for NBC.

3. QuickTime movies (for new program trailers)

4. AVI clips (also for upcoming series teasers)

Not to be outdone, the ABC site (*http://www.abc.com*, shown in Figure 3.10) makes good use of:

Figure 3.10
ABC TV's online presence.

1. Shockwave (for the falling stars on the home page)

2. Animated GIFs (to animate some text elements)

3. RealAudio (for interviews with stars)

4. QuickTime (to promote next season's shows)

Another heavyweight site:

http://www.cbsnews .com

Going to the URL *http://www.cnn.com* (Turner's CNN Interactive) for cool Web media is slightly less gratifying than browsing the ABC and NBC sites, but there are scattered QuickTime movies and audio clips available for downloading, as shown in Figure 3.11.

The scene at Fox is somewhat different. Organized into Netscape frames, the overall feel is much more interactive than the more text-based approach of CNN Interactive. Plenty of downloadable movies are available in the Fox Preview Theatre section (including some X-Files clips), and there are some scattered games, with various types of animation.

Also at this site is a home page for Fox Interactive, a sophisticated game and preview environment. This section uses Java to control the action in text-and-graphics

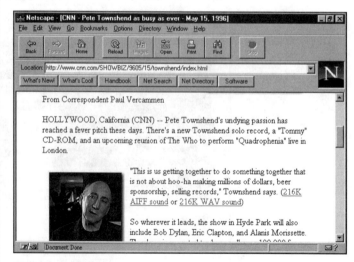

Figure 3.11

Download audio files from CNN Interactive.

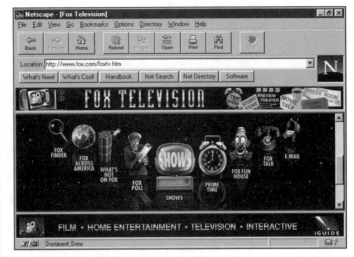

Figure 3.12

The Fox site.

interactive stories that are based on Fox movies and individual characters (such as Bart Simpson).

Not as obvious a presence on the Web are radio stations. A good example of a radio station with an online presence is San Francisco's KITS, also known as Live 105 (*http://www.live105.com*).

Figure 3.13

The What? Page at Live 105.

Among the Web media technologies in service here are:

1. Downloadable movies

2. TrueSpeech Audio

3. Live Webcasts

Recording Industry Sites

Record companies are also getting in the game. Rykodisc (*http://www.rykodisc.com*), for example, has built their site around streaming and downloadable audio clips from almost all of their artists, all within a very streamlined design.

Rykodisc's online multimedia arsenal employs:

1. Downloadable WAV audio clips

2. Downloadable MPEG audio files

3. RealAudio streams

4. Animated GIFs

5. Downloadable QuickTime and AVI movies

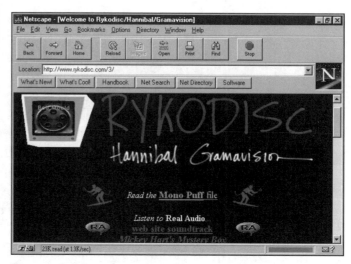

Figure 3.14

The Rykodisc home page.

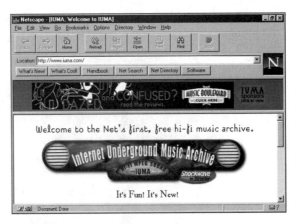

Figure 3.15
The IUMA site.

One of the first, if not *the* first, repositories of digitized musical works from unsigned bands was the Internet Underground Music Archive (IUMA). Over the last few years, IUMA has matured dramatically, and now reportedly commands substantial fees for designing Web sites for major labels.

If you browse to the main IUMA page (*http://www.iuma .com*), you can get a taste of the range of Web media they serve, currently including:

1. Shockwave movies

2. RealAudio streams

3. Downloadable MPEG and AU audio clips

Publishing Industry Sites

Independent CD-ROM publishers such as Blender often have related Web addresses (*http://www.blender.com*). Such complementary publishing vehicles can easily leverage multimedia assets already embodied on their associated CD-ROM products.

Figure 3.16

A page from the Blender site.

Blender's applied technology list appears to embrace:

1. Downloadable audio clips

2. Streaming VDO video files

3. Interactive stories

In the magazine world, periodicals such as *DV* (Digital Video) have built well-designed Web destinations to provide access to their back issues, and to also attract their audiences to late-breaking information in the professional markets they normally cover in print.

DV (*http://www.livedv.com*) takes this a step further by offering online tutorials and multimedia-enhanced reviews of new products that they normally cover in their paper magazine. Some of *DV*'s favorite enabling technology tools seem to be:

1. Shockwave

2. QuickTime

3. VDOLive

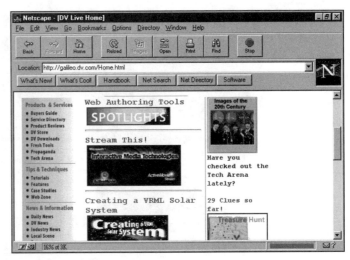

Figure 3.17

A scene from DV Live.

Some book publishers also caught the wave early—
especially the ones who produce books on these very Web
multimedia topics. However, the so-called *convergence*
phenomenon has linked the book industry at large to the
broadcast, movie, and computer industries in ways that
make publishing house Web sites inevitable.

A good example is The Coriolis Group (the publisher of
this book). The Coriolis Web presence, at *http://www*
.coriolis.com, is state of the art. There is so much advanced
Web technology going on at this site that it's hard to ab-
sorb it all in one visit.

When you tour the Coriolis Web premises, you'll experience:

1. Sophisticated Java applets

2. Animated GIFs

3. Programming contests

On the non-technical side, you can check out the address
maintained by HarperCollins publishers, shown in Figure
3.19.

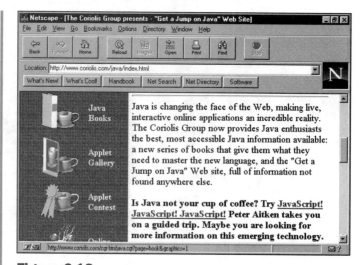

Figure 3.18

The Coriolis Group's Web site.

Lots of convergence tie-ins here which capitalize on various Web media strategies. Case in point: the audio book excerpts (downloadable WAV and AIFF files) available in the Harper Audio section (*http://www.harpercollins.com/audio*).

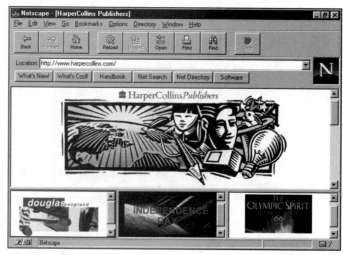

Figure 3.19

The view from www.harpercollins.com.

Original New Media Sites

The impact of streaming video, audio, and Web-based animation is even more profound on so-called *new media* publishers whose main distribution channel is the Web itself. One of the big challenges for such publishers is to make the technology as transparent as possible.

In other words, don't draw attention to streaming media as an end in itself or, worse yet, a mere novelty. Prepare your content as carefully as your budget permits, make it fit into your interface as efficiently as possible, then just serve it up on its own merits.

A site that seems to be following this philosophy is The Blue Wolf Network at *http://www.bluewolfnet.com*. (An extensive interview with John Barrows, the Blue Wolf Network's creator, is presented at the end of this book.)

The Blue Wolf's roster of applied Web sciences includes:

1. VRML

2. Java

Figure 3.20

Comic Belief at The Blue Wolf Network.

3. VDOLive

4. RealAudio

5. QuickTime

As this book goes to press, the number of active Web-centric new media publishers/broadcasters is growing rapidly. Since one screen shot is worth a thousand words, the following series of images and associated URLs should give you a good feel for the kinds of things people are doing with just VDOLive technology (not to mention the other types of Web-based media).

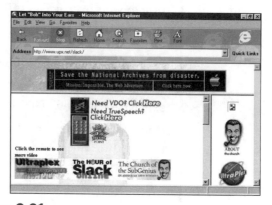

Figure 3.21

http://www.upx.net/slack

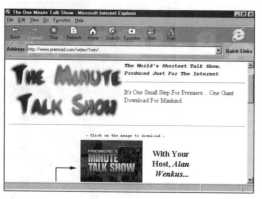

Figure 3.22

http://www.premrad.com/video/1min

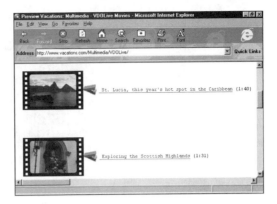

Figure 3.23

http://www.vacations.com

Figure 3.24

http://www.talentworks.com

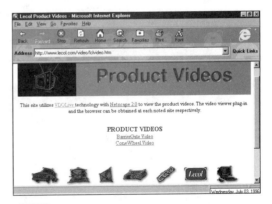

Figure 3.25

http://www.lecol.com/video/lclvideo.htm

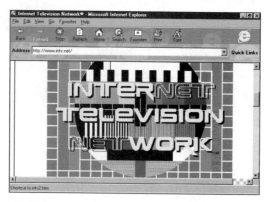

Figure 3.26

http://www.intv.net

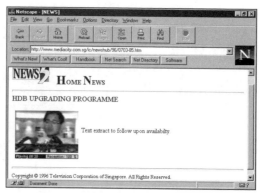

Figure 3.27

http://www.mediacity.com.sg/newshub/96

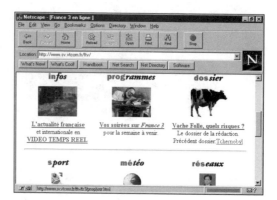

Figure 3.28

http://www.sv.vtcom.fr/ftv

Figure 3.29

The FOOTAGE.net site.

And, yes, it has occurred to a few stock footage companies that Web-based video is a good way to advertise their products. In fact, a site named FOOTAGE.net has assembled a meta-catalog of individual stock footage catalogs (*http://www.footage.net:2900*).

The medium of choice at the greater FOOTAGE.net installation seems to be downloadable QuickTime clips, although if you dig into it seriously, you might find other types of video files as well. Often, there are still image files (usually GIFs) available, made from individual frames of the respective movies.

Some of FOOTAGE.net's links.

Figure 3.30

The On Demand Stock Footage Server.

Some of the activities you can indulge in at
FOOTAGE.net are:

- Screening of clips (requires downloading first)

- Email individual stock footage companies directly

- Perform keyword searches

- Order catalogs and demo reels while online

- Order transcripts from a publication named *Journal Graphics*, a massive collection of historical broadcast records on CBS, ABC, CNN, NPR, and PBS

- Peruse government regulations about copyright issues involving stock footage

Copyright Issues

In one respect, copyright issues are just as uncertain and chaotic as they were in the first great CD-ROM era. Fortunately, while lots of silver discs are probably still being bootlegged in bad neighborhoods around the world, not too many legitimate publishers have done anything really stupid yet. Anyway, that's the devil we know.

The devil we know hardly at all is much more slippery. This one understands digital reproduction issues *and* broadcasting law. If you have legal experience in the digital media/CD-ROM industry, you'll already know to get permission (in writing, in advance) for anything you publish or Webcast that is not completely original.

The real bottom line is, if you have the slightest inkling that you're infringing on somebody's copyright, you probably are. If you think you can cut corners with clever digital alterations, cases like these have already been tried in court—and lost by the smug infringers.

If you want the complete story on this and related issues, the Net search engines can provide a wealth of information. Retaining a reputable attorney in advance of any significant publishing venture is also recommended (just ask any significant publisher).

Chapter **4**

Streaming vs. Downloading

Cool as it is, real-time streaming is not always the best way to deliver Web-based multimedia. All sorts of people (and programs) browse the Web, each with their own needs and delivery expectations, and it's only going to get worse.

Trying to anticipate those delivery expectations by offering various ways to play files may seem like a good idea at first, but such diversity has both practical and aesthetic consequences.

In this chapter, we'll discuss the differences between streaming and downloading. We'll also look at when streaming is preferable to downloading, and vice versa. As usual, the user is always right—even though he or she may not fully understand the options.

The concept of streaming is important when working with digital data—such as desktop multimedia.

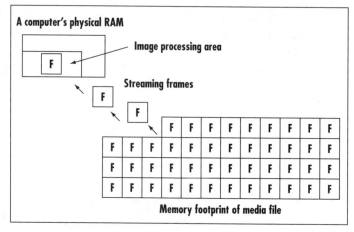

A computer's physical RAM

Image processing area

Streaming frames

Memory footprint of media file

Figure 4.1
Streaming a large file.

Stream On

As with most PC technology, it is important to have a context when you start slinging buzzwords. This is especially true for so-called *data streaming*, which is new for certain types of Web-based multimedia but not for multimedia in general.

Simply stated, streaming is a technique for processing data files (such as desktop video clips) which:

- are too big to fit completely into memory

- take too long to load prior to playback

- may be in a remote location, such as someone else's Web site

In other words, data streaming helps get multimedia files rolling on the user's PC as soon as possible. It is, however, exploited differently in the CD-ROM world than in the Internet world, as we'll see shortly.

A frame from a non-streaming movie.

The same frame streamed.

CUSeeMe: Better clarity, slower frame rates.

Web-based video conferencing software, like CUSeeMe, also streams data, but generally not from a server.

Local Data Streaming

Efficient streaming is crucial for good performance of any multimedia clip. In the CD-ROM world, this task is generally handled by the competing movie-playing engines from Apple and Microsoft: QuickTime and Video for Windows. As a movie plays, the following two cycles execute simultaneously and are repeated (more or less in the order shown) until the end of the movie file:

Cycle 1

- Read audio and video data from the CD-ROM

- Place the data into appropriate memory buffers

- Repeat the cycle if not at the end of the file

Cycle 2

- Read audio and video data from the buffers filled in Cycle 1

- Decompress the data (if necessary)

- Send the data to the screen and speakers

- Repeat the cycle if not at the end of the file

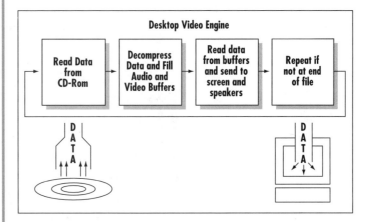

Figure 4.2
Streaming data from a CD-ROM.

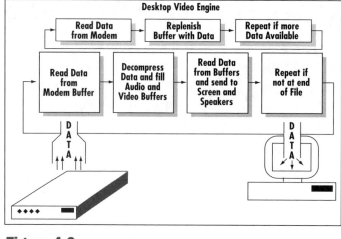

Figure 4.3

Streaming data over a modem.

A small bitmap— no need to stream.

The challenge for streaming routines is to always keep data in the buffers until the movie is finished playing. If the buffers don't run dry, playback will usually be smooth. Since audio buffers usually get top priority, you can assume deep trouble in the engine room when a movie's soundtrack breaks up.

Of course, not all moving images on personal computer monitors are under control of QuickTime or Video for Windows. Many CD-ROM products use proprietary streaming routines specifically developed for the image

Figure 4.4

Xing's Streamworks.

sequences they animate. Still, if those routines read large sound and image sequences from a CD-ROM (or a hard drive), execution cycles similar to those detailed above will likely be employed—with or without buffering.

Web-Based Streaming

Streaming data across the Web is much trickier. Not only is the software required to keep its audio and video buffers stocked with data, it must also manage data arriving from the modem—yet another buffering challenge.

Since all computer networks (and especially the World Wide Web) suffer from imperfect synchronization between clients and servers, this challenge can easily become a nightmare for programmers. The point here is that even *big* data buffers can run dry in two or three seconds, and such lapses are common with online connections.

Part of the excitement surrounding streaming media comes from its live broadcast feel. Just as important, however, is the instant gratification factor.

Web site developers needing a technical context for this new form of streaming technology should keep in mind two things:

- almost all multimedia data gets streamed in one way or another

- streaming from the Web does not necessarily imply recording

Figure 4.5
The current RealAudio player.

In other words, streamed movie frames are discarded as soon as they are played. Unlike recording with a VCR, you can't usually watch and record a clip simultaneously—at least not yet.

With this context established, let's now address some performance issues. We understand that real-world delivery rates of Web-based media are subject to the talents of the emerging hardware and software makers, but several overall principles still apply.

First of all, current performance levels for streaming desktop video correspond to QuickTime and Video for Windows circa 1992. This means:

- movie window dimensions of 160 x 120 pixels

- ten frames per second (or less, depending on Internet traffic)

Other factors can affect performance as well:

- *Quality of ISP service*
- *Peak vs. off-peak Internet traffic flow*
- *PC/OS prowess—discussed later in this chapter*

- bargain basement audio attributes (down to 8 KHz in some cases)

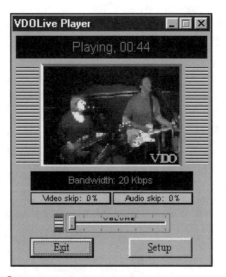

Figure 4.6
The current VDOLive player.

Figure 4.7
One of the initial players.

It is important to realize that brand new codecs have been developed to compress and play back Web-based media files. Furthermore, these new codecs have different priorities than the ones used to encode CD-ROM clips (such as Cinepak and Indeo).

For example, data integrity is now just as important as image clarity. Ensuring that an incoming media stream remains uncorrupted requires a sophisticated communications protocol—as well as more work for these new codecs.

A retooled existing codec is Indeo Video Interactive, a wavelet-based compressor re-designed from scratch to provide scalability.

Also, most of the new compressors employ some type of scalability. This allows a more powerful PC to get better-looking playback from a given media file than a less powerful PC. Similar approaches are used in new versions of existing CD-ROM codecs.

Because of the demands placed on these new codecs, the movies and sound files they present to the user are not yet as crisp as even the earliest QuickTime and AVI clips. As noted earlier, light Internet traffic at showtime helps close the clarity gap, but it is still quite obvious.

Figure 4.8
Another early contender.

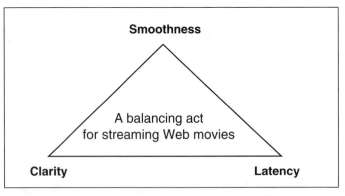

Figure 4.9

A balancing act for streaming Web movies.

Once again, codec designers must choose between smoothness and visual clarity. But now there is a third factor: latency.

The good news is that we are finally getting video on demand—or, more accurately, media on demand. If small movie windows remind you of QuickTime and Video for Windows in 1992, so should experiencing live desktop video on the Web for the first time.

Developer Positioning

One reason for the current state of streaming multimedia is that, as of this writing, the most visible development effort is being mounted by small, third party companies—as opposed to the likes of Apple, Microsoft, Sun, and Intel.

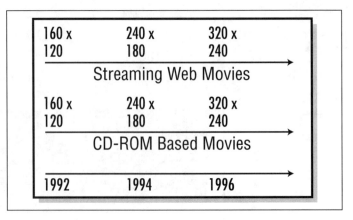

Figure 4.10

How desktop video frame size has increased.

The big players *are* developing products in the categories of video conferencing, high-end video on demand, and 3D/VRML (as well as sophisticated Internet software in general). None, however, yet go head to head with the real-time video streaming solutions from the existing crop of smaller third parties.

This situation may account for the original lack of hype for Web-based video. It may also account for the fact that software written by third parties will probably not be true enabling technology. In other words, certain key components will not be free—as opposed to Video for Windows and, finally, QuickTime.

Will the monoliths deploy their own solutions any time soon? If they do, it *will* be as enabling technology, or they haven't learned anything in the last five years. Unfortunately, since enabling technology entails a major disconnect from short-term profits, Apple Computer may not jump in for a while.

Microsoft, in retrospect, never even gave Video for Windows its full attention (as anyone who digs into VfW's internals can plainly see) so why should they worry about

Figure 4.11
Part of Apple's current solution.

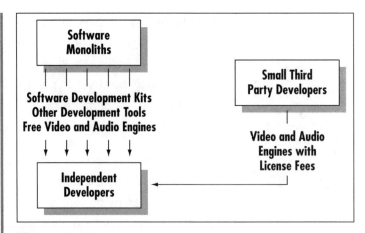

Figure 4.12

Enabling technology—small players can't provide it.

small players that they can seriously cripple simply by issuing a competitive announcement?

On the other hand, Microsoft is taking an extremely aggressive position when it comes to Web-based products. Its ActiveMovie Stream software, just being released as of this writing, seems to be an essential part of the assault.

Players like Macromedia pose less direct threats to small third parties, but for different reasons. Shockwave movies (made with Macromedia software) behave a bit like Web-streamed video, but they are actually local files that get downloaded prior to playback. We'll cover Shockwave movie preparation in a later chapter.

Configuring Your System

Just as in the early days of traditional desktop video, you must install specialized software to view and create Web-based multimedia files. And, because we are dealing with sophisticated technology, there are a few other issues to keep in mind as well:

First, each third party product is essentially a custom application or codec—as opposed to a whole new engine usable by other programs. Some are simply add-ins to browsers line Netscape Navigator and Microsoft Internet Explorer. This seems like a small point until you consider the roles played by QuickTime and Video for Windows.

Second, while you can download and install the viewer programs easily enough, the corresponding server software is quite a different story. If you are reading this book, you are likely just as interested in publishing Web-based movies as you are in consuming them. Unlike putting QuickTime and VfW movies on a golden master CD-ROM and having it replicated for publication, serving Web media requires a whole new type of investment—in hardware, software, and education. We'll be tackling these issues in the next chapter.

Finally, speaking of hardware, let's put some basic specs on the table now. We can use a 2×2 matrix: Macs and PCs across, clients and servers down. Note that these specs are not definitive, but can give a useful sense of scope

MAC Client	PC Client
System 7.1 on a Quadra	Windows 95 on a low-end Pentium
MAC Server	PC Server
System 7.1 on a PowerPC	Windows NT on a high-end Pentium

Figure 4.13

Mac and PC client/server requirements.

and perspective. In all cases, a 28.8 modem or better is assumed. Servers attached to ISDN, T1, and T3 phone lines usually need special modems and routing equipment.

Of course, many servers currently in use do not have Intel inside, such as the venerable Sun SparcStation, but these exceed our simple matrix and are covered elsewhere.

- *PC Client*—In general, Internet apps running under Windows 3.1 perform much worse than with Windows 95. Since Windows 95 only really gets going on Pentium machines, you pretty much need the Win95/Pentium combination (with 16 MB or more of RAM) to enjoy streaming multimedia on the Net.

- *PC Server*—All PC servers should be Pentiums, with lots of memory (at least 32 MB) and big hard drives (at least one GB). Since things get messy when servers crash or need rebooting, they should run Windows NT. Some vendors sell Win95 server solutions, but these will turn out to be short-term.

- *Mac Client*—Or the record, a Quadra 650 with 8 MB of RAM is a highly efficient Internet machine for the consumption of streaming desktop media. Properly configured, better hardware (such as the PowerMac) only gives better performance.

- *Mac Server*—Just as you would on the PC (Pentium) side, go where the power is: The PowerMac. A 9500 makes a perfectly adequate Web server, assuming lots of memory and hard disk space (at least 32 MB of RAM and several GB of disk space if lots of desktop media files will be served).

When Streaming Is Better

Until Web-based streaming media looks and sounds as good as what you can get from a CD-ROM, it is not going to replace traditional QuickTime and Video for

Windows movies. However, some of the applications for which streaming video currently *is* better are:

- Almost instant previews of better-quality VfW and QuickTime assets which are also available.

- Full length versions of longer performances, since traditional desktop movies placed on Web pages are usually only snippets from longer pieces.

- Interactive presentations, since downloadable files by nature can't be interacted with.

If this sounds like streamable video is essentially throw-away media, you may be on to something—but that doesn't necessarily diminish its value. Of course, this fits in with one popular view of multimedia in general, which is that it still provides more information than entertainment.

Chapter **5**

Streaming Video Production

This chapter concerns itself with the creation of Web-based video files. We'll concentrate on the most prominent solutions currently available, but point out up-and-coming products as well. If there are any glaring omissions, it's because market demand at the time this book was written was stronger for the products that *are* included here.

We'll start with VDOLive because it is a true video streaming technology which has made significant inroads with Web site developers. Although it is not pure enabling technology, VDOnet has marketed it aggressively and been responsive to its customers. By the time you read this, the Mac version of the player/plug-in should be in general release.

We'll also cover production of Shockwave movies—Macromedia Director animations which behave like streaming video in many ways, but which need to be downloaded first (albeit transparently). Like VDOLive, Shockwave has also made impressive headway in developer markets.

VDOLive

To get started, you'll have to purchase the VDOLive video compression and server administration software. Complete information, including a rate card, is available at their Web site (*http://www.vdolive.com*).

For tire kickers, VDO also distributes a lightweight package called VDOLive Personal Server, which lets you stream a maximum of two clips simultaneously from your Web site at no charge. Naturally, VDOnet expects you to purchase the heavyweight product once you're hooked.

As of this writing, a promising new streaming video product named VivoActive has just arrived on the scene. Check it out at http://www.vivo .com.

Since the Personal Server capture and compression programs have the same UI as the full versions of the applications, the production procedures that follow can be used by everyone—not just VDOLive retail customers. If you are thinking about using streaming video to enhance your Web site but want a demo first, download the Personal Server and follow the instructions below.

The VDO Capture and Compression Tools

Making streaming video files for public consumption entails two labor intensive processes:

*   Capturing and encoding with the VDOLive format

*   Maintaining those VDO clips on an HTTP server

Since up-to-date information on installing and maintaining VDO servers (both personal and retail) is best obtained

Figure 5.1
VDOnet does provide a free personal server.

from the latest versions of the product documentation—and at the VDO Web site—this chapter only deals with preparing VDOLive media.

Before getting started, let's perform a standard equipment check. System specs for working with the VDO tools are:

From a production perspective, there are effectively two options: the native VDO tools or Premiere for Windows 4.2 (since Adobe now supports VDOLive). However, even though many producers like to stay completely within Premiere, there are still some reasons to use the native tools—as you'll see shortly.

- Windows 95 or NT running on a Pentium with a minimum of 8 MB of RAM. (Actually, a Pentium machine is not mandatory—just highly recommended.)

- A 16-bit sound card (most models are supported). It's hard not to recommend the Sound Blaster 16.

- A video capture board that can grab uncompressed at 160 x 120, 15 fps. Some candidates here are the Intel Smart Video Recorder Pro or the FAST FPS 60, although more expensive cards will work well, too. Also, you can capture your video on the Mac and convert the resultant QuickTime files to the AVI format. This process is detailed in Chapter 15.

Capturing a Raw File

Assuming your capture gear is ready to go (and cabled correctly to your video deck), let's get ready to do a capture. From the Windows 95 or NT desktop, fire up the VDOLive Capture program. The user interface shown in Figure 5.2 should appear.

Note: Some ISA cards, like the ISVR Pro, may have problems with NT.

Figure 5.2
The VDO capture interface.

Play several seconds of your tape to check that the VDOLive Capture application is communicating with your video capture board. If they are cooperating, you should observe the videotape output in the monitor window of the capture application.

Now let's check some settings:

The VDO Capture Program user interface might look slightly different, depending on which capture card you are using.

1. In the *Options | Video Source* menu, set the option that corresponds to the physical connection between your capture board and video deck—usually S-Video or Composite. Choose S-Video (if possible) for better image quality, as shown in Figure 5.3.

   If you don't see any video in the program's monitor window, you could have the wrong option set here. If neither S-Video nor Composite produces a picture, try some different cables or test your capture card with another capture application to rule out hardware malfunctions.

2. In the *Options | Video* menu, verify the default calibrations of 160×120 (frame size) and 24-bit color, as shown in Figure 5.4.

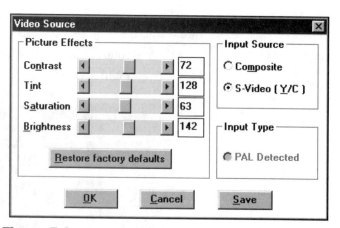

Figure 5.3

Choosing the input source.

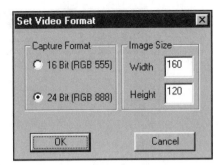

Figure 5.4

Setting the video format.

3. In the *Options | Audio* menu, confirm that defaults of 8 kHz, 16-bit mono are set, as shown in Figure 5.5. These values are specifically essential for the VDO *encoder* program, which we'll be working with after the clip has been digitized successfully.

   Desktop video experts will notice something interesting here: the 8 kHz audio rate. Obviously, this is not strictly MPC compatible, which carries major implications. More on that later.

For a Shockwave-like approach to streaming Web media, take a look at Gold Disk's Astound Web Player at http://www.golddisk.com.

4. In the *Options | Capture Settings | Set File* dialog box, enter the file name for the clip, as shown in Figure 5.6. Give it the .AVI extension (and remember to target it for a big hard disk).

5. In the *Capture* menu, select *Capture Video*. A dialog box like the one shown in Figure 5.7 will appear.

Figure 5.5

Setting the audio format.

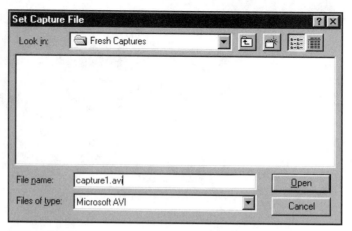

Figure 5.6

Naming your VDOLive clip.

Click *OK* or press your Enter key to begin digitizing. Many producers like to roll their tape first (starting a few seconds back), then click *OK* just in time. Others simply punch *Play* on the VTR, then summarily click *OK*. It's a personal thing.

6. To end the capture, hit the Enter key. The digitized clip is now saved on your hard disk. If you haven't used any other digitization programs (like Microsoft's VidCap or Premiere's capture facility), you may want to practice this operation a few times before digitizing anything crucial. Once you're comfortable with it, we'll move on to the compression process.

Another Web video technology too new to give adequate coverage here: CoolFusion from Iterated Systems, available at http:// webber.iterated.com/ coolfusn/ cf_home.htm.

Figure 5.7

Starting the actual capture process.

Compressing a Raw VDO File

To compress the just-captured clip, we need the VDOLive Clip program. This application comes with the Personal Server and the retail VDOLive tool collection. Its primary user interface is shown in Figure 5.8. The procedure that follows describes the most straightforward way to use the program, although there is certainly room to experiment once you get familiar with it.

If clip editing is needed, the video and audio tracks must be edited separately. To cut video frames, click on the first frame in the sequence, then shift-click the last frame in the sequence. All the selected frames should now have a blue border. To remove the sequence, click Cut in the Edit menu. You can edit the audio track in the same manner.

1. From the *File | Open* menu, select the clip to be compressed. Some of its video frames and a partial audio track will appear in the main interface.

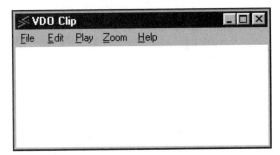

Figure 5.8

VDOLive Clip's user interface.

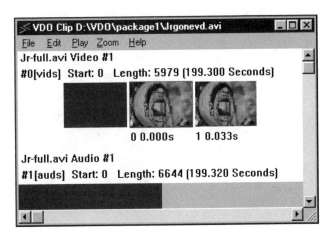

Figure 5.9

A first look at a clip to be compressed.

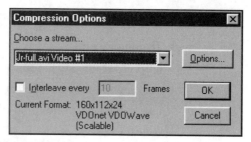

Figure 5.10

Choosing the compression options.

2. In the *File* menu, click the *Driver options* item. The *Compression Options* dialog box will appear.

3. Select the item labeled *Video #1* (this label is preceded by the name of the uncompressed file), then click the *Options* button. The *Video Compression* dialog box will appear, as shown in Figure 5.11. Select the item *VDOnet VDOWave (Scalable)* from the *Compressor* combo box. Put a check in the box labeled *Key Frame Every* and enter 60 in the associated text field.

4. Click the *Configure* button, which brings up the *Rate Control Configuration* dialog box. A good strategy for now is to use a high number like 64 or 128 (the VDOLive documentation gives some reasons for this), then click *OK*.

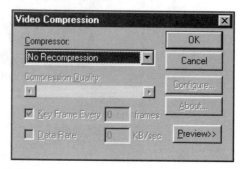

Figure 5.11

Selecting more compression options.

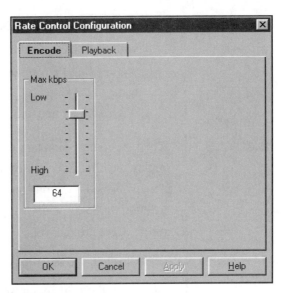

Figure 5.12
Setting the encoding rate.

5. Back in *Compression Options*, select *Audio #1* from the same box as *Video #1*.

Another new Internet video product, though more on the video conferencing side, is FreeVue, at http://www. freevue.com.

6. Check the *Interleave every* box and enter 10 in *Frames*, as shown in Figure 5.13.

7. Click the *Options* button. In the *Sound Selection* dialog box, select the *VDOWave 1* codec. Since the only available settings are 8 kHz/16-bit/mono, click *OK* to return to the *Compression Options* dialog box, then click *OK* again to exit *Compression Options*.

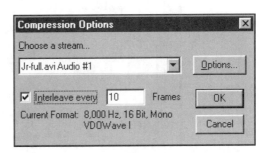

Figure 5.13
Setting the interleaving rate.

8. At last, we're ready to encode the uncompressed clip with the VDO compressor. From the main menu, select *File | VDOencode*. You'll be prompted for the name of the target file, then encoding will begin. Job status will be updated in the Clip program's title bar.

When the compression task is finished, you'll be prompted to play the clip. This is useful for confirming that the file is well-formed, but you can also simulate playback at different modem speeds with the Clip program's preview option. Here are the steps:

1. Close all the open movie files.

2. From the *Play* menu, select *Rate Control*.

3. Instead of *Encode*, click the *Playback* tab.

4. Select a bit rate to simulate, then use Clip's *File | Open* menu item to load the VDO encoded file for testing.

5. Repeat this procedure at enough standard bit rates (28.8 kbps, 56 kbps, etc.) to get at least a rough idea of real-time playback. If you are happy with the performance, your VDO clip can be considered ready for prime time—as in posting on your server.

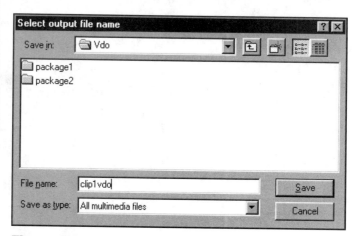

Figure 5.14

Choosing the target file name.

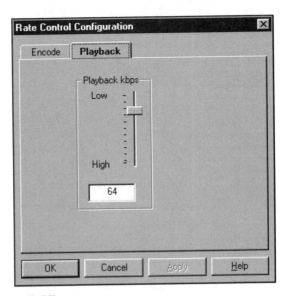

Figure 5.15

Selecting the playback speed.

Capturing and Compressing with Premiere

Working with VDO files under Premiere 4.2 for Windows is a bit less complicated—at least for Premiere users. You can use Premiere to capture a clip to your hard drive, but

Don't worry that you cannot specifically set the target sampling rate to 8 kHz. This will be done automatically as Premiere and the VDO codec work together. As specified above, you must be using version 4.2 of Premiere for Windows.

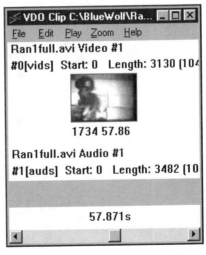

Figure 5.16

Testing the VDO file.

you'll have to save that clip back out as uncompressed. Then you'll need to re-import the uncompressed file and compress it with the VDOLive compressor.

If you're still following this, the next step is a standard *Make Movie* using VDOWave as the target video compressor, as shown in Figure 5.17. (Note: If you are working with the retail VDO tools, make sure to use the VDOWave I Audio codec for the best sound quality. The Personal Server tools only allow you to use the VDOWave II codec.) The finished file will be just as good for uploading to your Web site as the same movie made with VDO Clip.

Shockwave

As noted earlier, Shockwave is Macromedia's way of making a Director movie play on a Web page. To make things as easy as possible for Web developers, Macromedia provides a single conversion tool named Afterburner. This program takes normal DIR files as input and outputs so-called "shocked" movies (with the default DCR extension) ready for embedding in an HTML document.

There are two major issues here:

As of this writing, Shockwave is only supported by the Netscape Navigator browser (for both Windows and the Mac).

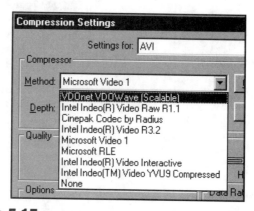

Figure 5.17

Choosing VDOWave as the target video compressor.

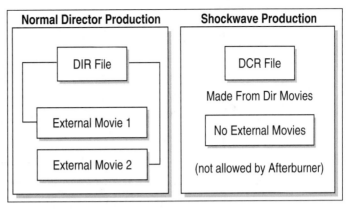

Normal Director Production	Shockwave Production
DIR File	DCR File
	Made From Dir Movies
External Movie 1	No External Movies
External Movie 2	(not allowed by Afterburner)

Figure 5.18

Afterburner has some limitations.

1. As of this writing, video clips (like QuickTime and AVI files) cannot be contained in a DIR file, and therefore cannot be contained in a shocked movie.

2. Shockwave is not (yet) a true streaming solution, even though it tries to act like one. When you click on a shocked movie hot spot, the whole DCR file is downloaded to your local system in the background before it plays. In other words, there is a wait involved.

Yet another new contender: ACTION, an MPEG Web video technology from Open2u. Download it from http://www.arasmith.com/action.

All this being said, it is still possible to make Shockwave movies that approximate a video experience. They tend to be of short duration, with small frame sizes and only 8-bit

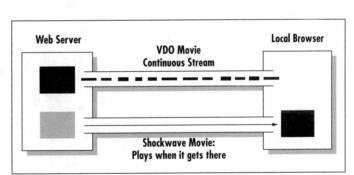

Figure 5.19

The difference between Shockwave and VDOLive.

color, but they can have sound and their own interactive hot spots—just like plain old Director movies.

The following section provides a step-by-step process for creating these movies in Director and getting them onto your Web site. The video frames and audio track in the example are exported from an AVI clip so that the finished shocked movie is as video-like as possible. Most Director movies (as opposed to the QuickTime or AVI movies they play) are more computer-graphics oriented.

Making a Shockwave Movie

Let's start by producing the raw materials:

While VidEdit is not the only tool available for breaking up a movie into serialized bitmaps, it is perhaps the simplest.

1. Choose an AVI clip to make into a shocked movie and open it with the Video for Windows developer tool VIDEDIT.EXE. The movie in Figure 5.20 has a frame size of 120 × 160.

2. Select (for this example) 20 consecutive frames. These frames will constitute the animation sequence in your final shocked movie. Use VidEdit's frame

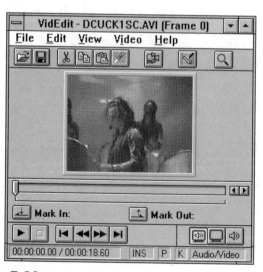

Figure 5.20

Viewing a movie in VidEdit.

Figure 5.21

Selecting frames using Mark In and Mark Out.

scrubber and *Mark In/Mark Out* controls to set the selection.

3. Click *File | Extract* to get to the *Extract File* dialog box. Drop down the *List Files of Type* combo box and select *DIB Sequence*.

4. Select the output directory for the DIB sequence in the *Directories* list box. Enter a base file name for the sequence and click *OK*. If your base file name is, for example, MYSEQ, VidEdit will name the output files MYSEQ00.DIB through MYSEQ19.DIB.

5. To extract the audio track for the sequence, select *Microsoft Waveform* from the *List Files of Type* combo box, enter the file name for the resulting WAV file, choose a target directory, and click *OK*.

You now have everything you need to start building the Director movie.

With our media components assembled, we can now proceed to the Director phase of this production.

MovieStar, a QuickTime plug-in from Intelligence at Large, is another new Web technology worth looking at. Surf to http:// www.beingthere.com.

1. Open Director for Windows (this example uses version 4.0).

2. From the *File* menu, click *Import*.

3. In the *Import File* dialog box, navigate to the directory where the DIBs and the WAV file were stored by VidEdit.

4. Click *Import All*. Director's Cast window should fill up with all the individual DIB files in the directory. You'll probably have to import the WAV file separately.

5. Click the title bar of the Cast window to give it the focus, then choose *Select All* from the *Edit* menu (or type Control + A).

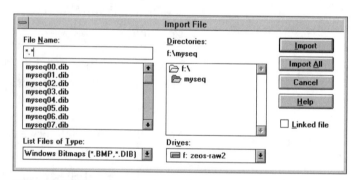

Figure 5.22

Finding your DIB files.

Figure 5.23

Viewing your DIB files in Director's Cast window.

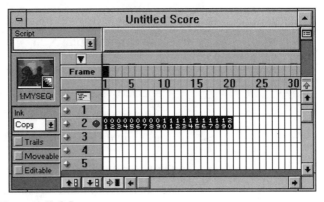

Figure 5.24

Setting up the score.

6. Depress the Alt key while dragging the selected Cast members to the Score (the Alt key makes them line up horizontally).

7. Make sure each movie frame DIB is flush against the upper left corner of the Director stage.

8. Drag the WAV file Cast member to a position in a different Score row but in the same Score column as the first member of the DIB sequence.

9. Duplicate the WAV Cast member 19 times (one less than the total number of DIBs) and arrange the copies

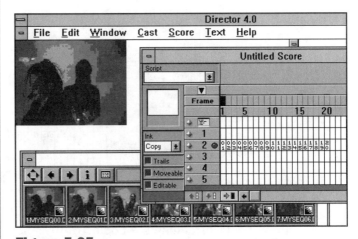

Figure 5.25

Make sure your frames are properly aligned.

Again, detailed instructions on how to plan and execute shocked movie productions can be found on the Macromedia Web site.

horizontally over the rest of the DIB sequence, as shown in Figure 5.26.

10. Play the movie to confirm that it behaves as expected, then save it as a normal DIR movie. This movie should be able to play from start to finish and then stop, with the audio rough-synchronized.

You now have a DIR movie ready to convert with Afterburner. Clearly, this movie is quite short, does not loop, and has no interaction built in. These features could be added quickly by an experienced Director programmer, but would take up too much space to detail here.

Assuming you have downloaded Afterburner from the Macromedia Web site, here's how to use it to process your freshly-made DIR movie:

1. Double click on Afterburner from the File Manager.

2. Navigate to the target DIR file in the file selection dialog box that appears and click *OK*.

3. Choose a target directory and file name in the *Save As* dialog box, then click *OK*. The saved DCR file should be ready for posting on your Web site.

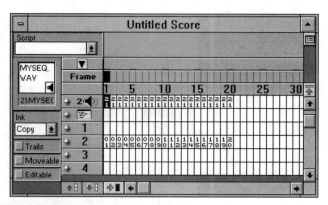

Figure 5.26

Arranging the copies of the audio cast members.

To see a shocked movie in action that was made using the basic approach just described, surf to http://www.downrecs.com/rollo.html.

Rollo

Click here to play this movie

Putting a Shocked Movie on Your Web Site

Chapter 11 covered the basics of embedding media—such as shocked movies—in Web pages, but from a general HTML perspective. Using that model, let's now do it specifically for our freshly converted DCR file, then move it to the server.

1. In your HTML file, add the following lines (note that a GIF is specified as an alternate graphic if the user does not have the Shockwave plug-in for his or her browser):

```
<CENTER>
<H2>MY SHOCKWAVE MOVIE</H2>
<P>
<EMBED src="dcr/shocked.dcr" WIDTH=160
  HEIGHT=120 >
<NOEMBED><IMG src="art/shocked.gif"></NOEMBED>
</CENTER>
```

2. Put the edited HTML file on your Web server.

3. Move the DCR file to your server in the directory indicated by the lines just added to the HTML script—in this case /DCR, right off the home directory for the HTML file. (Remember to upload it as raw data if you are using the Mac Fetch program.)

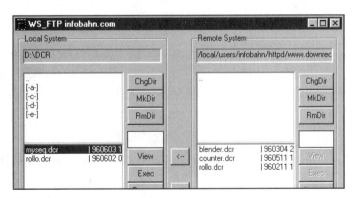

Figure 5.27
Uploading a file to the server.

4. Test the shocked movie live; tweak it until it performs as desired. As noted above, all it will do at this point is play through once and stop. There are certainly lots of sophisticated Shockwave movies deployed across the Web, but most of them look like animations—which they are. Until Director supports embedding of real desktop video in DIR movies, that's the way it will stay.

QuickTime Live

One thing Mac-based Web developers will have noticed is that, so far in this chapter, there has been almost no mention of QuickTime. This is because, strictly speaking, Apple does not yet have a streaming version of that technology.

As of this writing, based on what's available at their various Web sites, here's what Apple does have to offer:

- QuickTime Live—This appears to be coverage of cool events in Hollywood, the multimedia community, and the music business. Many QuickTime (and other media) files are available to download, and often they provide Web addresses for actual "live" coverage of key events.

- QuickTime Conferencing—Most developers know that QTC is still a key technology for Apple. The original application of QTC, however, was the LAN— as opposed to the Web. Both network environments support TCP/IP packets, but time-based media like QuickTime can perform a lot differently on the Web than on a local area network. In general, QTC's focus is *high bandwidth* video conferencing—not the lower world of dial-up 28.8 Web surfing.

According to the readme file for QuickTime TV, you'll need bandwidth equal to or greater than 128 kbps (such as with two-channel ISDN or Ethernet), although it does work with a 28.8 modem (at about one frame per second).

While QuickTime Live is a formidable technology, it is not Apple's response to streaming video solutions in the Windows camp. Apple certainly does have a viable Internet video technology, but it fulfills different customer needs and requires high-end hardware.

- QuickTime TV—If you download the free software at the URL *http://qtc6.quicktime.apple.com/qtc/qtc.live.html*, you can tune in to streams coming from user-specified Web addresses using a stand-alone program or a browser helper (as opposed to clicking on an item in a Web page and *starting* a stream from a server). Some streams to tune into are: tv.apple.com:5001, tv.apple.com:5004, and tv.apple.com:5006.

According to Apple, an advanced QuickTime plug-in for Netscape Navigator is imminent. With the help of some new software called QuickStart, a movie played from a Web page using Netscape 3.0 will start playing when enough of it is received to make playback possible. What happens system-wise after that is unclear, but the plan is clearly to make existing QuickTime movies perform as much as possible like real streaming video.

It is significant that Apple is not yet forcing their multimedia authors to recompress their existing video assets. This is worth noting for two reasons:

- It saves those authors a fair amount of work.

- It keeps the video quality high.

Figure 5.28
QuickTime Live's coverage of the Grammy Awards.

Figure 5.29

A QuickTime Internet broadcast.

If you've seen the video quality of most VDOLive clips, you'll quickly grasp this point. The association of QuickTime with poor image quality is something that Apple definitely does not want to happen.

Key Topics:

- **Using the RealAudio encoder**

- **Setting up the RealAudio Server**

- **Trying out the RealAudio Personal Server**

Web-Based Audio

As we learned in the first wave of the multimedia revolution (the CD-ROM years), the role of sound cannot be overstated. It is critical and complex, and worth all the time and effort producers and software developers can afford to spend on it.

Think of it this way: If a desktop movie clip drops a video frame, no one may ever notice. However, if the audio breaks up, even for a fraction of a second, whatever spell your audience is under will likely be broken immediately. This is especially true for music.

In the current wave of the revolution (the Internet era), Web-based streaming audio debuted well and continues to improve. RealAudio, the present industry leader, is successful because users find it easy to use and of acceptable quality (despite grumblings from some self-appointed technology critics).

RealAudio's competitors (Xing and TrueSpeech, among others) also perform well and provide viable alternatives.

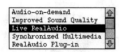

This chapter focuses on RealAudio production techniques for three reasons:

- RealAudio's substantial penetration of the multimedia heartland

- its impressive technical track record

- its overall ease of use

Acquiring the Software

RealAudio is the brainchild of Progressive Networks. All pertinent information about the company, as well as its various products, may be obtained by visiting the Progressive Networks Web site at the address *http://www.realaudio.com*.

As you'll see when you arrive there, several software packages are available. We'll assume you have already installed the RealAudio Player 2.0 software on either your PC or your Mac (or both) and are now ready to move on to the encoding and server side applications.

Progressive Networks claims to have over 4 million copies of its RealAudio Player in circulation. Some supported browsers: Netscape, AIR Mosaic, Cello, EINet, WinWeb, Internet MCI Navigator, Spyglass, Microsoft Internet Explorer, Quarterdeck Mosaic, NetManage WebSurfer, and NetCruiser 2.0.

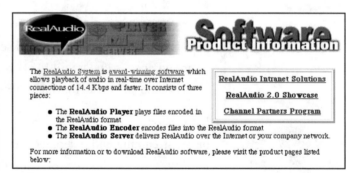

Figure 6.1

The RealAudio site.

Figure 6.2

The RealAudio Player download site.

RealAudio Encoding Tools

Progressive Networks seems to create and distribute tools with desktop producers in mind. As of this writing, free RealAudio encoders are available from their Web site for Windows 95, Windows NT, and the Mac (both 68K and PowerMac).

The Windows RA encoder takes WAVs and several other file types as input. Source file formats for the Mac include AU, AIFF, SND, and SD2 (Sound Designer II). You can easily create audio assets on one platform (like the Mac)

Two extra features are offered by the Mac-side RA encoder:

- *a utility for exporting directly into RA format from SoundEdit*

- *Apple scriptability—for encoding big batches of RA files*

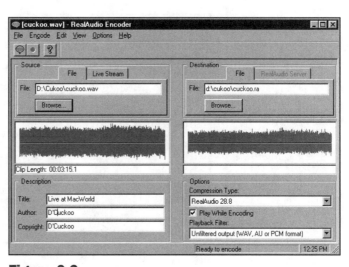

Figure 6.3

The Windows RealAudio Encoder.

and encode them on another (like Windows 95) because most of these formats are industry standards, and tools exist to translate between the different formats.

You can get a detailed production guide at the RA Web site, but let's go step by step through a typical encoding session now. This will provide a basis for concentrating on the more important quality issues that follow. We'll use the Mac encoder, but the Windows product is functionally the same (though a bit more elaborate).

Encoding on the Mac

Note that there are no user calibration controls on either the Mac or the Windows RA encoder. All audio processing (as opposed to compression) must be done prior to using the RA encoder.

Also note that with Netscape 2.0 you can embed RA clips in your HTML documents, so the user can play a stream without bringing up the RA Player. This is covered in detail in Chapter 11.

1. Double click the program item to bring up the RA encoder's main interface (after downloading and running the installer), as shown in Figure 6.4.

2. Click the *Input* button, then select the source file from the pop-up list box, as shown in Figure 6.5.

3. Fill in the *Title, Author, and Copyright* fields with appropriate data, then select your target *Encoder* data stream from the pull-down menu (28.8 or 14.4).

Figure 6.4

The Mac RealAudio Encoder main user interface.

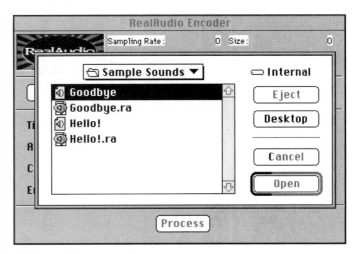

Figure 6.5

Selecting an AIFF source file.

Progressive Networks is wise to distribute the RA encoding tools separately. If the tools were bundled with the retail server software, prospective producers would have a much harder time test driving the technology.

4. Click the *Process* button, then edit the name of the RA output file in the *Save encoded file as:* field, as shown in Figure 6.6.

5. Click the *Save* button. A progress bar will track the encoding time until processing is complete.

6. Close the RA encoder, then click on the newly encoded file to bring it up for inspection and playback

Finished RA files cannot be referenced directly in HTML scripts. Instead, HTML scripts contain references to RAM files, which in turn point to the actual location of the RA files on the server. This is covered in detail in Chapter 11.

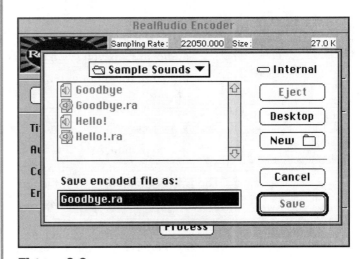

Figure 6.6

Selecting an RA target file.

with the RA player. The quality of the RA file played locally should be the same as when it is streaming (assuming reasonable Internet traffic).

When you think about it, super-small audio files are valuable all by themselves, even without streaming capability. In other words, you could post RA assets for download only and offer, say, a whole musical performance in under 500 KB.

In general, a 28.8 RealAudio file is about 1/10 the size of the WAV file or AIFF file from which it was compressed (assuming the attributes of the WAV or AIFF were 22 KHz/8-bit/mono). 14.4 RA files are even smaller.

Getting the Best Quality

According to the Progressive Networks documentation (and common multimedia sense), the best sounding RealAudio streams are encoded from the highest quality sources, such as DAT tape and audio compact discs.

It's pretty hard to argue with this advice, but it needs to be placed in context. Two key questions are:

- Will your audience know the difference between audio streams you slave over and those which are arguably rougher but require far less production effort?

- How long will those RA files be available to your online audience?

The first issue involves a value judgment, but you'll have to make one at some point. For example, an audio stream like Brian Cooley reading the news on clnet radio (*http://www.cnet.com*) needs the highest production values possible. clnet has clearly made this investment, since the RA

If you're recording live performances, professional caliber equipment is highly recommended, especially the microphones. You might even want to hire some audio engineers to get the best performance possible from the equipment.

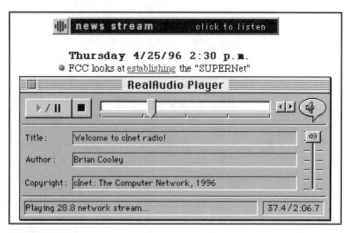

Figure 6.7

The clnet Radio page.

If you have the audio CD of a musical composition you want to encode as an RA file, a useful tool is SmartSound (get it at http://www.sonicdesktop.com). SmartSound will convert an audio CD track to a sound-only QuickTime movie, which can then be converted to an AIFF or WAV file. Because you don't have to capture audio using SmartSound, your source audio tracks should be nearly noise free.

clips sound very much like AM radio. The tight delivery doesn't hurt either, which is enhanced by the mint production.

On the other hand, content that is noisy by nature may sound effectively the same after encoding, regardless of whether the source is a CD or a cassette tape. In fact, trying to clean up such content often has a negative effect.

It's like working with talking heads vs. pans and zooms in the desktop video environment. Content shot specifically

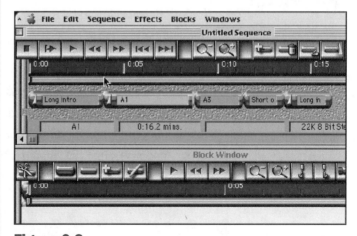

Figure 6.8

The SmartSound user interface.

for encoding with Cinepak can look very much like television—in a quarter screen window. Footage from real life usually compresses less efficiently, but why worry if you do the best you can and your audience likes it?

The second issue raised above also has important implications. If the RA files on your site change frequently, and you are not competing with traditional broadcasters (where production values *would* be important), how do you justify layers of extra production costs for assets that serve limited functions?

Clearly, a lot depends on the capabilities of your production studio. The more processing you can do prior to final RA encoding—for the assets that will truly benefit—the better. But don't sweat it (at least not for a while yet) if you've got great content and only limited facilities.

RealAudio Production Strategies

Presented below is a field-tested guide to producing good quality RA files. The items covered first should be considered mandatory for any RealAudio production/encoding session. Further down the list are things to consider if time and budget permit.

See the section in Chapter 8 on audio hardware if you plan to process your analog audio files on their way to the sound card (as opposed to after they're captured).

Two good Web sites for even more information on this subject are the RA home pages (see the document entitled *Getting the Best RealAudio Sound—http://www. realaudio.com/help/content/audiohints.html*) and the Hyperstand section at the *New Media* magazine site (*http://www.newmedia.com*). Look for the document *Getting Real with RealAudio* by Rudy Trubitt and Tim Tully.

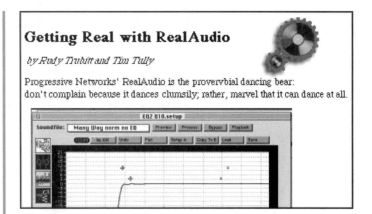

Getting Real with RealAudio

by Rudy Trubitt and Tim Tully

Progressive Networks' RealAudio is the proverbial dancing bear: don't complain because it dances clumsily; rather, marvel that it can dance at all.

Figure 6.9

Some guys who've been there.

Recording the Analog Signal

Keep in mind that the 14.4 version of RealAudio was developed primarily for the delivery of speech, while RA 28.8 is good enough for transmitting many kinds of musical performances. Progressive Networks claims you can get AM radio quality with RA 28.8, but the jury is still out.

1. As mentioned earlier, start with the best quality analog source. This means using the audio CD or DAT version rather than the cassette version (assuming you have a choice).

2. Set all your levels carefully. Make the input volume as high as possible without clipping (going in the red).

3. Unless you're already tweaked, capture the clip several times at different input levels and play it back each time. If possible, look at its wave form with an audio file editor to make sure you're using all available amplitude (but not clipping).

Using a Desktop Audio Editor

1. All audio files submitted to the RA encoder should be 16-bit and have a sampling rate of 22.050 KHz. Up-sampling from existing desktop audio assets with lesser attributes is not necessary, but freshly recorded audio clips should be captured this way.

2. Not all audio editing tools offer normalization, but they should. In general, it's a good idea to normalize any clip you use in a multimedia application, but it should always be the final step in any processing cycle. In other words, don't normalize until you have gated, compressed, and equalized your clip (these procedures are covered below). If possible, only go up to 95 percent of the full normalization range.

3. If noise gating (a.k.a. expansion) is available on your audio editor, and it has a range control, set it initially to around 5 to 10 dB. Process the file at this setting, then keep readjusting it (and reprocessing the file) until you like the results.

4. Assuming your editor supports compression, try various settings from 2:1 to 4:1. This will help cut down on audio artifacting. If you are creating RA 14.4 streams you may want to use slightly more compression than 4:1, but experimentation is recommended. Remember that music will suffer more than speech.

As noted in more detail in Chapter 9, a good professional Windows audio editor is Sound Forge 3.0, from Sonic Foundry. A widely used Mac tool is SoundEdit 16, a Macromedia product.

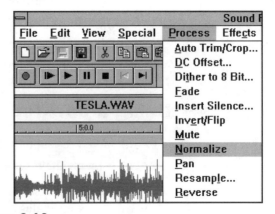

Figure 6.10
Applying normalization with Sound Forge.

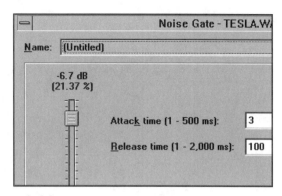

Figure 6.11

Calibrating a noise gate.

5. Most sound editing apps have some type of EQ (equalization) capability. Because the RA encoder tosses out a relatively high percentage of high-end audio data, it is a good idea to boost a clip's midrange. Frequencies from 1.5 KHz to 3.0 KHz are excellent candidates for fattening up, by +2dB to +4dB. Do not boost any frequencies above 4 KHz unless you want to add distortion. Once again, trial and error is king, especially if you have many different kinds of content.

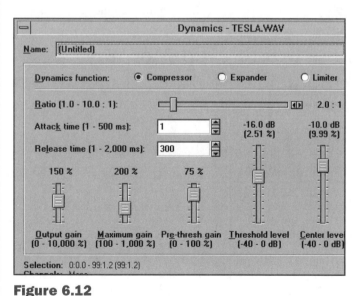

Figure 6.12

Adding compression to the mix.

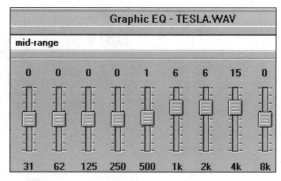

Figure 6.13

Enriching a clip's midrange.

If you're wondering how to put these procedures together in ways that make sense for projects with different quality requirements, Trubitt and Tully (from the New Media/Hyperstand site noted above) offer the following advice:

The Basic Approach

1. Capture the audio clip.

2. Normalize it (at 95%).

3. Submit it to the RA encoder.

A Better Way

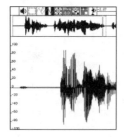

1. Capture the audio clip.

2. Equalize it (as described above).

3. Apply compression (also as above).

4. Normalize it (at 95%).

5. Submit it to the RA encoder.

Walking with the Tall Dogs

1. Capture the audio clip.

2. Equalize it.

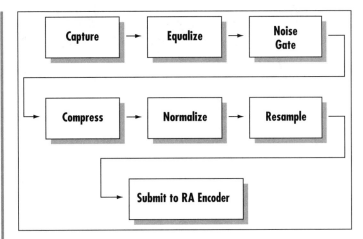

Figure 6.14

A serious processing cycle.

Some microphone tips from Tim Tully:

- *Use the best mic you can afford.*
- *Keep away from subtle noise makers like computer fans, air conditioners, etc.*
- *Keep the mic close to the speaker's mouth, but not too close or you'll get the proximity effect. This can be reduced if your mic has a low-cut switch.*

3. Noise gate it (as described above).

4. Apply compression.

5. Normalize it (at 95%).

6. Change the sampling rate to 8 KHz (not everybody recommends this).

7. Submit it to the RA encoder.

The RealAudio Personal Server

Between the RealAudio Player and the full-blown RealAudio Server lies a product called the RealAudio Personal Server, which delivers up to two simultaneous RealAudio streams across the Web (or over a local area network). Platforms that currently support RA Personal Server are Windows 95, Windows NT, and the Mac.

Progressive Networks will provide you with the means to download and run the Personal Server software after you complete an online questionnaire. The retail product is

Microsoft Windows 95   Mac OS

Supported platforms.

RealAudio Personal Server Beta Application

The RealAudio Personal Server requires Windows 95, Windows NT, or Mac OS 7.5.x.

Please complete and submit this form to apply for a beta copy of the RealAudio Personal Server. All applicable fields and questions MUST be completed for your application to be valid.

Figure 6.15

Applying for the RA Personal Server.

priced at $99, although the online documentation for the product currently refers to it as a beta.

Web site managers curious about RealAudio's general performance characteristics will get an excellent feel for things by acquiring the RA Personal Server and testing their RA-encoded clips through the channels the Personal Server provides. It's nowhere near as potent as the big RA Server, but it's not meant to be.

Setting up the RealAudio Personal Server

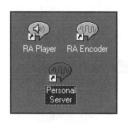

We'll assume you have encoded some RealAudio files in general accordance with the production strategies detailed earlier in this chapter. The next step (short of test driving or purchasing the big RealAudio server) is to install the Personal Server software on your Web server hardware.

As noted above, only Mac and 32-bit Windows versions of the program exist to date. This means, of course, that you can only run Personal Server on a computer that supports one of these operating systems. If your regular Web server is not an Intel-based machine or a Mac, you'll need to use a workaround.

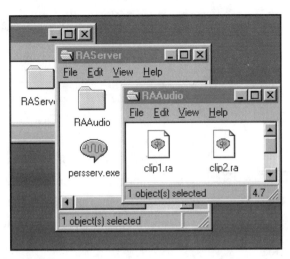

Figure 6.16
RealAudio clips.

One workaround method, detailed below, lets you establish a dial-up connection between your local Personal Server computer and your regular remote WWW server. As long as your Personal Server is running and connected to your remote Web server, users can access your RA clips—provided you tell them the address of your Personal Server.

The instructions that follow will get the Personal Server up and running on your local Windows 95 machine, assuming you are able to make a normal connection to your remote Web server with your browser or an FTP tool.

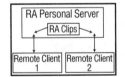

1. Download and install the Windows 95/NT version of the Personal Server.

2. Put the RA files you want to serve in a directory underneath the Personal Server base directory. We'll call the clips to be served CLIP1.RA, CLIP2.RA, and CLIP3.RA.

3. Establish a connection to your Internet service provider.

4. Double click the Personal Server program icon. The program won't come up unless you have an active connection to your Internet service provider.

Note: The default name of the sub-directory used to store Personal Server's RA clips is RAAudio, although you can easily change it by clicking the Setup button.

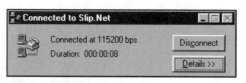

Figure 6.17

Connected to an ISDN line.

Files ready to
stream.

*If your Web server
was running NT, you
could easily config-
ure the Personal
Server to serve RA
clips from your Web
pages (just like the
big RA Server), but
you could only
provide two clips at
a time.*

5. When the main interface of the Personal Server appears, you are ready for business. Keep the address that appears in the *Local Host* text field handy—you'll need to supply it to any prospective client who wants to make a connection.

Let's switch over to the client. Our example is Mac-based, even though it would be functionally the same on a Windows machine. The first thing you'll notice is that there is no Web browser involved here—just the RA player application. Here's how it works:

1. Establish a connection with your ISP.

2. Fire up the Mac RA Player (if you don't have an ISP connection established, this will start one).

3. From the *File* menu, select *Open Location.*

Figure 6.18

The main Personal Server user interface.

Figure 6.19

The RA Player—unconnected.

4. In the *Open Location* dialog box, key in the address supplied to you by the Personal Server administrator (at the machine where the RA clips are stored). Follow this address with a forward slash and the name of the RA file you want to hear. For example:

```
pnm://sf-asc-44-193.dialup.slip.net/clip1.ra
```

5. Wait a moment while CLIP1.RA is buffered, then sit back and enjoy the performance.

Figure 6.20

Opening a RealAudio file.

Figure 6.21

An active RealAudio player.

If you want to hear clips 2 and 3, reinvoke the *Open Location* dialog box and specify each of the clip's file names.

The RealAudio Server

One of the great things about the main RealAudio Server is that you can test drive it prior to making an investment. To order an evaluation copy of the software, go to the Progressive Networks site and fill out their online application form. They'll provide you with an address for downloading the server software, and email you an ID string to insert in the server configuration file.

Another great thing about Progressive Networks is the depth of their Web site. It's worth spending time going through it to see the different uses for RA technology.

While Progressive Networks has made their products quite easy to use, there are many different types of Web servers out there. Fortunately, the installation process tends to be generic—although users with just Mac or Windows experience can hit the wall quickly when trying to set up *any* software on a Unix system (and vice versa).

What follow is a series of steps for installing the RA Server on a Web server running the BSDI operating system (a flavor of Unix). To add an extra layer of perspective, we'll do everything remotely via FTP and Telnet operations.

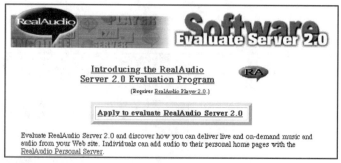

Figure 6.22
The RealAudio Server 2.0 Evaluation Program.

The intent is to give you an idea of the scope of this exercise, not dwell on every platform-specific detail. At some point you will probably need the help of a system administrator—assuming you're not one yourself. The bottom line is, don't waste time if you do hit the wall; server administrators deal with this stuff every day. Here's the breakdown:

1. Download the compressed server software package to your local system. In this case, the file is named BSDI_TAR.Z (already we're into Unix) and is about 7 MB.

2. Download and read the associated documentation at least once.

3. FTP the compressed file to your Web server. Take a minute to think about where it will fit best in your Web server's overall directory structure.

4. Telnet into your Web server.

Here's where you begin to appreciate the compartmentalization of programming for the Web. As suggested in other chapters, a book of Unix commands may come in handy about now.

5. Navigate with your FTP tool to the directory where you deposited the compressed RA Server package.

6. Uncompress the BSDI_TAR.Z file using the Unix *uncompress* command.

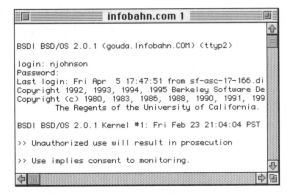

Figure 6.23

Logging on.

An installed RA
Server directory.

*Note that the ID
string may be close
to 80 characters.
Also, you might want
to back up the origi-
nal SERVER.CFG
file first.*

7. Use the Unix *tar* command to decompress the resultant BSDI_TAR file into its executable and ancillary files, which are automatically placed into an embedded directory tree. The RA Server is now essentially set up.

8. FTP the SERVER.CFG file back to your local machine. Using a text editor, carefully cut and paste the ID string (from the Progressive Networks email) into the SERVER.CFG file, then FTP it back to your Web server.

9. Start the RA Server as a Super User (or get the server admin to do this for you). If this doesn't work, definitely get the admin involved. Make sure the RA Server gets restarted whenever the server itself is rebooted.

10. If the RA Server starts successfully, fire up your Web browser, go to your site, and click on some RA files to see if they play, assuming you have put some in your Web pages. (This process is described in Chapter 11.)

11. If you know the RA Server is running, but you're getting error messages, make sure to double check the spelling on all your RealAudio and RAM files, as well as their directory placement, before contacting the administrator.

Key Topics:

- **Working with MIDI files and mods**

- **Using client pull and server push animations**

Get the streaming news here.

Chapter **7**

Other Types of Web-Based Audio/Visual Media

The types of multimedia posted on your Web site can reflect the identity of the site itself. For example, if you offer streaming audio and video, it suggests you appreciate instant gratification. Or, if your content is presented for downloading only, you may be perceived as more of an archivist or a shopkeeper.

Of course, such generalizations don't apply for sites just getting started and experimenting with all their options. Or it may be simply a matter of budgeting, since many of the prominent streaming solutions have license fees attached. Still, once you refine your goals and settle in as a player, the media you traffic in will significantly reflect your online philosophy.

Where is this leading? To the idea that, despite one's best efforts to make Web form and Web content agree, some types of media may never conform to any specific publishing model—even though there is no question of the perceived value such media types bring to your site. It's a harsh world.

The categories of media we're referring to include MIDI sequences, mods, exotic types of animation, and anything else off the main multimedia beat that produces some type of multimedia-*like* experience on your Mac or PC.

Midigate—a Web browser helper application.

As with desktop video movies, most of these "exotic" files will usually be composed of just data. You can, of course, post their respective player applications for users to download—especially if the players are shareware or freeware.

If this sounds like non-sampled media (for lack of a better term) is somehow inferior, it's definitely not. Sophisticated MIDI sequencing applications were in use long before the days of QuickTime, Video for Windows, and even Windows itself (at least as we know it today).

In some cases, you might even find yourself distributing DOS-only software. Just because you get it with a Web browser doesn't mean it runs under Windows!

Actually, MIDI is an official component of the MPC spec. It is also a well-entrenched and supported standard on the Mac, and a kosher QuickTime component type.

Address: http://w3.one.net/~jlambert/music/index.html

File	Size	Song	Note
aomm.zip	41K	Always on my mind. PSB	4 Channel ProTracker MOD
blt.zip	76K	Bizarre Love Triangle. New Order	4 Channel ProTracker MOD; TrueFaith near end.
bltlong.zip	174K	Bizarre Love Triangle. New Order	4 Channel ProTracker MOD; uses stereo effects, samples fr[o] song.
boring.zip	75K	Being Boring (REMIX). PSB	4 Channel ProTracker MOD; chords and bassline.

Figure 7.1

You can get some mint mods at this site.

The problem is, MIDI has not evolved as quickly as the audio and video components of QuickTime and the Microsoft time-based media engines.

Another type of near-multimedia experience, server push, is not based on a site's multimedia assets at all. Instead, it is controlled by a combination of HTML and CGI code, and is highly dependent upon the capabilities of a user's browser and modem.

It is worth remembering that the Web was not really built to accommodate multimedia—especially Microsoft Windows multimedia. If it sometimes feels like things are being retrofitted, they are.

What the user sees is generally a simple animation, such as the sequence at the top of the home page at *http://www.suck.com* (Figure 7.2 shows that page's HTML code). The effect, however, can be just as memorable as a ShockWave movie or a streamed video clip—depending on the skill of the animator.

In fact, some types of dramatic visual effects may be orchestrated with HTML code alone (aside from the obvious ones like blinking text and quickly changing background colors). Letting a browser do as much work as possible is almost always a good strategy.

The balance of this chapter will cover the deployment of non-sampled multimedia data files (such as MIDI sequences). It will also look at how to trigger visual and

```
<!--the suck logo-->
</pre>

</pre>
<p align=center><img src="/suckpush/nph-suckpush.cgi
CK"><h5 align=center><i>"a fish, a barrel, and a
smoking gun'
1996. <i>Updated every weekday.</i></h5>

<!--the suck fish section-->
<table>
```

Figure 7.2
The HTML for the disappearing Suck logo.

audio events on your Web pages without engaging streaming media files.

Working with MIDI Files

People with no fondness for MIDI often have trouble understanding it. Because MIDI sequences cause computers to play music, they are sometimes confused with digital audio files, which is exactly what they are *not*.

QuickTime supports MIDI (sort of).

MIDI is an acronym for Musical Instrument Digital Interface. A MIDI file is an encoded series of instructions that trigger audio events in devices attached to computers. (Macs, of course, can play MIDI sequences using their *internal* audio hardware.)

Until recently, to hear anything that sounded like real music you had to invest a fair amount of money (and time) in external equipment: drum machines, synthesizer modules, keyboards and other input devices for recording MIDI sequences, reverb and EQ boxes, and so forth. All of this hardware was connected with special MIDI cables, and all of the separate audio output had to be mixed together. Some units stored samples of real instruments (like drums), while others used oscillators to generate musical tones on the fly. If you had cash and patience, you could squeeze out some cool sounds.

Now, finally, the MIDI hardware jungle is thinning out. MIDI pros will soon be able to cache the sound samples formerly held in external boxes in PC memory, provided they have a high-end machine with enough RAM or a high-end sound card. All mixing and signal processing will be done digitally by the PC, and the results will be stored on a hard drive (as opposed to a tape cassette).

If you are looking for a good MIDI sequencing product to help you compose your own MIDI music, Cakewalk Home Studio by Twelve Tone Systems (800-234-1171) is an excellent place to start.

So much for the MIDI professionals. In the consumer world, MIDI still sounds like an arcade game soundtrack (i.e., robot music). Not that this is bad, just that you should adjust your expectations if you plan to incorporate MIDI technology into your Web site.

There are two practical ways to get started using MIDI:

- Post MIDI files for download only.

- Designate a MIDI file on your server to be copied to the user's machine and start playing as background music when that user visits a particular page on your site.

Posting MIDI Files for Downloading

1. If you haven't done so already, convert the format of your MIDI files to a .MID extension (a.k.a. General MIDI). Most retail sequencer software allows you to save into this format. If you are using someone else's MIDI files, and are not an experienced MIDI musician, ask the third party composer to do this for you.

2. Create an icon that identifies MIDI files when you anchor them in your HTML scripts (optional).

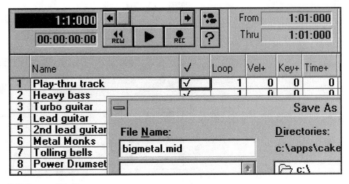

Figure 7.3

A glimpse of Cakewalk's user interface.

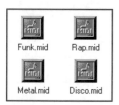

Sample MIDI file icons.

Some PC sound cards come with simple MIDI sequencers as bonus products. These programs are usually good for creating MIDI tunes that will only be played through a PC sound card.

A sample MIDI directory.

3. Edit your HTML code to include references to your MIDI files.

4. Agonize over whether you want to provide a custom MIDI player application. If so, reference it in your HTML script somewhere near your MID file references. In the Internet Explorer for Windows 95, the default player of MID files is the Media Player. In Netscape Navigator 2.0, there is no default MIDI player defined for either platform (Windows or Mac).

5. Decide if you want to give instructions for configuring the custom player as a helper app. This will involve instructing the user on how to change his browser options and set up the player to recognize a new MIDI MIME type. As noted above, this is more of an issue on the Mac (at least for now). All it really does is ensure that MIDI files downloaded later get played automatically.

6. Create a MIDI directory on your server, probably at the same hierarchical level as your digitized video and audio clips (optional).

7. FTP everything over to your server: MIDI files, custom player, and edited HTML files.

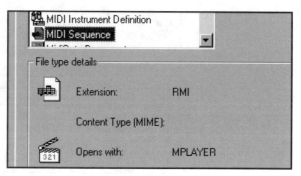

Figure 7.4
Configuring the media player to play MIDI files.

You can just as easily specify a WAV file to work with the *<BGSOUND>* tag on a given page. Some people use long MIDs for their home pages and short WAVs for arriving at minor pages.

Note that, as of this writing, the *<bgsound>* tag only works with the Microsoft Internet Explorer.

HTML code for a WAV file.

8. Do as much testing as your schedule allows. The Internet Explorer should open and play any legal MID file you click on once the file is downloaded. Netscape will probably just ask you where you want to save the file named *filename.MID*.

Playing MIDI Files in the Background

This process is much easier than posting MIDI files for downloading (at least in the Windows world). It also makes for easy previewing of the MIDI files you are offering for downloading, if you are willing to add a few extra pages to your site. Here's what to do:

1. Modify the HTML scripts for all your musical pages to include the tag **<bgsound src="/sounds/ mysound.mid">**. A similar script is shown in Figure 7.5.

2. Copy the MIDI files for your musical pages to the MIDI file directory on your server.

3. Copy the edited HTML scripts for your musical pages to your server.

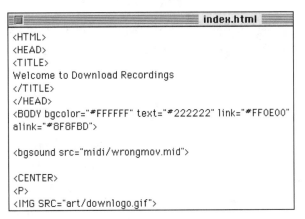

Figure 7.5

The HTML code that will play a MIDI file in the background.

Microsoft Web pages (big surprise) make liberal use of MIDI files playing in the background. Check out http://www. windows95.com.

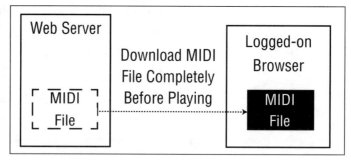

Figure 7.6

The non-streaming nature of MIDI files.

4. Surf to your musical pages with the Internet Explorer to make sure they are truly musical.

5. Remove all background MIDI music as soon as your visitors start complaining. Either that or pay a professional MIDI musician to create something good.

If you're wondering whether any kind of streaming is going on here, the answer is no. MIDI files are generally small enough to download quickly and store in a browser's cache—just like HTML documents and static picture files like GIFs and, to some extent, JPEGs.

Mods

Most people are less informed about mods than they are about MIDI, even though mods (short for modules) evolved as a reaction to MIDI's limitations. A Yahoo search on mods will dredge up plenty of background information on them, as well as links to sites overflowing with mod files.

One informative place to visit right away is http:// home.interlynx.net/ ~rwerner/ether/ modsdir.html.

A mod is a hybrid of a MIDI-like triggering sequence and a bunch of smallish digital audio samples—all stored in a single file. A custom program is needed to play a mod, since the file type is not supported natively by Windows or the Mac. Custom applications are also needed to create and edit mods.

Figure 7.7

A mod editor in action.

Many mods actually sound quite good. Prior to the popularity of the Web, mods were distributed via electronic bulletin boards and a kind of musical underground sprang up around them. Unlike MIDI sequences, mods sound the same wherever you play them. Go get some and see.

A mod is an excellent example of a non-streaming, non-standard multimedia file. They are cool enough to distribute even if you specialize in streaming multimedia, and compact enough to begin playing relatively quickly if you provide a mod player program for your visitors to configure as a helper app.

Assuming a truly streamable version of QuickTime (and QuickTime for Windows) is on the way, it will be interesting to see how MIDI tracks are handled in the new version. Since robust support for MIDI is lacking in the current version of QuickTime, the streamable version may turn out to be a wasted miracle (as far as MIDI is concerned).

To perform this configuration in the Mac 2.0 Netscape Navigator, a user would:

1. Pull up the *Options/General Preferences* dialog box.

2. Click the *Helpers* tab.

3. Click the *New* button.

4. In the *New MIME type* dialog box, key in "audio" for *Mime type* and "x-mod" for *Mime subtype*.

5. Click *Browse* and navigate to (and select) the *mod player app*.

```
alt.binaries.sounds.d
alt.binaries.sounds.erotica
alt.binaries.sounds.midi
alt.binaries.sounds.misc
alt.binaries.sounds.mods
alt.binaries.sounds.mods.d
alt.binaries.sounds.movies
alt.binaries.sounds.music
alt.binaries.sounds.samples.music
```

Meanwhile, back at the usenet.

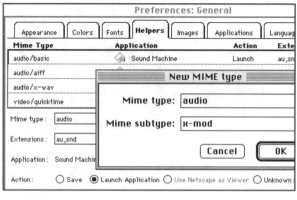

Figure 7.8

Configuring a mod helper app in Netscape.

6. Key in "mod" in the *Extensions* field.

7. Check the *Launch Application* radio button.

Working with Non-Streaming Animation

As mentioned earlier, it is possible to make images move on your Web pages without the benefit of add-on technology, such as streaming video or Java. We'll cover these techniques here as foils for the add-on solutions, and also because they have substantial value in their own right.

The two basic categories that these animation techniques fall into are usually referred to as client pull and server push. The former is the least elegant, but you can do it all with HTML and static images. Server push involves CGI or Perl programming, but can produce more attractive results. Some interesting things can be done with *just* HTML, but they tend to be fairly high on the pure novelty scale.

Reminder: CGI scripts reside on your server and handle things like hit tracking and user input management, as well as server push operations.

Client Pull

Nobody really uses this technique for anything except parlor tricks. Technically speaking, it provides a conceptual

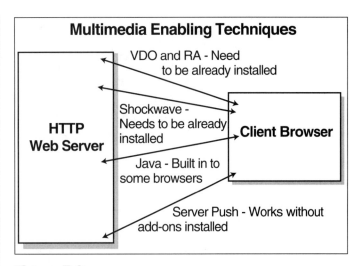

Multimedia Enabling Techniques

VDO and RA - Need to be already installed

Shockwave - Needs to be already installed

HTTP Web Server

Client Browser

Java - Built in to some browsers

Server Push - Works without add-ons installed

Figure 7.9

The beauty of server push.

counterpoint to server push, but that's about the extent of its real usefulness. Plus it's slow, full of flicker, and steals control from the user. It also piles up the user's back-arrow stack. In other words, if you want to return to where you were before the client pull started, you might have to click your browser's back arrow button more than a few times.

Client pull does its magic by utilizing a special HTML tag to jump to another page after a specified interval without receiving user input. The tag is essentially

```
<META HTTP-EQUIV=Refresh CONTENT="X;
URL=http://www.mydomain.com/test/pullme.html">
```

where X is the number of seconds to wait before automatically jumping to the specified URL. You can toggle back and forth between two pages, round robin through a larger series of locations, or even start somewhere and just end up somewhere else, watching what amounts to a flicker-laden slide show along the way.

If you do want to use client pull animation on your site, a model to work from is presented below. We'll assume the

The <META> element can do more than enable client pull operations, but it is new with HTML 2.0 and is not guaranteed to work with older servers. Note that it goes in the <HEAD> section of an HTML document.

```
<HTML>
<HEAD>
<Meta HTTP-EQUIV=Refresh Content="10;
URL=http://www.downrecs.com/
        pullme1.html">
<Title>PullDemo</Title>
</HEAD>
<P>
<img src="pullme1.gif">
<P>
<BODY>
  .
  .
  .
```

Figure 7.10

The heart of a client pull page.

goal is to click on a link in Page A, which will take us to page B. Once at Page B, a client pull will take us to Page C. Another pull on Page C will take us back to Page B, and a cycle will commence.

A good client pull example is available at http://www. earthlink.net/ ~lyndaw/open.html.

1. Construct an HTML document named PageA.html that contains the code in Listing 7.1. Create a pair of complementary graphics (for example, a sad face and a happy face) named sad.gif and happy.gif. Make sure the address of your actual site is used instead of the made-up site name in this example.

2. From your text editor, save PageA.html as PageB.html, and then again as PageC.html. Remove the line **<img src="sad.gif">** and the line containing the phrase, "Click here to break the cycle." from PageA.html.

3. Open PageB.html. Replace the word PageB.html in the **<HEAD>** section with the word PageC.html.

4. Still in PageB.html, replace the line **<img src= "sad.gif">** with **<img src="happy.gif">**.

5. Put all the files (the three HTML documents and the two GIFs) somewhere appropriate on your Web site. Make sure it works before adapting it for anything more ambitious.

Listing 7.1

```
<HTML>
<HEAD><META HTTP-EQUIV=Refresh CONTENT= "3"
   URL=http://www.mydomain.com/test/PageB.html">
<TITLE>Pull Demo</TITLE>
</HEAD>
<P><P><P>
<img src="sad.gif">
<P><P><P>
<BODY>
<a href "http://www.mydomain.com/test/PageA.html">
   Click here to break the cycle </a>
</BODY>
</HTML>
```

Server Push

How fast do the frames play in a server push? That depends on the speed of the user's modem, Internet traffic conditions at the time, and the size of the frames.

Many sites depend on this technique (as opposed to client pull). In fact, it is often considered the only viable alternative for Web page designers who need to provide *some* sort of animation for as many visitors as possible—specifically those without ShockWave (or a similar add-on technology) already installed. The Netscape browser (version 1.1, at least) is also required for server push support.

First, the good news. Depending on the skill of the animator, server push animation can look pretty darn slick, although it does help if the images are small (preferably no more than 10 KB). Unlike client pull, the current page does not change, reload, or even flash.

The problem is, you can't implement server push animation with HTML alone. At some point you have to create a server-based CGI script, which means writing a C/C++ program or some Perl code. Such dependencies makes some Web designers nervous. Many quickly dismiss themselves as mere mortals and have fun pretending to glaze over at the thought of doing actual programming.

This is one of the drawbacks of Web programming still being highly compartmentalized (as we'll discuss later).

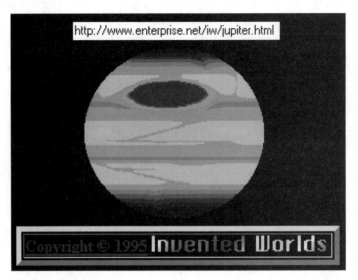
http://www.enterprise.net/iw/jupiter.html

Copyright © 1995 Invented Worlds

Figure 7.11

A cool server push page.

For an experienced C/C++ developer or Perl programmer, writing a CGI program is a relatively easy task—given the specialized knowledge required and (for C ++) a development environment, like Microsoft's Visual C++.

For Web sites without C/C++ or Perl programmers on staff, it simply becomes a business decision:

- Hire a contractor to write CGI scripts made to your specifications, or

- Allocate the time to study Perl or buy and learn an entry-level C compiler so you can modify public domain CGI programs for your particular requirements. After all, if you are working with HTML, you are already writing code.

Following are the generic steps for setting up a server push using a Perl script. As noted earlier, this is a fairly platform-dependent operation so you will likely need the help of your server administrator at some point.

For one of the most lucid and comprehensive explanations of how server push works, surf to http:// bakmes.colorado.edu/ ~bicanic/altindex .html

1. Make sure your Web server has Perl installed by Telneting in and typing "whereis Perl" at the command line. If Perl is on the system, the path to it will be returned. Most Unix systems come with a Perl interpreter.

2. Create the images (GIFs are generally best) you want to animate, such as the series of frames in the left column.

3. Procure a CGI script. For starters, you could use the free one provided at *http://bakmes.colorado.edu/ ~bicanic/altindex.html*. This one requires that you create a separate text file that enumerates the images you want to animate, plus a few other simple details. The code from that file is given in Listing 7.2.

Listing 7.2

```
#! /usr/bin/perl
#
# Nick Bicanic 1995
# nick@never.com
#
# Use this program freely but please attribute it to me.
#
# A really small animation program for gifs alone -
# nothing else.

# The program does take an argument, so it's invoked
# with:
#
# <img src=testing.cgi?file.txt>
# where file.txt is the ASCII file which stores the
# gifs in the order you want them animated.
#
# The only problem is that both this script and the
# gifs and the text have to be in the same directory
#
$|=1;    # Thank you Achille
print "HTTP/1.0 200 Okay\n";
print "Content-Type: multipart/x-mixed-
    replace;boundary=sometext\n";

print "\n--sometext\n";
```

The frames in our server push example.

```
open(imagelist,@ARGV[0]) || die "Cannot open
    @ARGV[0]: $!";
while (<imagelist>) {
        chop $_;
        print "Content-Type: image/gif\n";
        print "\n";
        open (sendgif, $_);
        print (<sendgif>);
        close sendgif;
        print "\n--sometext\n";
}
close(imagelist);
```

4. Edit the HTML document that contains the server push. The syntax for this particular example will be something like:

```
<img source="/cgi-bin/nph-gifs.cgi?mygifs.txt">
```

FTP the CGI script, the edited HTML page, the GIFs, and the ancillary files to your Web server.

5. Perform the configuration tasks on the server side, such as making the CGI script executable by third party Web browsers. You can do this yourself in a Telnet session by executing *chmod 755* on the CGI script, but otherwise ask your server admin for help. Also, not all Web servers handle CGI operations in the same way, which is why you will likely need assistance from the server admin at some point.

Again, these are generic steps, but they do define the scope of implementing a server push on your site.

Multipart GIFs

If you want to read the technical history of the multipart GIF, check out http://home.mcom.com/comprod/products/navigator/version_2.0/gif_animation/index.html

Finally we come to what might please most of the people all of the time (given the acknowledged constraints of the environment): the multipart GIF (also known as GIF89a). If you place a multipart GIF in an HTML script it will play all of its frames when the user loads that page in his or her browser, just as with a normal GIF. On a fast machine this can almost look like passable animation—with no sound.

The only catch is that the user must have a compatible browser, which basically means Netscape Navigator, although we can likely expect this facility from Microsoft Internet Explorer soon. Nothing else is needed (like Java or a CGI script), since the action happens at the browser level.

To make a multipart GIF, you need to use a GIF-specific tool, several of which are available as shareware or freeware on the Web. Two good ones are:

- GIFBuilder (Mac) at *http://iawww.epfl.ch/Staff/Yves. Piguet/clip2gif-home/GifBuilder.html*. Freeware.

- GIF Construction Set (Windows) at *http://www. mindworkshop.com/alchemy/gifcon.html*. Shareware.

Both apps are very easy to use, but we'll use the Mac-based GIFBuilder for the following example:

1. Before you start the program, get your GIFs in a row. If you are animating frames from an existing QuickTime or AVI movie, you can output them from Director or Premiere (or even VidEdit), then convert them to GIFs with Photoshop. Put them all in a separate directory. Better yet, use GIFBuilder's *Convert* Option to convert a QuickTime movie to a finished GIF89a—if you have enough memory.

2. Fire up GIFBuilder. Its main UI will look like the one shown in Figure 7.12 (no GIFs are added to the process list yet).

3. Choose *File|Add Frame*, then navigate to the directory where you stashed the GIFs.

4. Add the GIFs one by one until they're all listed in the main UI.

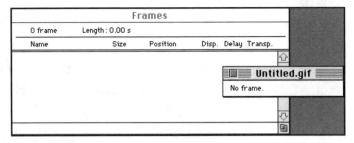

Figure 7.12

GIFBuilder's main user interface.

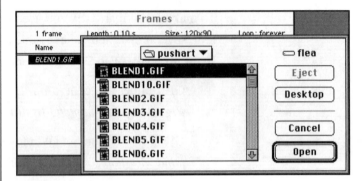

Figure 7.13

Adding GIFs to be processed.

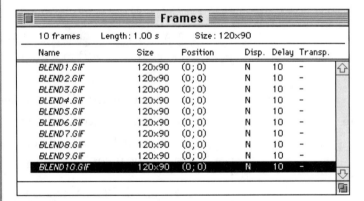

Figure 7.14

GIFs ready to be processed.

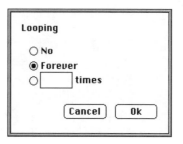

Figure 7.15

Setting the loop factor.

You can also go directly from QuickTime movies to GIFs with a program named SmartDubbing, available at http://www.xs4all.nl/~polder.

5. If you want your animated GIF to loop at showtime, highlight the last GIF in the list and click *Options|Loop*. Enter the number of loops you want in the *Loop* dialog box.

6. Click *File|Save As* and enter a name for the new animated GIF, then save the file.

There are many other options in GIFBuilder's menus worth exploring (if you don't care to read the documentation), but the above instructions will produce something you can put up live right away. To anchor your new GIF89a in an HTML script, just do it the old fashioned way:

```
<IMG WIDTH=120 HEIGHT=90 SRC="images/mygif89a.gif" _
    BORDER=0>
```

That's all there is to it. Read the documentation that comes with the program for performance tips and recommendations.

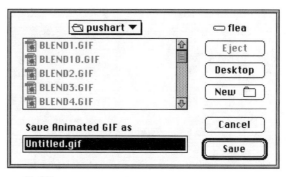

Figure 7.16

Saving the multipart GIF.

Key Topics:

- **Seeing the system as a whole.**

- **Which platform is better for digitizing— Mac or PC?**

- **How good is good enough?**

Chapter **8**

Hardware Tools for Web Media Creation

Two issues surface immediately in any serious discussion of digitizing media for the Web:

- Is the Mac (or PowerMac) still the best platform for this process?

- Is *pretty good* an acceptable quality standard?

The short answer to number one is that media files (especially video) are best digitized on the platform on which they will be played back. Of course, things are never that simple, since Web servers normally stream the same media files to *both* Macs and PCs. A better concern, which this chapter addresses, is whether Windows machines can digitize media that looks good on both PCs *and* Macs.

The second issue is even more provocative and deserving of a detailed discussion, which this chapter also provides. Because new multimedia capture and storage equipment hits the market monthly, I'll concentrate on categories of hardware tools (with appropriate suggestions for proven brand name gear) as opposed to specific products.

Abstract Components

Any multimedia digitizing station can be broken down into four generic hardware components:

- *CPU*—The computer itself. In general, a PC or a Mac.

- *Capture Card*—The device that digitizes the analog video or audio. Mostly needed for video media.

- *Mass Storage Volume*—Usually a large-capacity hard disk. Used for temporary storage of raw digitized media.

- *Media Source*—The deck or camera that the media plays from at capture time, such as a VCR or a DAT player.

Somebody's day job.

With most PC digitizing systems, you can capture better quality clips than you can play back (on other PCs). This is because most capture cards have on-board circuitry for video compression/decompression. PCs without such capture cards must use software-only decompressors, such as Cinepak and Indeo.

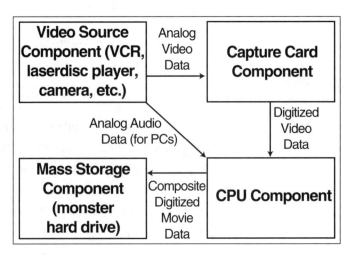

Figure 8.1

Components of a media capture system.

If your Mac or PC system incorporates all of the above components, you should be able to produce good-quality desktop digital media—provided you also have the appropriate capture and post-production software (covered in the next chapter).

The CPU Component

Mac desktop producers have long had the luxury of using video decks that are controllable with single-frame accuracy from the Mac itself. Such pinpoint control is not yet commonplace on Windows machines.

The role of the CPU is to synchronize the activities of the capture card and the mass storage device. In the early days of QuickTime and Video for Windows, many PCs and Macs (such as 386s and sub-Quadras) were unsuitable for production-quality digitizing, but this has changed now that Pentiums and PowerMacs are common and affordable.

When choosing a computer to use with a capture station, there are several important things to keep in mind:

- The more powerful your machine, the more time you will save—especially when compressing your freshly digitized raw files into either streaming or CD-ROM-compatible formats.

- Some high-end Macs have video capture capability built in, which can eliminate the need for a separate video capture card.

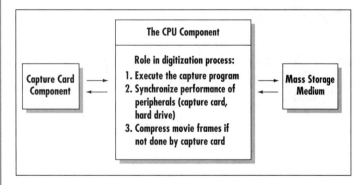

Figure 8.2
The role of the CPU.

On a PC you will need a separate sound card. The Sound Blaster 16 is currently so popular and trustworthy that you can't go wrong with it. If you have the money, however, higher-end cards like the Turtle Beach line are definitely worth looking into.

The Capture Card

This is the component category where most of the controversy (Mac vs. Windows) originates. In fact, there seems to be a perpetual arms race in this product area *regardless* of platform. At the high end are solutions like Data Translation's Media 100 (Mac), which starts at over $10,000, and the DPS Perception (Windows) which currently goes for about $3,500 on the street.

Many people believe that the new all-digital video cameras will eliminate the need for the video capture process. Unfortunately, as any professional video editor will tell you, things are not that simple.

These Cadillac boards are mainly designed for outputting digital video files back to videotape, although CD-ROM producers like them for the excellent quarter-screen QuickTime and AVI files they capture.

For digitizing streaming video files, however, such a high-end card may be overkill. We'll discuss the *good enough* perspective later in this chapter. If you need to go shopping, consider Windows cards such as the Intel Smart

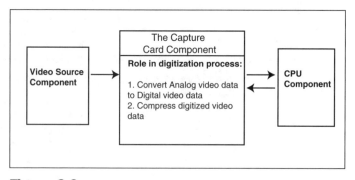

Figure 8.3

The role of the capture card.

Video Recorder Pro (somewhere in the $500 range) or the FAST FPS/60 for around $1,000.

On the Mac side, the Video Spigot and SpigotPower boards from SuperMac, among others, have good reputations at comparable prices.

In the middle of the Mac spectrum are the workhorse cards used by most producers of CD-ROM video clips: the Radius VideoVision Studio and the RasterOps/Truevision Targa line, among others.

A few sources of capture card shoot-out articles: DV (Digital Video), New Media, and Multimedia World. Each of these magazines also has a Web site for additional information.

The things to look for in a capture card are directly related to the card's role in our abstract component scheme. In the old days, you had to spend a lot of money for a card that wouldn't create a bottleneck in your system. Today, the system bus itself is often the bottleneck, at least in non-PCI machines.

The bottom line is, if a board can capture up to quarter-screen images at 15 frames per second with good to excellent 24-bit quality, it is a fine candidate for inclusion in a Web-video digitization station.

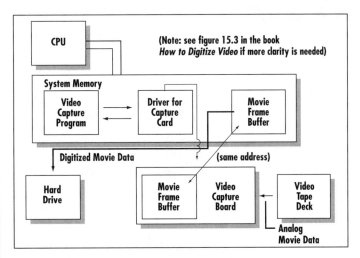

Figure 8.4

How a capture card works.

Mass Storage Devices

The role of the mass storage component in our abstract system is to store data captured and encoded by the digitizer component. Of course, mass storage capacity is also needed for media files *after* they have been compressed, but not nearly as much space is required.

For the most part, we are talking about monster hard disks here—external SCSI drives that start at roughly 1 gigabyte and go up from there. Such devices have suffered drastic price cuts in the last few years, and will get even cheaper as Zip and Jaz drives (fast, high capacity *removable* storage devices) proliferate.

Mail order companies like Club Mac (1-800-CLUB-MAC) can get 1 and 2 GB (and larger) external SCSI hard drives to you overnight by FedEx.

As in CD-ROM production, the basic rule is either your drives are big enough to hold your raw captures or they're not. For Web media, it will be safe to think in 1 GB units (at least for a year or two) at around $300 or so for a 1 GB drive.

As noted above, the data communications protocol that ties almost all mass storage devices together—and to their CPUs—is SCSI (Small Computer Systems Interface). Don't be intimidated by terms like Fast-Wide SCSI,

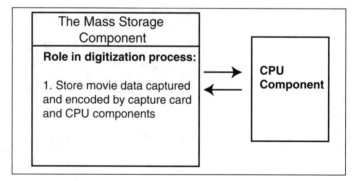

Figure 8.5

The role of the mass storage component.

SCSI-3, or even FireWire (SCSI's hot new competitor). Today's SCSI-2 systems and drives are fine for Web media production.

Note: Under native DOS, SCSI hard drives cannot have partitions larger than roughly one gigabyte. Windows 95 and NT have much greater limits, depending on how they're configured. Macs have essentially a 2 GB limit.

Good news: SCSI has finally been tamed in the DOS and Win95 worlds, regardless of the lingering horror stories. An unbeatable SCSI manager for DOS/Win31 machines is Adaptec's EZ-SCSI (*http://www.adaptec.com*). On the Mac, SCSI has always been academic.

More good news: Most external SCSI hard drives can be reformatted back and forth between Mac and DOS without much trouble. In cross-platform development, this feature can be a real benefit to digital media handlers—provided they know what they are doing. One good strategy is to keep all your external SCSI drives formatted DOS and let your Mac see them with a program like Formatter Five.

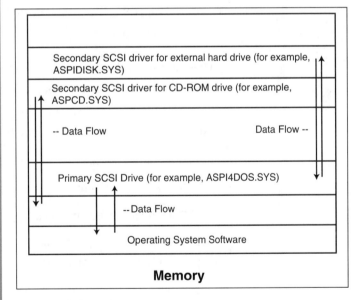

Figure 8.6

How SCSI works in DOS machines.

The Analog Media Source

The analog media source comes in many flavors: VCR, VTR, Camera, DAT Player, LaserDisc Player, and so on. Just as varied are the tape quality standards inherent in these devices: VHS, SHVS, Hi8, and Betacam. Also, don't forget the digital standards: D1, D2, D3, and the newest ingenue, Sony's consumer digital format.

Features to look for in a video camera:

- *Image stabiliza-tion*
- *Manual control of exposure and focus*
- *White balance*
- *Color sensing*
- *Title creation*
- *Lots of zooming levels*
- *Good image resolution*
- *Remote control*

These days, media files included in retail CD-ROM titles are generally captured from Betacam SP (video) and DAT (audio) decks. Web site designers are following suit with the downloadable media they offer, but it remains to be seen whether the lower video and audio quality of streaming assets will tempt them to relax their standards.

Let's face it, there's job security in insisting on Betacam, but those decks are expensive and not getting cheaper. Maybe we'll see a revived interest in fresh, raw content captured on Hi8 cameras and posted quickly on ever-changing Web pages.

There are several excellent books in print that cover the desktop video waterfront (not the least of which is *How to Digitize Video*, published by John Wiley & Sons, Inc., ISBN 0-471-01440-0) and include tips on how to handle

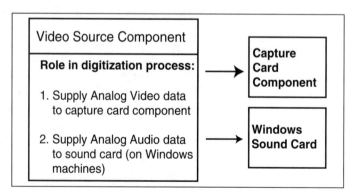

Figure 8.7

The role of the video source component.

tape and equipment—as well as how to shoot video for digitization. This subject is worth a quick summary:

1. Keep your takes short, assuming you know what you want.

2. Edit in the camera (keep unnecessary footage to a minimum).

3. Move in for close-ups before shooting (as opposed to panning and zooming). Full-frame motion doesn't digitize well.

4. Use a tripod whenever possible. Human frailties don't digitize well either.

5. Try to shoot your subjects against static backgrounds.

6. When recording Hi8, never start recording at the beginning of a cartridge. Always go two to three minutes in.

7. Never record at slow tape speeds.

8. Always use headphones when capturing audio with video.

9. Always mic your subjects separately—as opposed to using the camera mic (not doing this just once will make you a believer).

Keep in mind that the caliber of the analog source component has no bearing on the ability of the capture station to physically capture movies—unlike most other components.

Figure 8.8
More than adequate for the job.

Audio Gear

As the maxim goes, much of what you see is what you hear. Multimedia producers are acutely aware of this phenomenon, which is why games like *Myst* are so successful. The same principles are now being applied in the online world.

Compared to video capture cards, there are only a few board-level products dedicated solely to digitizing audio. The ones that do exist are mainly on the Mac side and are typically high-end (such as the Sound Designer II from ProTools), although several sophisticated PC solutions are shipping, such as the Turtle Beach products.

Most sound processing is done to the analog audio signal prior to digitization, and to the captured audio file through software tools, which are covered in the next chapter. If you intend to deliver as full and clean a signal as possible to your audio capture tools, you should consider the following list of equipment:

- *Amplifiers*—Appliances that boost (or lower) the volume of an audio signal. The trick is to do it cleanly, without also boosting the noise level. In a chain of audio gear, this would come right after the source.

It's hard to ignore the fact that many people enjoy working completely on-screen, no matter what they're doing. Digital audio tools are currently so powerful, and streaming audio currently so artificial sounding, that just getting a pretty good analog signal digitized will be enough—at least for a while.

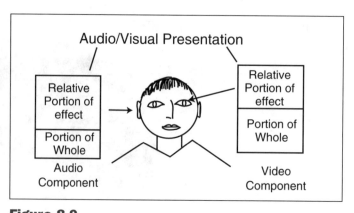

Figure 8.9

The effect of audio vs. video.

Not included in this list, of course, are special effects gear, such as phasing and 3D sound equipment. Such effects will shortly be standard on CD-ROMs. How soon they'll migrate to Web sites is hard to predict.

If you want really great audio, you can add impedence converters, specially shielded cables, and so on. These extras actually do make a difference.

- *Equalizers*—These devices partition the audio spectrum into discrete frequency bands that you can calibrate separately. Good for reducing noise and eliminating unwanted frequencies altogether.

- *Limiters/Compressors/Noise Reducers*—Limiters and compressors keep the high end of an audio signal from distorting, although compressors do it more intelligently. Both are very useful in processing audio about to be digitized. Standard analog noise reducers do just that, reduce noise, but are only useful in all-analog systems.

- *Mixers*—Used for mixing multiple audio sources into a single, well-balanced signal suitable for digitization or delivery to the above equipment. Good for adding background music and ambient sound.

A final word: Professional sound designers insist on using at least some of the gear described above, and you can't argue with them. Most desktop videographers, on

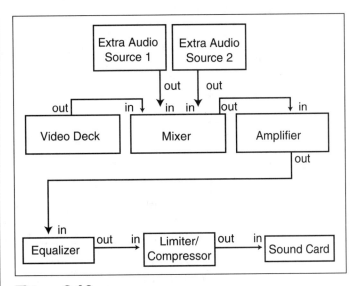

Figure 8.10

Order of FX boxes.

the other hand, carefully calibrate the audio controls in their video capture software and don't look back.

Which Platform Is Better?

As noted at the beginning of this chapter, the above question is almost irrelevant. True, the Mac was the superior digitization machine during the first phase of the multimedia revolution—and may be for a while yet—but it is no longer dominant. In fact, creators of new video technologies (such as VDOLive) have developed for Windows first.

One factor that should help you to determine your favorite platform is how easily you can move your assets to the other platform. Assuming you don't have a LAN, this is often a matter of swapping SCSI hard drives and CD-ROM players.

Generally speaking, Windows programs handle AVI movies (and WAV files) in a consistent and predictable manner, and those files look and sound best when captured under Windows with high-quality equipment. Such equipment is now affordable and readily available.

Consequently, the question becomes how to make movies that look good on Windows *and* the Mac. The answer is not straightforward. Tools do exist for converting from AVI

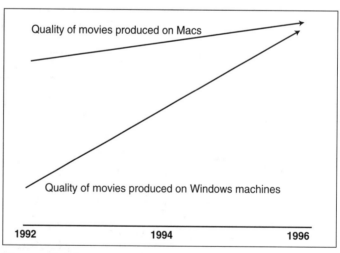

Figure 8.11

Quality/Time lines—Mac vs. Windows.

to QuickTime (and vice versa), but they are imperfect and often require the use of additional tools to finish the job. Also, some problems (like gamma level) can never be fixed for both platforms simultaneously.

How big a problem is it to make cross-platform movies? Not as big as it sounds. Companies developing software that streams video are doing it for Windows now and for the Mac if they can afford it (and can find enough qualified Mac programmers), but they don't seem unduly worried.

In the long run, the most successful players will be those who make a point of being cross-platform developers.

New manufacturers of Windows capture cards keep coming out of the woodwork, while Mac digitizing boards keep coming down in price. With a few minor exceptions, no one seems interested in developing dedicated cross-platform conversion software.

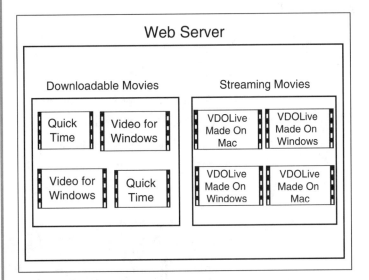

Figure 8.12
Mixed platform files on Web sites.

Producers of Web-based multimedia have better things to worry about than an outdated holy war. Choose your tools, make your investment, and start digitizing.

How Good Is Good Enough?

The way you answer this question says more about your personal ethics than your video aesthetics, but it's important to ask now that movies are starting to look worse instead of better (of course, we're talking about *streaming* movies here). Don't worry, it's essentially rhetorical anyway.

It will be interesting to see if the quality of downloadable media goes up substantially—as a balancing factor to the low quality of streaming media. This could happen as soon as MPEG reaches critical mass.

The big unknown is whether the new streaming software will do such a hatchet job on high-quality raw video that it won't matter whether the raw file was captured from Beta or VHS. The same question applies for audio files—is DAT required?

The safe answer is the standard garbage in/garbage out dogma, but the eye and ear are the truest judges of quality, and so far it's not an easy call. As you experiment with the new compressors, you'll have to judge for yourself, but you might come away with some new aesthetics.

Figure 8.13
A raw frame.

Figure 8.14
A streamed frame.

What are the implications here? Can we all just digitize from VHS and 8mm (for streaming video) and audiocassette tapes (for streaming audio) and forget about it—at least until streaming technology gets to the next quality level? It sort of fits with the general feeling of uncomplicated publishing and actually having fun on the Web.

The CD-ROM industry is filled with video and film industry refugees obsessed with very high quality video and with hardware companies that cater to the high-end, high-quality market. Fortunately for the film buffs, they are getting gratification—in the CD-ROM world. Maybe they'll linger there a while before migrating to the online world.

Final Note: No special gear beyond what is described in this chapter is required for creating streaming media. The real work is done with software tools.

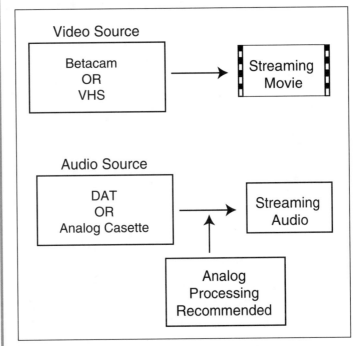

Figure 8.15

Analog preprocessing of audio.

Key Topics:

- **Windows-based applications**

- **Mac-based applications**

Software Tools for Web Media Production

The last chapter discussed Mac and PC *hardware*; this chapter deals with *software* tools for producing Web-based media files. Fortunately, these tools (and their hardware counterparts) have matured tremendously since the early days of QuickTime and Video for Windows.

No longer do you need a bunch of standalone programs to help you on the journey from capture to final compression—although some people still prefer to work that way. For many desktop producers, Adobe Premiere (for both Windows and the Mac) is now sufficient for all of the dirty work involved with digitizing video and audio content.

Still, creating desktop video and other types of multimedia files remains a highly tool-centric process—as opposed to working within a more integrated framework like an office

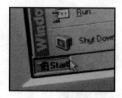

productivity suite or a Windows programming environment. The purpose of this chapter is to pull together a short list of applications for Web media production that have earned the respect of veteran developers.

Please note that this chapter is not meant to contain a definitive collection. In fact, it may seem something of a hodge-podge if you are just getting into desktop media production. Some of the tools that I endorse are heavyweight products from major players (like Adobe). Others are simpler, single-purpose applications from smaller companies. In one or two cases, shareware is recommended.

The approach I've taken in this chapter is to discuss Mac and Windows products separately, and then to organize them generally by function: capture, editing, post-production, special effects, and so on. Software that addresses so-called cross-platform issues also gets special attention, for obvious reasons.

Traditional multimedia authoring software (the kind used for CD-ROM titles) is specifically *not* covered here. Also, products like Macromedia Director and Shockwave are covered in other chapters.

Fortunately, several powerhouse tools, like Adobe Photoshop and Premiere, come in both Mac and PC versions, with nearly identical user interfaces. Adobe has worked hard to keep these products in synch—a great help for cross-platform developers.

Adobe Premiere	Microsoft VidEdit	Microsoft VidCap
Adobe Photoshop		
SoundEdit 16	**Multimedia Producer's Desktop Environment**	Debabelizer
Sound Forge		
Apple MoviePlayer	Movie Shop	Movie Cleaner Pro

Figure 9.1

And these are just the basics.

MacOS

Note: *Working with uncompressed media files that stay huge even after processing (like converting a raw QuickTime file to a raw AVI file) can take its toll simply in file transfer times (not to mention the extra storage space required).*

An important distinction: If you are producing traditional multimedia files for *downloading* from a Web site, all the standard tools and techniques for creating CD-ROM-based video and audio assets still apply—depending, of course, on how many MB of media data you want to force your guests to download. However, if your goal is to produce *streaming* multimedia files, you will only be able to use standard tools up to a point (at least until those tools are upgraded). Somewhere in your production scenario you will have to encode your assets with the new streaming compressors.

In general, these streaming compressors want their source media as rich and raw (compressed) as possible prior to the encoding process. This has several implications, depending

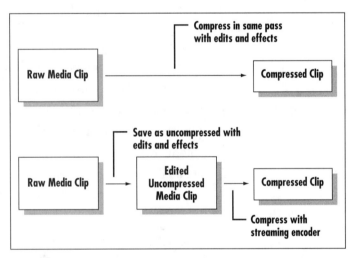

Figure 9.2

Editing streaming media may require an extra step.

on the particular streaming codec (VDOLive, Xing, etc.). We'll get into the specifics for each of these in the appropriate chapters. For now, it is important to realize that (in a bizarre reversal) many of the files you output from, say, Premiere may soon be highly *un*compressed, as opposed to trampled by Cinepak. But don't worry—the streaming compressors will trample them even more.

Microsoft
Windows 95

Windows Software

Windows software for multimedia production has improved the fastest in the last few years (as compared to the Mac and other multimedia software). This is not surprising, given the proliferation and standardization of Video for Windows and QuickTime for Windows in the market and the developer community.

Most experienced developers would just as soon forget the 1.X versions of Adobe Premiere and Photoshop for Windows, and only recently has a stable version of Director for Windows been available for native authoring (yes, in Windows) as part of a reliable, overall production strategy. Not that dependable tools didn't exist in the early days— just that sophistication *and* stability did not usually ship in the same package until well past the 1.0 versions.

Almost all programs that run well under Windows 3.1 will work just fine under Windows 95 and Windows NT. For best results, you should reinstall your programs under Win95 if you upgrade to it from a Win31 system.

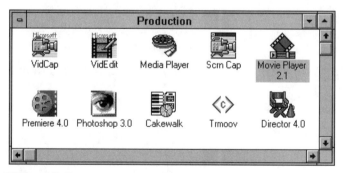

Figure 9.3

Some of the available Windows software.

Adobe Premiere for Windows

Currently at version 4.2, Premiere for Windows is considered adequately stable and provides an almost complete environment for making movies on your PC, including a capture facility. Many capture boards are, in fact, designed to work specifically with Premiere. As of this writing, Adobe has announced support for the VDOLive codec—great news for Web media producers.

If you haven't used it before, Premiere's user interface is intuitive and easy to master, with the same feature set as the 4.2 Mac version. You can import both QuickTime and Video for Windows movies, and output in either format as well. The program is so powerful, in fact, that I cannot do it justice in a single page.

Performance tip: Premiere works even better with Windows 95, especially Premiere version 4.2 (which is 32-bit). On certain big jobs, Premiere for Windows 4.0 can hang when running on Windows 3.1—a problem that seems to go away with the Win95/Premiere 4.2 combination. For more information, contact Adobe at (415) 961-4400.

While Premiere for Windows makes great AVI movies, it is always a good idea to take QuickTime clips made with it back to a Mac for a reality check. In fact, opening those movies with MoviePlayer and doing a Save As from there is an even better idea.

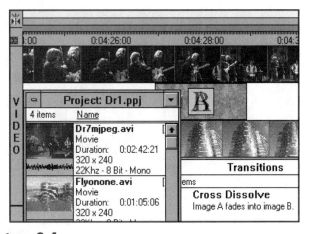

Figure 9.4

The Premiere for Windows user interface.

VidCap   VidEdit

Media Player

Note: Please see the Mac software section for a description of Adobe Photoshop. As noted earlier, however, Photoshop for Windows is a vital part of any Windows media production facility.

VidEdit and VidCap

According to Microsoft, the Windows 3.1 (16-bit) versions of these two complementary programs are as old as the hills. While 32-bit versions do now exist, you can only get them by subscribing to the Microsoft Developer Network (MSDN). Sources for the 16-bit apps include Microsoft's FTP site and the temporarily discontinued JumpStart CD-ROM, also published by Microsoft.

Next to Premiere, VidCap and VidEdit are probably the most widely-used programs for capturing and compressing video under Windows, despite the fact that many Mac developers have never heard of them. Some people prefer these apps just because they don't want to spend $500 or so for Premiere.

Most high-end Windows capture cards include proprietary capture programs as part of the package. If you can make the card work with VidCap instead, you'll likely be less frustrated in the long run—assuming you are making Web or CD-ROM movies and do not need to output to videotape.

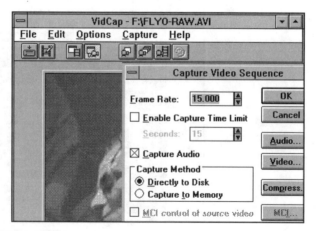

Figure 9.5
The VidCap user interface.

MPC Level 2
Specifications
CPU: 486-25
RAM: 4 MB
Hard drive: 160 MB
Monitor: 640 x 480
SVGA
Sound Card: 16-bit
CD-ROM: 300 kbs

VidEdit (VidCap's companion program) is vastly under-rated. Hidden in VidEdit's modest user interface are facilities for cropping, scaling (re-sizing), creating palettes, replacing audio and video tracks, and importing/exporting other types of multimedia files (like bitmaps and FLC clips). Straight-ahead tasks like compressing raw captures are a snap once you do it a few times.

One thing to remember is that relatively simple apps like VidEdit seem to only work with media files that conform to so-called MPC specifications—such as 8-bit/22.05 KHz/monaural audio attributes. These specs are not meaningful in the Mac environment.

In other words, a streaming media file encoded with, say, 8 KHz audio cannot be loaded or output by VidEdit. You can, however, do most of the other processing (cropping, scaling, frame rate adjustment, etc.) with VidEdit prior to submitting the file to the program that encodes it with the streaming codec.

The VidEdit user interface.

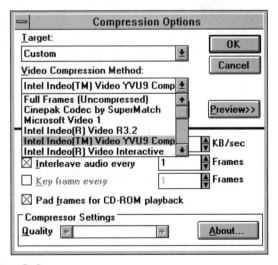

Figure 9.6

VidEdit's compression options.

Media Player

As new types of movies are introduced under Windows 95, clicking on one in a file list is not guaranteed to invoke the standard media player. It all depends on how your system is configured.

Media Player is the quick and dirty way to simply play a Windows multimedia file, such as an AVI movie or a WAV audio clip. On a standard Windows desktop, clicking on an AVI or WAV file in the file manager will invoke Media Player and load that particular clip for playback. If you select the appropriate MCI driver, you can also play back streaming media, such as VDOLive clips, for local testing. Windows 95 has its own (32-bit) version of Media Player.

Sound Forge

What Premiere is to desktop video, Sound Forge is to Windows-based desktop audio. And, as in my capsule description of Premiere, a couple of paragraphs cannot adequately communicate the full extent of Sound Forge's capabilities and power.

Details worth knowing are that Sound Forge can do both sophisticated audio capture and post-processing—including high-quality down-sampling and noise reduction. It can also translate among most known audio file formats

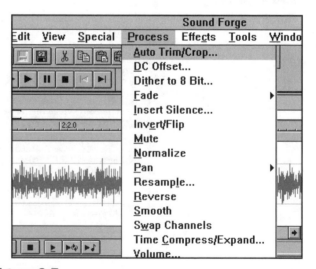

Figure 9.7

The Sound Forge user interface.

(including Mac formats). For more information, contact Sonic Foundry at (608) 256-5555.

Mac Software

For symmetry, I'll organize Mac applications for multi-media production like their Windows counterparts, although I understand that the Mac tool arsenal is much richer and arguably more potent. To reiterate, my goal is not to be exhaustive, but to recommend essential products for producing both traditional and streaming media.

Adobe Premiere

This product originated on the Mac before QuickTime for Windows and Video for Windows were even released—even though Adobe's strategy seems to be to keep the Mac and Windows versions in numerical synch (currently v4.2).

If you are a professional developer, you need this solution for both CD-ROM and streaming multimedia production. As on the Windows side, high-end Mac capture boards—

Custom tools for doing interesting things with Quick-Time movies come from many places, including the AppleLink archives, CompuServe (for example, GO MACMEDIA) and Apple's own developer subscription service.

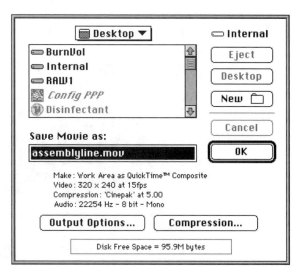

Figure 9.8

Premiere's Make Movie dialog box.

Adobe

and their proprietary software—are now being specifically manufactured to work within Premiere's user interface.

Technical note: While Premiere for Windows can import and output both QuickTime and Video for Windows files, the Mac version only deals with QuickTime files (although it will flatten them for Windows). For more information, contact Adobe at (415) 961-4400.

Adobe Photoshop

Photoshop can be hard to learn for newcomers, even more so than Premiere. The rewards are great, however, once you get good at it. Probably the best way to get started is to buy one of the many Photoshop books available on the market.

Like Premiere, Photoshop is the reigning heavyweight in its field. Nearly any still-image file that will decorate a Web page or be imported into a Premiere movie project can be processed with confidence in Photoshop, using either the Mac or Windows version.

Photoshop is such a powerful program, in fact, that it can seem overwhelming at first. Once you get the hang of it, however, you'll get productive fast.

MoviePlayer and ConvertToMovie

MoviePlayer and ConvertToMovie are the simple movie-playing and editing apps associated with the run time

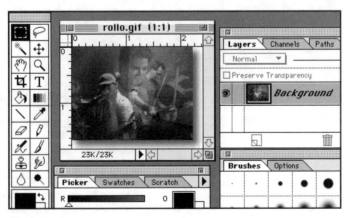

Figure 9.9
Part of Photoshop's user interface.

MoviePlayer provides the best way to ensure that a QuickTime movie will play on a Windows machine. Do a Save As on the movie, and then check the boxes as shown in Figure 9.10.

A dialog box in ConvertToMovie.

version of QuickTime for the Mac. They are free, but you generally have to procure them online or from a friend.

Clicking on a movie file in a Finder window will usually invoke MoviePlayer (if the movie is a MoviePlayer document according to its file type and creator tags). With the 2.0 (and higher) version, you can obtain detailed information about the properties of a QuickTime clip; cut, copy, and paste frames; add and remove audio and video tracks; and save the clip for playback on the Microsoft Windows desktop.

ConvertToMovie is one of the least-complicated ways to recompress a QuickTime clip, and can also be used for cropping, scaling, palette creation, and a few other tasks (like VidEdit on the Windows side). Unfortunately, ConvertToMovie is somewhat useless for anyone who uses Premiere on a regular basis.

MovieShop vs. Movie Cleaner Pro

In the first golden era of QuickTime, not everybody had Premiere. Production often took the form of capture with

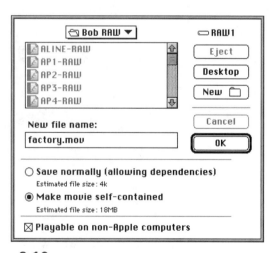

Figure 9.10

Flattening with MoviePlayer.

The power of
MovieShop.

*Like MovieShop,
Movie Cleaner Pro
has a very useful
batch processor—
just right for com-
pressing a folder full
of movies overnight.*

MovieRecorder (now retired), rough edit with MoviePlayer, and final compression with a third party app (written by George Cossey) called MovieShop.

Apple has alternately supported and downplayed MovieShop, but it remains a warhorse of the desktop video industry, especially for quarter-screen (and smaller) QuickTime clips. In many producers' opinion, the best version is 1.14, if you can find a copy. A guide to using it effectively can be found in the book *How to Digitize Video*, ISBN: 0-471-01440-0.

Interestingly enough, and in spite of the long shadow cast by Premiere, a possibly worthy successor to MovieShop has appeared on the scene: Movie Cleaner Pro, developed by Terran Interactive. This dedicated application has some advanced features that give it at least a temporary edge over similar features in Premiere, including high-quality smooth-ing, gamma filters, and the ability to have a guaranteed high-rez last frame (great for movie credits). For more information call Terran Interactive at (408) 278-9026.

Notably missing in this chapter is a discussion of special effects software, such as morphing tools. Many good ones

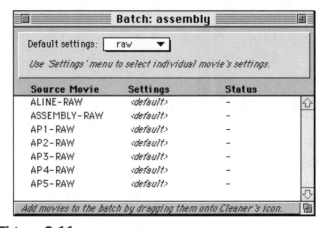

Figure 9.11

Batch encoding with Movie Cleaner Pro.

do exist, although they are not necessarily key elements in day-to-day production environments. Most multimedia trade publications run frequent features devoted to this class of software.

SoundEdit 16

Macromedia's SoundEdit 16 is an audio file editor of the same class as the Windows app Sound Forge. One of its more handy features is the ability to open a movie file and just work on its soundtrack, as opposed to stripping off the soundtrack beforehand.

All the essential functionality is there: down-sampling, normalization, EQ, noise reduction, and so on. All of the popular file formats are supported for importing and outputting. More sophisticated (and more expensive) Mac sound tools are available, but this is the one to start with. For more information call Macromedia at (415) 252-2000.

Other Useful Mac Production Tools

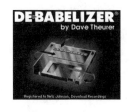

The following tools are also highly recommended:

- *DeBabelizer*—The Swiss Army Knife of bitmapped graphics converters, especially for batch operations.

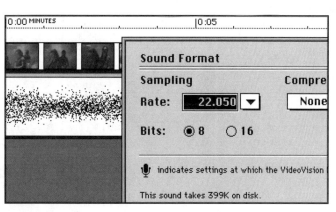

Figure 9.12

Part of SoundEdit 16's user interface.

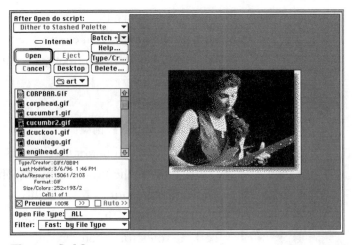

Figure 9.13
DeBabelizer rules!

Developers swear by this program. Ignore it at your own risk. We need one for Windows. For more information call Equilibrium Technologies at (415) 332-4343.

- *After Effects*—Premiere on steroids, and at a commensurate price. Sworn *at* by people without the patience to learn its initially obtuse user interface. Broadcast pros who know how to get great results from it swear *by* it. For more information call Adobe at (206) 470-7000.

- *GrabGuy*—Considered old news by modern desktop producers, this program controls a high-end video deck to make multiple passes over a tape, digitizing frames at very high quality—as opposed to making a single pass and capturing to motion JPEG. Hard to find these days.

Note: When converting from AVI to QuickTime, or vice versa, you'll get the best overall results by doing the conversion with uncompressed files, then compressing on the target side after the conversion.

Cross-Platform Production Software

If you need to convert from QuickTime to AVI, or vice versa, you can see why I said earlier that this is a tool-centric world. While Premiere for Windows certainly has this capability, the problem is that it wants to recompress the file as well as change its file format.

A proven Windows program that converts without recompression is TRMOOV.EXE, available at the Web site *http://www.downrecs.com*. On the Mac side, there is a pair of Microsoft apps (one for each conversion direction) that can be extracted from the file QTAVI.ZIP in the CompuServe forum WINMM, Library 4 (GO WINMM).

TRMOOV is quite useful for converting Cinepak encoded clips (and other movies compressed with codecs supported by the source *and* target platforms). The Mac apps—VFW Converter and AVI to QuickTime Utility—are indispensable for developers capturing on the Mac but needing to produce streaming media for a Windows-only solution, such as the current version of VDOLive.

As you upgrade your Windows or Mac (or cross-platform) studio to accommodate the demands of streaming asset

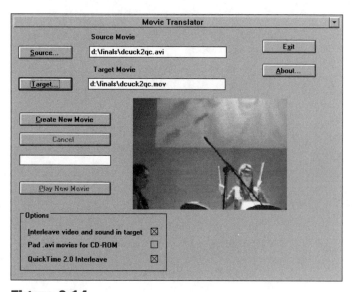

Figure 9.14
The main TRMOOV dialog box.

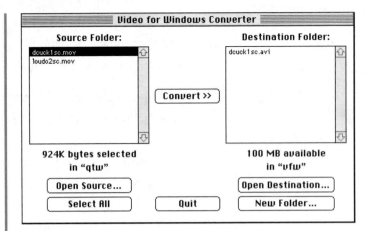

Figure 9.15

The VfW Converter user interface.

preparation, you will likely find more and better applications that will save you time and effort. The ones presented in this chapter have made their mark in the first wave of new media production. Many more are sure to follow.

An overview of the programming issues involved in managing multimedia on a Web site.

Key Topics:

- **Differences between Web and CD-ROM software development**

- **Programming for streaming vs. download-only environments**

The VDOLive player.

Chapter 10

Programming for Web-Based Media

Developing software for delivery of Web-based media requires skill in several areas of programming. Familiarity with multiple languages and various operating system command sets is usually essential also, as is knowledge of different *modes* of programming. This applies for both streaming and non-streaming media, and for both Macs and PCs.

In general, computer programming for the Internet as a whole remains highly compartmentalized (which is why experience with several programming modes is important). This is especially true for Web sites that stream multimedia files or offer them for download.

Let's put things in context: use your browser to view the HTML source code for a random Web page. The complexity of this HTML code does not suggest the programming expertise needed to integrate it (and its dependent media files) into a Web server environment.

Sooner or later you will need to Telnet to a Unix server. Without some knowledge of Unix commands, you'll have a hard time doing anything productive. A good reference is Unix Commands by Example (cover shown above). ISBN: 0-13-103953-9

Note that we include here such diverse programming activities as Java development in C++, FTP, operations and Telneting to servers with Unix commands—as well as basic HTML scripting. While these activities may be diverse, each qualifies as a form of programming.

As a result of all this compartmentalization, programmers new to the World Wide Web are generally unprepared for soup-to-nuts Web site development (and maintenance). Fortunately, the additional programming skills are not hard to acquire. And, if you work on just a single part of a large Web venture, you may be able to get by with just one development language.

```java
import java.awt.*;
import java.applet.*;

public class MyGraphicsApplet extends Applet
{
    Image image;
    public void init( ) {
        image = getImage( gatDocumentBase( ),
            "images/image42.gif");
    }
    public void paint( Graphics g) {
        Rectangle rect = bounds( );
        g.drawImage( image, 0, 0, rect.width,
```

Figure 10.1

Some Java code.

```
#VRML V1.0 ascii

DEF BackgroundColor Info {
    string "0.9 0.5 0.5"}
Perspective Camera {
    position 0 -70 -290
    orientation 0 1 0 3.14
    focalDistance 5
    heightAngle 0.785398}
Rotation {
    rotation 1 0 0 1.5705   #SFRotation
PointLight {
```

Figure 10.2

Some VRML code.

However, if you engineer a whole project yourself or integrate the work of others, you risk becoming a generalist. Experiencing this mixed blessing as a CD-ROM developer is bad enough—going through it again as a Web programmer can cause even greater ambivalence!

Generalists Rule

The good news is, such generalism has become highly marketable. For example, plenty of Mac people still don't know (or care) how to partition DOS hard drives. On the other hand, most DOS developers have yet to use the superior Mac QuickTime tools. Solving problems in both camps is key when creating cross-platform Web media.

Even more important, most professional Web page designers (HTML coders) will continue to need the help of C++ programmers and system integrators to get their Web sites into stable orbits on the Internet—at least until

Generalists like to visualize. Maintaining a media organizational chart, either hanging on your wall or electronically, will help you keep it all in your head.

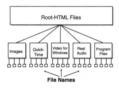

Organizing your Web media files.

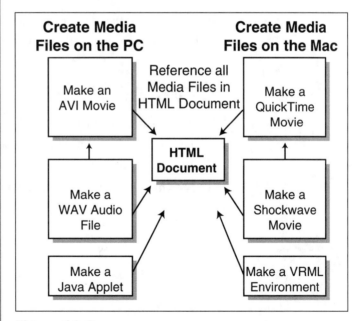

Figure 10.3

Web site production chores.

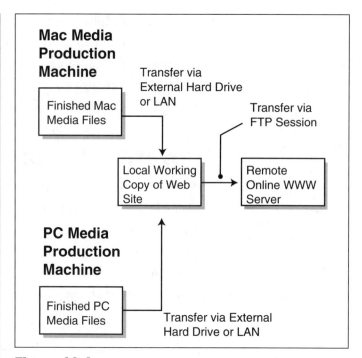

Figure 10.4
Moving Web media files around.

they acquire all the compartmentalized knowledge and skills necessary to do it themselves.

Crucial Skills

To launch and maintain any sophisticated or commercially viable Web site, you will need to work confidently in at least the following languages and environments (or be ready to hire other programmers who can fill in the gaps):

- HTML

- C and C++ (for CGI scripts, Java applets, etc.)

- Visual Basic Script/JavaScript

- VRML

- Windows, Macintosh, and Unix OS commands

The wide range of skills needed for competent Web site construction contrasts with the smaller knowledge base necessary for professional CD-ROM production. Remember that we are not talking about vertical knowledge in a particular software development area, but rather horizontal experience across multiple programming environments.

In the CD-ROM world, assuming you are the developer in charge, your tool kit can easily contain either an authoring language (such as Macromedia Director) or proficiency in an integrated programming environment (such as Microsoft Visual C++) or both. Experience in burning CD-ROMs also tends to make customers happy, as does the ability to write, say, an installation program.

Parallel Worlds

In Web site development, sophisticated HTML scripting is roughly analogous to authoring with Director for CD-ROM production. Both programming environments provide ways to create consumer goods suitable for delivery on personal computer desktops.

It's a fact: Whether spent in Web or CD-ROM development, many of a programmer's otherwise productive hours can be spent just keeping track of all the media files.

```
<BODY bgcolor="#FFFFF"texts="#22222"links="#FF0E00"li
alink="8F8FBD">
<CENTER>
<IMG WIDTH=470 HEIGHT+101 SRC="art/musihead.gif"BORDE
<H@>Life in A Blender</H2><P>
<NOEMBED><IMG src+"art/blender.gif></NOEMBED>
<EMBED WIDTH=160HEIGHT=140 src="dcr/blender.dcr">
</CENTER><HR>
<H2>QuickTime video clips <FONT SIZE=3>(10- TO 15-sec
exerpts)</FONT></H2>
<P><DD><A href="qtw/blender.mov">Daddy Gets Lost</A>,
QuickTime movie<P><HR>
<H2>Full-length RealAudio clips<H2>
<DD><A HREF=ra/Imancake.ram>Little man Cake</A><BR>
```

Figure 10.5

HTML spaghetti with media sauce.

For more control, Web page technicians can use lower-level languages for dealing with CGI script requirements and building Java applets. Similarly, CD-ROM developers often use C++ to build Xobjects to work with Director applications.

Unfortunately, the similarities end here. While you can essentially author and test a CD-ROM on a single computer (strict quality assurance issues aside), the programming model for day-to-day Web site development involves substantially more equipment. Also, as noted above, a much greater *breadth* (as opposed to depth) of experience is required on the part of the programming team.

No one's saying Director and Visual Basic programming is easy—just that their environments are more self-contained.

Would You Like Fries with That?

Here's an example: A developer adds notation for a streaming movie to a Web page text file using a word processor. Some more-complex HTML code is also needed to display a static image in case someone's browser can't recognize imbedded multimedia files. Finally, a tag is added for a downloadable QuickTime movie several megabytes in size, for which the streaming movie acts as a trailer.

To download the QuickTime movie, a user must first enter a password in a corresponding text field. The entered password is processed and approved (or not) by a program residing in the server's CGI-BIN directory before the user can start the download.

Another literary reference: Teach Yourself CGI Programming with Perl in a Week—ISBN: 1-57521-009-6.

Because this is a proprietary Web page, the developer chose to write the CGI program from scratch in C (hardly rocket science but a potential problem for non-C programmers). Many Web designers still contract this task out or design around it.

Not only did the developer write the program, he or she actually had to *test* it (probably repeatedly). At the very

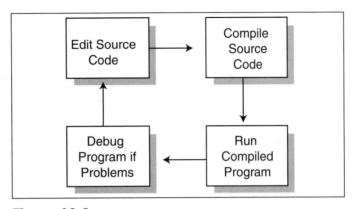

Figure 10.6

The standard software development cycle.

least, this involved substantial time and effort FTPing files to the server and possibly changing the file attributes with a Telnet program. If you don't have the patience for the standard edit-compile-test-debug cycle required in C++ programming, you might want to stick to HTML coding.

Each *individual* task mentioned above is not especially daunting and can be undertaken and mastered in turn. However, even multimedia programmers are not automatically equipped to handle the complete range of tasks specified (and implied) in the scenario above.

Where the Action Is

A good way to organize your hardware is to start with three basic machines:

- *Multimedia production*
- *Web programming and testing*
- *Server (if your server is local)*

The first part of this chapter focused on clarifying the general subject of programming for the Web. Still, despite the many facets of Web development, a basic question remains: How do I get my multimedia files attached to, imbedded in, or referenced by my Web pages to make my content available for consumption by visitors to my Web site?

To keep things organized, we'll answer this question in several phases. First, it depends on whether you want to stream your media or just offer the files for conventional downloading. Basic strategies for each approach are presented

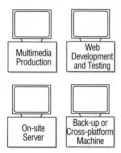

below. Advanced coverage is provided in the next several chapters.

Note that offering streaming media generally requires the installation of specialized software on your server. If your server is a Unix machine and you are a Windows or a Mac programmer, you will quickly see how truly compartmentalized things can get. In the scenarios that follow, this point will hit home often.

Programming Overview: Downloadable Media

Coding Web pages for visitor downloads only seems easy. The HTML part is straightforward enough, but the real grind is in making sure it all works. Also, some page layout time is needed so that your visitors are clear on what they're about to download, how big the thing is—and if they have time to get a cup of coffee while the download happens.

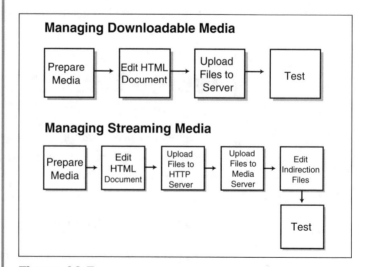

Figure 10.7

Streaming media management: new challenges.

Here's a common procedure:

1. Edit your HTML document to include a reference to a media file, say a QuickTime movie.

2. If you have your movie ready to go, and you are working on a Mac, fire up Fetch (the shareware FTP tool) and open a connection to your server—assuming it is remotely located.

The Fetch user interface.

3. Move the media file to your server, generally in a movie folder one level below the root folder for your HTML documents.

4. Deposit the edited HTML document into the server.

5. Close Fetch and invoke your browser. Surf to your site and click the reference to the movie. Wait to see if things go smoothly.

6. Repeat steps 1 through 5 if you are dissatisfied with the process, which happens more often than not.

On the Windows side, a solid FTP tool for transferring media files is WS_FTP.

If your Web pages already contain static art, and you are used to FTPing those art files to the server yourself, the procedure outlined above will be academic. If you haven't communicated directly with your server yet, you should get ready for a serious learning experience.

One you have such server-side maintenance down cold, you can concentrate on fine-tuning the media references back in your HTML documents. For instance, some Web page designers like to make hot spots out of frames from their movies. Others like to offer both QuickTime and Video for Windows versions of the same clip, as shown in Figure 10.8. As usual, overkill is in the mind of the beholder.

Figure 10.8

A site offering both QuickTime and AVI movies.

Programming Overview: Streaming Media

This is where things get interesting. In fact, the differences between Web sites that stream media and those that don't are often matters of budget as much as available programming expertise. Streaming technologies like RealAudio and VDOLive cost significant money to license. Fortunately, there are less-expensive alternatives like ShockWave, Java, and VRML, but they do not do true media streaming.

Here's the overview:

1. Prepare your media files. Third party solutions like VDOLive and RealAudio normally provide processing tools to re-encode AVI and WAV files into their respective third party formats. Unlike with QuickTime and Video for Windows, these preparation techniques are not yet fully cut and dried.

2. Edit your HTML documents to accommodate all your media types. HTML scripting for VRML and

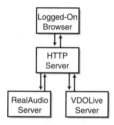

Streaming media can be spread across multiple servers.

Java objects will take many HTML authors into deep water right away, never mind the lower level coding for the VRML and Java objects themselves.

3. If you haven't already done so, prepare your server by creating the ancillary files required to direct visitor requests for media to the server where the media is actually stored—not necessarily the same server that holds the HTML file. This assumes you have already installed the streaming software engine.

4. Start testing. If you don't have your server in the same room, you may be messed up before you even get started, at least when you first install any new streaming software. Once your server is properly configured, you should be able to add new media and do limited maintenance via Telnet sessions, but don't rely on this.

5. When things get hairy, try designing around the problem as opposed to getting too wrapped up in the standard debugging process. These tools and technologies are still too new for there to be only one way to do things.

A generic Telnet session.

Figure 10.9

Shockwave in action.

Of course, general performance will always be an issue.
As a Web programmer, you can legitimately blame the
companies that develop the software that does the actual
streaming, but you will still be responsible for some
things—many of them downright subjective. At least
with HTML coding you probably won't have to deal with
outright crashes.

Chapter

11

Key Topics:

- **Invoking helper applications for media playback**

- **Embedding media references for playback using plug-ins**

- **Scripting Shockwave and VRML references**

Adding Media References to HTML Scripts

One of HTML's key features is its extensibility. Web browser software companies (such as Netscape) benefit from this extensibility in at least two important ways:

- Such companies can distribute new browser products without worrying too much about new ad hoc data types referenced in standard HTML scripts.

- More importantly, a browser manufacturer may create proprietary HTML reference tags so that third party developers can add increased functionality (and thus value) to the Web sites they work on—assuming the site visitors use that company's browser.

If new data types and browser capabilities become de facto standards (and other browser companies decide to support them), these proprietary conventions usually get integrated into new versions of the official HTML specification. After that, everybody benefits.

The catch, of course, is that only Company A's browser can handle Company A's HTML extensions until competing browsers are either specifically retrofitted or are generally upgraded to conform to a new HTML spec (assuming the new spec has Company A's extensions). Netscape is famous for creating its own HTML extensions, which are usually very useful to the Netscape faithful.

Click here to play this movie

In general, HTML extensions allow for new types of Web page formatting, such as tabular layout and online forms which process user data input. They also make possible the presentation of new kinds of embedded objects—such as multimedia files.

The current version of the official HTML spec is 3.0, which will soon be incorporated into all major Web browsers and includes many of the 2.0 extensions. As most multimedia veterans know, diverging standards are both the bane and the fuel of the industry.

This chapter explains how to add media references to HTML scripts. The goal is to make it easy for a user to click on a Web page hot spot, then immediately consume a media clip (either as a stream or as a download-first file). We'll also look at HTML's relationship to Shockwave and VRML (Virtual Reality Modeling Language).

A media reference can be added to an HTML document in two fundamental ways:

- As part of an anchor tag, such as

  ```
  <A HREF=".../VDOFILES/myclip1.vdo">
  ```

- As an embedded file using HTML's **<EMBED>** tag.

In the first case, a helper application will play the specified media clip—myclip1.vdo—as soon as it starts streaming into the browser from the Web server (assuming the helper app is properly installed). In this example, the helper is the VDOLive standalone player.

In the embedding case, the clip will usually play on the face of the Web page via a browser plug-in (as opposed to a helper app), assuming the browser recognizes the **<EMBED>** tag. If the browser recognizes the **<EMBED>** tag, custom controls should appear on the screen to regulate its behavior. The **<EMBED>** tag was first supported by the Netscape 2.0 extensions.

The two cases above obviously refer to streaming media. For download-only clips, the syntax is basically the same as in the first model, but the helper app plays the clip after it is downloaded. A good example is a standard AVI clip that gets downloaded first, then is automatically played by the Windows Media player.

Referencing RealAudio Clips in HTML Scripts

Let's put things in context. As demonstrated in Chapter 6, streaming audio files compressed with the RA Encoder are immediately ready for uploading to a Web server and referencing in an HTML script—although not *directly*, as you'll see in a minute. Since the standard file extension for such clips is .RA, we'll refer to them as RA files from now on.

If you plan to serve RA files from your own Web site, you'll need to have the RA Server or Personal Server installed and correctly configured on your Web server computer. You'll also need to have your RA files on the Web server, in a place where the RA Server software can access them at showtime.

Finally, you'll need to create some helper filers, which need the extension .RPM or .RAM, depending on whether

Once the RA Server software is installed on the server, it is generally referred to as the PN Server.

they'll be imbedded or played with the RA standalone player (we'll call them RPM and RAM files, naturally).

These RAM and RPM files are what actually get included in your HTML script. They provide the geographic glue between the PN Server and your RA files. In fact, that's all they do. Here's an example of a generic RAM/RPM file:

```
pnm://www.coolserver.com/coolclip1.ra
```

What's implied by this syntax is that the RA clip named coolclip1.ra is in a directory one level below where the PN Server (a.k.a. the RA Server) is installed. This is all happening on the physical server that is the host for *www.coolserver.com*. It's confusing at first, but then it gets clearer.

If you make a reference to an RA file directly it will just be downloaded—maybe not a bad idea in some cases.

Both the RA file and the RAM or RPM file for a given RealAudio clip need to be present on your Web Server, but only the RA file needs to be in a directory under the PN Server. The RAM or RPM file should be in a directory off the home directory for your HTML files. Remember, the RAM or RPM file *points* to the RA file.

Invoking the RA Player

With these relationships in mind, let's work through some real-life scenarios. We'll start with the common event of invoking the standalone RA Player when a user clicks on a link to an RA clip on a Web page. We only need to employ RAM files in this example.

1. Edit your HTML document to include references to the RAM files that correspond to the RA files you want the user to hear. The HTML fragment in Listing 11.1 shows the proper syntax. Figure 11.1 shows how the actual page looks, based on the script fragment.

QuickTime video clips (10- to 15-second excerpts)

Kitten Packs a Rod, 1.1 meg flattened QuickTime movie.

Full-length RealAudio clips

Kitten Packs a Rod
Easy Eggs
Little Man Cake
Motherlode

Figure 11.1

Part of "Life in a Blender's" home page.

Listing 11.1   Referencing an RA File with a RAM File

```
<HR>
<H2>Full-length RealAudio clips</H2>
<P><DD><A HREF=ra/kitten.ram>Kitten Packs a Rod</A>
  <BR>
<DD><A HREF=ra/easyeggs.ram>Easy Eggs</A><BR>
<DD><A HREF=ra/lmancake.ram>Little Man Cake</A><BR>
<DD><A HREF=ra/mothrlod.ram>Motherlode</A><BR>
<H5><A HREF=http://www.realaudio.com><IMG src=
  "art/real-aud.gif" BORDER=0 ALIGN=MIDDLE HSPACE=6>
  Don't forget your RealAudio player!</A></H5>
<HR>
```

Because of how RA file referencing works, you can point to a RAM file on someone else's site and have the clip play when a user browses your site—as long as your Web server is configured to handle the RA MIME type.

Note that all of the RAM files referenced in the HTML code are expected to be in a directory named ra under the home directory for this HTML file. When a user clicks on one of the clip titles displayed in the Web page, the RA Player should come up and start playing the clip, as in Figure 11.2. Because these are *streaming* clips, there is no need to warn the user about their file sizes.

2. Create and edit the RAM files referenced by your HTML script. In this case, the contents of the four files referenced are:

```
kitten.ram = pnm://www.fakedoom.com/kitten.ra
easyeggs.ram = pnm://www.fakedoom.com/easyeggs.ra
lmancake.ram = pnm://www.fakedoom.com/lmancake.ra
mothrlod.ram = pnm://www.fakedoom.com/motherlod.ra
```

Figure 11.2

Playing the RA clip Easy Eggs by Life in a Blender.

3. Transport your edited HTML script to your Web server.

4. Transport your RAM files to the appropriate directory under your domain's base directory on your Web server—in this case ../ra.

5. Transport your RA files to a directory just below the one where you have installed the PN Server. The default name for this directory is *rafiles*. Remember to check that your FTP tool doesn't change the upper and lower case letters in both your RA and RAM file names.

6. Make sure your Web server's PN server is running, then fire up your browser and surf to the page you just upgraded and test it out.

Embedding an RA File

This is where RPM files come in. As of this writing, the software that makes embedding RealAudio clips possible is available only as a beta plug-in from Progressive Networks (available at the PN Web site—*http://www.realaudio.com*). The principles and scripting syntax, however, are not likely to change significantly by the time the retail product comes out. Also, as of this writing, the only browser that supports embedded RA clips is Netscape Navigator (version 2.0 and above).

The HTML code for making embedded RA files play from a Web page is a bit more complex. The up side is that Web site developers have more options in the number and placement of the on-screen controls that can be used to regulate playback of an RA clip.

Note that your Web server has to be configured to recognize RPM files as compatible with the MIME type audio/x-pn-realaudio-plugin. This is not as hard as it sounds, especially if your server is already configured to recognize RAM files. Your server administrator can easily take care of it if you're not up for the task.

Let's step through another real-life example, just as we did when we invoked the standalone RA Player. Be aware that not all of the style and control elements available for customizing the behavior of embedded RA files will be used in this example. A complete listing of these elements is available at the Progressive Networks Web site.

1. Edit your HTML document to include references to the RPM files that point to the RA files you are embedding. The HTML fragment in Listing 11.2, taken from the Progressive Networks sample pages, shows the scope of the additional scripting required.

Xing's StreamWorks solution for streaming audio bypasses many HTML issues by employing CGI (Common Gateway Interface) scripts. It's always interesting to go to sites that use other technologies, such as TrueSpeech and Voxware, and see how they're doing it by viewing the HTML source for those pages.

Listing 11.2   Adding Play and Stop Buttons

```
<A NAME="example1">
<B>1) Play and Stop button only</B></A>
<P>
<EMBED SRC="audio/jazz.rpm" ALIGN=BASELINE WIDTH=40
    HEIGHT=20 CONTROLS=PlayButton CONSOLE="jazz2">
<EMBED SRC="audio/jazzs.rpm" ALIGN=BASELINE WIDTH=40
    HEIGHT=20 CONTROLS=StopButton CONSOLE="jazz2">
<NOEMBED><A HREF="audio/jazz.ram">Your browser
    doesn't support plug-ins! Play the audio using
    the helper application.</A></NOEMBED>
<BR>
<B>Richard Simon - Ray Brown Your Head</B>
```

As in the previous example, all of the RPM files referenced in the HTML code fragment above are expected to be in a directory (this time named *audio*) under the home directory for the HTML file. The way this page appears to the user is shown in Figure 11.3.

Note that while there is no hot-linked file name to click on to bring up the RA Player, there is a simple line of text identifying the clip. All of the behavior of the clip is controlled by the Play and Stop buttons. (Remember, this is a very simple example.)

Also note the **<NOEMBED>** element. This provides a graceful way to switch tactics if a user's browser does not support embedded media types. As you can see by the RAM file reference in the **<NOEMBED>** part of the code, Plan B is to display the hot-linked clip name and let the user click it to bring it up in the RA Player.

2. Create and edit the RPM files referenced by your HTML script. Content-wise, they are just like RAM files:

```
pnm://www.domain-name.com/filename.ra
```

3. Put your edited HTML script on your Web server.

4. Put your RPM files in the audio file directory just under your domain's base directory on your Web server.

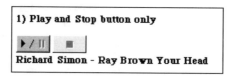

Figure 11.3

Minimal controls for an imbedded RA clip.

A cool way to add background music to a page is to embed an RA clip and assign it the AUTOSTART= TRUE control.

5. Put your RA files in a directory just below the one where you have installed the PN Server. Again, check that your FTP tool doesn't change the upper and lower case letters in both your RA and RPM file names.

6. If your PN server is running then invoke your browser and go to the page you just upgraded to see if it looks the way you want it to.

As mentioned above, this embedding example only suggests the flexibility you have when exploiting the RA plug-in from your HTML scripts. Beyond the basic **WIDTH** and **HEIGHT** parameters lie the more interesting attributes, such as **CONTROLS** and **CONSOLE**. Plenty of good examples are available at the Progressive Networks Web site, but its worth mentioning some key features here.

CONTROLS: Lets you embed specific controls from the standard RA Player interface, such as the control panel, volume control, and status bar. Coding **CONTROLS=All** gives you the whole RA Player. The script fragment above only includes **CONTROLS** for the PlayButton and the StopButton.

CONSOLE: This element is used to link two or more embedded items together. In the example above, the PlayButton and StopButton **CONTROLS** work in tandem due to the **CONSOLE="jazz2"** setting. Specifying **CONSOLE="_master"** connects a given plug-in to all the other plug-ins on that page. Once again, be sure to refer to the Progressive Networks home page for complete and up-to-date technical specs in these areas.

Referencing VDOLive Clips in HTML Scripts

Once you get used to it, the real work involved in adding media files to Web pages is not the scripting, but the media creation, testing, and transportation of files to your Web server.

The way HTML scripts reference VDO clips is very similar to the way RealAudio references them. If you want to invoke the VDO Player when a user clicks a VDO hot link (like an icon or a movie title), assuming the user does not have a VDO plug-in, the HTML syntax is very straightforward:

```
<a href="http://www.coolserver.com/vdofiles/
   coolclip.vdo> Click here to watch coolclip</a>
```

On the other hand, if you want to use a VDO plug-in, you can get more control over how the user sees and interacts with the online page and the embedded movie—but only if you are willing to do a little extra scripting. As of this writing, big surprise, the available plug-in just works with Netscape Navigator 2.0 +.

As with RealAudio, if you want to serve VDO clips from your site, you'll need the VDO Server or Personal Server properly set up, configured, and running on your HTTP server hardware. Your VDO movies (in AVI format) will need to be on your physical server also, in a directory where the VDO Server has access to them.

And, once again, you have to build some helper files. This time they take the extension .VDO. Like RealAudio RAM and RPM helpers, VDO files make the connection between the VDO Server and your VDO movies. Here's an example of a generic VDO file:

```
vdo://www.coolserver.com/vdoclip1.avi
```

A good way to interpret this line is to imagine the VDO clip named vdoclip1.avi resident on a VDO server (in effect, a virtual server, since it's all software) located within the domain *www.coolserver.com*, which is located on a physical server *somewhere*. vdoclip1.avi is one level down from the directory where the VDO server is installed.

The VDO clip file needs to be resident on your physical server, in a directory under the VDO Server. The VDO helper file will likely be in a directory under your HTML files, but not necessarily. As with RealAudio, the helper file *points* to the actual media file.

Invoking the VDO Player

Let's put this into practice. Lots of ambitious Web sites are using VDO technology with good results, mainly because setting it up (at least on the HTML side) is pretty straightforward. Any time you visit a VDO-enabled site, you should view their HTML source and see if anyone's got any new ideas.

1. Edit your HTML document to include references to the VDO files that correspond to the AVI movies you want the user to view. The HTML fragment in Listing 11.3 shows the proper syntax. Figure 11.4 shows the actual page, based on the script fragment.

Listing 11.3   Referencing an AVI Clip with a VDO File

```
<center><br><h3><blink>FOR YOUR VIEWING PLEASURE!
    </blink></h3><br>
<img src="./images/livevideo.gif">
<br><br>Visitors to our official web site can now
    view Sawyer Brown via VDOLive! The player you
    will need to view the footage is free and
    downloadable from the Internet. Enjoy and
    please let us know what you think.<br>

To download your copy of <A HREF=
    "http://www.vdolive.com/download">VDOLive Video
    Player</A> click here.<br>
<img src="./images/SBlivevideo.gif"><br>
<a href="http://www.vdolive.com/vdofiles/
    sawyer_brown.vdo" >Please click here to view a
    Sawyer Brown video</a>
```

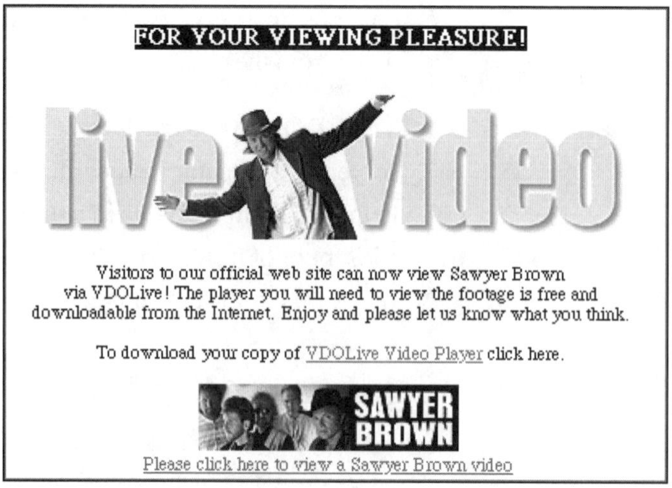

Figure 11.4

Part of Sawyer Brown's home page.

Note that the VDO file referenced in the HTML code for the Sawyer Brown site is in a directory named vdofiles at http://www.vdolive .com, although the HTML file itself is at http://www.acton .com/country/ sawyerbrown.html.

When a user clicks on the highlighted text *Please click here to view a Sawyer Brown video* (without a VDO plug-in), the standalone VDO Player application should automatically come up and start streaming the clip shown in Figure 11.5.

Figure 11.5

Playing a VDO clip by Sawyer Brown.

2. Create and edit the VDO files referenced by your HTML script. In this case, the contents of the file sawyer_brown.vdo is probably something like:

```
vdo://videoserver.vdolive.com/movies/
    sawyer_brown.avi
```

3. Transport your edited HTML script to the appropriate directory on your Web server.

4. Transport your VDO files to the appropriate directory on the appropriate Web server.

5. Transport your VDO-encoded AVI files to the appropriate directory on the machine where you have installed your VDO Server. Remember to check that your FTP tool doesn't mess up the upper and lower case letters in both your file names.

6. Make sure all your servers are running, then fire up your browser and surf to the page you just upgraded and test it out.

Embedding a VDO File

The plug-in technology available for VDOLive movies is not yet as robust as that for RealAudio clips, but it does provide a decent alternative to the standalone VDO player. As usual, only the Netscape browsers (Mac and Windows) currently support plugged-in VDO clips, but look for this to change sooner than later.

As you might expect, the HTML script for making an embedded VDO movie play from a Web page is more verbose, but the result is much less pedestrian. You'll see this as we work through the steps involved in getting a VDO movie plug-in up and running:

1. For each movie you want to play, edit your HTML page to add a reference to the VDO file that points

to the AVI file you are embedding. The partial HTML script shown in Listing 11.4 illustrates the flavor and size of this exercise.

Listing 11.4 Adding VDOLive Movie Support

```
<EMBED SRC="http://www.vdolive.com/vdofiles/
    sawyer_brown.vdo"
autostart=true loop=true stretch=false width=160
    height=128>
<NOEMBED> <a href="http://www.vdolive.com/vdofiles/
    sawyer_brown.vdo"> Your browser doesn't support
    plug-ins! Play the clip using the helper
    application.</a></NOEMBED>
```

In this example, the dimensions of the video frame are 160×112, since both height and width must be multiples of 16 (this is enforced by the VDO compressor at encoding time). The extra 16 rows at the bottom are used for displaying messages such as "Loading" and "Playing".

When stretch is true, the size of the video frame adjusts to the size of the plug-in window. When stretch is false, the video is centered in the designated area.

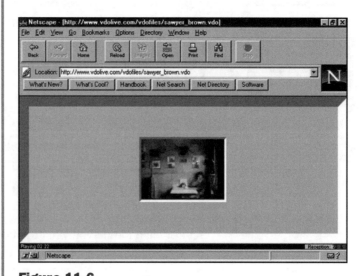

Figure 11.6
An imbedded VDO clip.

You'll notice the **<NOEMBED>** *element. As we have seen, this allows for bailing to the stand-alone player if the browser in question does not support embedded media. Also note how the syntax for the VDO file is the same for both cases, and it's up to the browser to sort things out.*

2. Create and edit the VDO file(s) referenced by your HTML script. Let's assume we're using the same movie as in the non-plug-in example:

```
vdo://videoserver.vdolive.com/movies/
    sawyer_brown.avi
```

3. Move your edited HTML script to the appropriate directory on your Web server.

4. Move your VDO files to the appropriate directory on the appropriate Web server.

5. Move your VDO-encoded AVI files to the appropriate directory on the machine where you have installed your VDO Server. Check that your FTP tool doesn't change the upper and lower case letters in your file names (if your Web server is a case-sensitive Unix machine).

6. Make sure that all your files are in place (there are a fair number of them, as you can see) and start testing. You may want to have someone else do this for you after a while, since they may better simulate the behavior of an actual user.

Embedding Shockwave Movies in HTML Scripts

Some types of Web media don't have standalone players. Good examples are Shockwave movies and VRML worlds. We'll focus on VRML in a moment, but for now we'll concentrate on Shockwave. As of this writing, the only way to reference a shocked file in an HTML script is with an **<EMBED>** statement via Macromedia's Shockwave plug-in.

Shockwave movie production and server configuration is covered in detail in Chapter 5. In the instruction list that

follows, we'll be working with an Afterburned Director movie (a DCR file) all ready for posting on a Web server (note that no helper file is needed). Let's get started:

1. In your HTML file, add the following lines:

```
<CENTER>
<H2>Rollo's Kitchen</H2>
<P>
<EMBED src="dcr/rollo.dcr" WIDTH=160 HEIGHT=140>
<NOEMBED><IMG src="art/blender.gif"></NOEMBED>
</CENTER>
```

2. Put the edited HTML file on your Web server.

3. Put the DCR file on your server in the directory indicated by the lines you added to your HTML script (in this case /dcr, right off the home directory for the HTML file). The Shockwave movie will appear to the user like the picture in the left column, ready to play. If the user's browser doesn't support the Shockwave plug-in, he or she will see a GIF image instead.

4. Test it live until it works as planned.

*There are some other control elements besides **WIDTH** and **HEIGHT**, described in the technical materials at the Macromedia Web site, but not many. With Shockwave, the point is to get the movie running in the browser and let the user interact with it there.*

Embedding VRML Worlds in HTML Scripts

When you're poking around in VRML space, it's easy to forget that the world you're in may just be an object plugged into an HTML page (assuming you got there via the Web). But that's actually all it is—from an HTML scripting point of view—despite the dramatic experience it can provide:

```
<a href="../vrml/main.wrl">BLUE'S JOINT</a>
```

Because this is not a book about VRML, it would be misleading to begin a discussion of it here. What we need to do is put VRML in context relative to HTML and Web

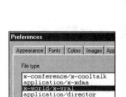

Defining a VRML Browser MIME Type.

browsers. A good place to go for more information are the search facilities at the Netscape and Microsoft Web pages (*http://www.netscape.com* and *http://www.microsoft.com*).

The heart of VRML is the VRML browser. A VRML data file (the data that describes a particular VRML world) is a text file with tightly formatted descriptions of all the individual objects that will be visible to the user in the on-screen world.

In general, if a user has a VRML browser installed, his or her Web browser will be configured to run that VRML browser whenever a world file is downloaded (as a result of clicking on a hot link). The world will likely take over the screen at that point, but when the user exits the world they'll likely be back at the Web page (although some worlds are connected to other worlds with HTML-like links).

In theory, it's like clicking on a movie link and having the movie helper play the movie. Because it's VRML, however, the perceptual shift is much greater and can make you think that you've left the Web page far behind.

Plug-ins Are Go!

Audio/Video

Image Viewers

3-D and Animation

Business and Utilities

While VDOLive, RealAudio, Shockwave, and VRML solutions like Live3D have received lots of attention by being there first and being highly publicized, many more such technologies are on the way. Just take a look at the fast-growing third-party plug-in gallery at the Netscape site.

As this chapter was written, Apple Computer announced a QuickTime plug-in for the Netscape 3.0 browser. According to Apple, flattened QuickTime movies will now start playing in a Web page before they are completely downloaded. Is this true streaming? Probably not, if POQTM (plain old QuickTime Movies) files are involved. However, it will be interesting to see how this product evolves.

Even though Microsoft is also greatly extending the capabilities of its next-generation Web browser(s), the most visible new technologies will likely continue to come from third parties, at least for a while. A good place to monitor such activities is Browserwatch at *http://www.browserwatch.com.*

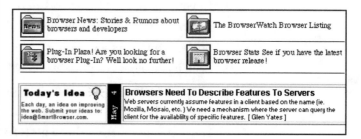

Figure 11.7

The Browserwatch site.

Chapter

Key Topics:

- **Java**

- **ActiveMovie Stream**

- **VBScript and JavaScript**

Programming Languages for Web-Based Media

As noted in Chapters 10 and 11, programming for the Web takes many forms, many of which do not overlap or have much in common. Editing HTML scripts is programming. So is constructing a Perl routine. So, too, is performing a Telnet session with your remote server.

The type of programming we'll focus on in this chapter is more rightly referred to as *software development*. Professionals in this environment work with low-level programming languages like C++, and also with slightly higher-level tools such as Microsoft's Visual Basic or Borland's Delphi—to name just a few. Java falls into this category as well.

As a producer of Web-based media (and perhaps some of the code which makes that media perform), you need to at least be aware of the issues in software development which can affect the future of your own site and the customer sites that you help maintain.

If you have considered a Web site as the proving ground for your first serious programming experience, okay, but make sure the project is on a non-critical path. Professional-level software development skills are not learned in a year, much less a month.

Low-Level Languages

The most common low-level language these days is C. More specifically, it's C++, which is considered the weapon of choice for doing anything lean and mean under either Windows or the Mac—not to mention with Sun machines. Microsoft, Borland, and Mac-centric companies like Metrowerks and Symantec all make sophisticated C++ software development products (like Visual C++ and Code Warrior).

Point of view is everything here. If you told one person you were doing Internet development in C++, he or she might assume you were building a Web browser. Another person might think you were working on a search engine or a firewall. C++ is versatile and powerful enough for each of those tasks, and more.

Other low-level languages (like Pascal and the even lower Assembler) are certainly capable of supporting Internet product development. But C++, because it is so eminently usable under Windows, the Mac, and Unix, will get almost all of our attention in this chapter.

C++ rose to fame as a so-called "object oriented" language. While most serious programming tools need to be able to create reusable software objects to remain viable, this is not necessarily desirable for all software development. Object oriented programming, however, is well suited to the Web.

In the context of adding multimedia assets to a Web site, the most visible place where C++ meets the Web is Java (at least for the moment). Java applets are produced in a C++-like development environment using Sun's Java compiler. Those applets can then be placed on Web servers and referenced in HTML scripts.

Building a Java Applet

Bookstores that carry programming guides are overflowing with books on Java. The way the industry hypes it, you'd think all non-Java programmers were just plain losers. One good thing about Java, though, is that experienced C ++ programmers can get up to speed fast. For Web site producers who are *not* C++ programmers, this is one of the big downsides—unless they plan to hire C++ programmers.

Below is a recipe for getting a taste of the Java development process, regardless of whether you're a C++ programmer or not. The goal is to get the tools, make a simple applet, and put that applet in a Web page and on a server in as short a time frame as possible.

The early versions of the Java compiler were just stand-alone, command-line apps. Whole development environments, similar to Microsoft's, are now finally becoming available.

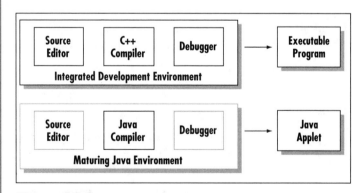

Figure 12.1

The Java development environment.

1. First, note that (at the time of this writing) there are fewer Java development tools for the Macintosh than for Windows. On the Microsoft side, only Windows 95 and NT are supported. Check Sun's Web site for the appropriate Sun operating systems (*http://www.sun.com*).

2. Get the Java compiler. Many of the Java books out there come with a version of it, but the best place to go is Sun's Web site. Sun is on the fast track with their Java development tools, so it's hard to predict how the Java compiler will be delivered as time progresses. It should always be available at the Sun site in some form, however, whether as a free beta or a retail product.

   In this demonstration we'll assume you have procured the program JAVAC.EXE (the compiler) and have installed it and its associated code libraries on your hard drive. To keep things as simple as possible, we'll be running the compiler from a command line in Windows 95.

3. Select a simple test program from a Java reference book or from the online Java demo pages, if you have downloaded the product from their site. A Java source code file normally has the extension .java, as in the file name MyTestApplet.java.

   Because of the nature of this exercise, we actually use a program named MyTestApplet.java. All it does is display a GIF file on the screen and play an audio clip, but you can use it as a real test program

Note the liberal use of long file names in the Java environment, a reminder of the Unix environment where Java was invented.

Figure 12.2

An up-and-coming project from NeXT.

if you're following this recipe. The source code is provided in Listing 12.1.

Listing 12.1   MyTestApplet.java

```java
import java.awt.*;
import java.applet.*;

public class MyTestApplet extends Applet {
    Image iImage;
    AudioClip acAudioClip;

public void init() {
        iImage = getImage(getDocumentBase(),
            "MEDIA/GIF1.GIF");
        acAudioClip = getAudioClip
            (getDocumentBase(),
            "MEDIA/AU1.AU");    }

public void paint(Graphics gObj) {
        Rectangle rRect = bounds();
        gObj.drawImage(iImage, 0, 0, rRect.width,
            rRect.height, this);
        acAudioClip.play();
    }
}
```

To see what other people are doing with Java, try searching on the keywords sample Java programs in Alta Vista.

4. Put the Java source code file in the same directory as the Java compiler (and its ancillary files). Let's assume the name of that directory is BIN, which it probably is by default if you did a standard installation of the Java development tools.

5. Open an MS-DOS window on your Windows 95 desktop by clicking *Start | Programs | MS-DOS Prompt*, as shown in Figure 12.3. You may want to maximize this window for a better sense of orientation. We're working in this mode so we can see any error listings.

6. Change the current directory to wherever BIN (mentioned above) is in your directory tree. In this example, the full path to BIN is C:\DEV\JAVA\BIN. For testing locally before posting to the server, create a subdirectory off of BIN named MEDIA.

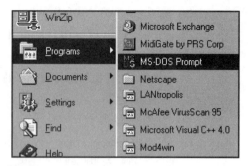

Figure 12.3

Opening an MS-DOS window.

7. At the command line, key in:

```
javac MyTestApplet.java
```

The Java compiler will now process the source file. If there are no errors, the program compiled successfully and is ready to test locally. If there are problems, you will see the errors listed immediately below the compiler invocation.

8. The Java compiler will produce at least one binary object from each Java source file you give it. In this case, the compiler should have spawned a file named MyTestApplet.class. This is the file that we'll be referencing in our HTML document. Minimize the MS-DOS window for now.

Figure 12.4

Successful compilation.

James Gosling · Bill Joy · Guy Steele

The Java™ Language Specification

The Java Series

...from the Source™

9. Produce a GIF file named GIF1.GIF and an AU file named AU1.AU (based on the media specified in the Java source file). A tool like Sound Forge, described in Chapter 9, can output AU files— Sun's answer to WAV files. Put these files in the MEDIA directory you created under the BIN directory. Nothing fancy needed here, just anything you want to see and hear in this test run.

10. Create an HTML document identical to the Listing 12.2. We'll call this document MYTESTAP.HTML. After we test it locally, we'll transfer it to the server. Remember to reference this file in some other existing HTML file on your site so that you have a way to get to it with your browser.

Listing 12.2   MYTESTAP.HTML

```
<html>
<head>
<title>My Test Applet
</title>
</head>

<body>
<h1>My Test Applet</h1>
<p>
<hr>
<p>
<applet code=MyTestApplet width=200 height=200>
</applet>
<p>
<hr>
<p>
</body>
</html>
```

11. Put this HTML file in the BIN directory. Open a window on the BIN directory from your Windows 95 desktop and click on the file named MYTESTAP.HTML. This should invoke Netscape Navigator (assuming you have it installed) which will then load the document MYTESTAP.HTML.

If things are going as planned, you should see the words APPLET MYTESTAPPLET RUNNING at the bottom of your browser first, followed by the GIF.

Don't be alarmed if all you see is a gray box for a few seconds. Eventually you'll see the GIF file you supplied (and possibly hear your AU file) when the GIF gets painted. Click on the gray box with your mouse if too much time goes by.

12. If the above local test was successful, you can now move these files to your Web server for real-world testing. Using your FTP tool, copy the applet and the file MYTESTAP.HTML to your HTML documents' home directory on your server. Do the same for the existing HTML file that references MYTESTAP.HTML. Remember to FTP the applet as raw data.

    If you don't already have a subdirectory named MEDIA on your server, create one and put the GIF and AU test files you created in it. Remember this is just a quick example for getting a simple Java applet up and running and you can delete these test files as soon as it's over.

13. Fire up Netscape Navigator (Mac or Windows) and surf to the live MyTestApplet page on your

Figure 12.5
MyTestApplet live.

server. If you transferred everything correctly, the applet and the media files should play just like they did in the local test.

James Gosling, the lead developer of Java at Sun.

The purpose of this exercise was to acquaint you with the bare essentials of Java software development and media integration. This is not a book about Java; if you want to learn more, you should invest in some good Java programming books. By the time *this* book is published, a much better suite of Java development tools should also be available from Sun.

C++ programmers used to working in Microsoft's Visual C++ environment may feel slightly disjointed at first. This should change relatively quickly as Sun improves the development toolset with better source editors, debuggers, and project management facilities.

One thing Web site producers need to monitor is how well Java handles multimedia data types like streaming video and audio. Part of the high-level theory behind Java is that it moves small objects and pieces of larger objects to the user's local machine without the user noticing. This

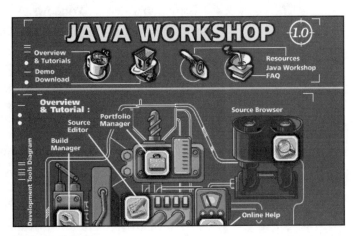

Figure 12.6
Sun's Java Workshop.

is a different strategy from the streaming techniques used by RealAudio and VDOLive.

Again, point of view is key. Java programmers probably don't think exactly like commercial Web site developers, who must look at all the options for incorporating audio and video media assets. Also, like Netscape products, Java is a competitor to Microsoft's Web solutions, even though Microsoft has announced support for it.

True, Java is powerful and diverse (the HotJava Web browser is written *in* Java!), but it requires a substantial investment in time and money to make it serve you well. For making media play in Web pages, it should be considered just one of several options.

ActiveMovie Stream

Another Web programming area that is becoming a hotbed of software development centers around Microsoft's ActiveX and ActiveMovie technologies—specifically ActiveMovie Stream (ASF, which stands for ActiveMovie Stream Format). ActiveMovie is considered to be the successor to Video for Windows. ActiveX is essentially the next generation of OLE (Object Linking and Embedding).

Recently announced and demonstrated at industry events, ActiveMovie Stream is Microsoft's challenge to existing Web-based streaming products like VDOLive, Xing's Streamworks, and RealAudio. Because ActiveX technology in general leverages off the mature and powerful OLE, its incubation was relatively short.

The way things are shaping up, ASF movies will likely be played from Web pages rich with Visual Basic scripts— as opposed to simple HTML code—which makes creating those Web pages a lot more similar to traditional software development.

Here's what's currently available for developers interested in Microsoft's ActiveMovie Stream:

- Plentiful technical marketing literature. It's worth reading and revisiting for updates.

Figure 12.7

The final frontier?

- Endorsements from other major software companies

- Alpha- and beta-level tools for creating ActiveMovie Stream clips, complete with sample movies and applications to play them. Note that this is all 32-bit software and not supported by Windows 3.1.

Note: All of the areas in /advtech are worth regular monitoring at http://www. microsoft.com, such as /internet and /int-dev. Also, try http:// www.windows95 .com.

If you go to the Web site at *http://www.microsoft.com/ advtech/activemovie/download.htm*, you can download the following three items:

- The ActiveMovie Stream editor

- The ActiveMovie Stream Add-On kit (sample media and applications)

- The underlying code libraries that support this technology

Let's run through a sample hands-on session with the ActiveMovie Stream editor. Remember, it's still very early in the game with this product, but you'll at least get a sense of how it is being positioned. Also remember that this is pre-release software and prone to unpredictable behavior—such as crashes. It may seem confusing at first, but if you think about what the program is trying to do as you work with it, things will begin to clear up. As noted earlier, we'll be running this app on the Windows 95 desktop.

1. Start the editor, then choose *File | New*.

2. Click on *File | Save* to save your new project file (with the file extension .ASP). You'll be prompted with a dialog box for a target directory, which will be used to hold all of the media you add to your project.

3. Bring up the *Add Files to Project* dialog box by executing the sequence *File | Add Files*.

4. Note that you can only import still images (such as BMP, DIB, GIF, RLE, and JPG files) and WAV audio

Note: you can also drag the media files from a folder in the Windows 95 Explorer (file manager) to the lower part of the editor's UI, instead of using File\Add Files.

Figure 12.8

The ASF Editor's main user interface.

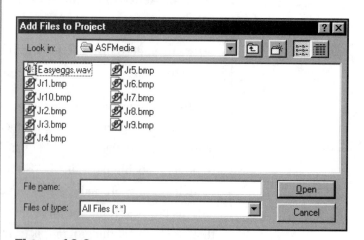

Figure 12.9

Adding media to an ASF project.

clips. We'll discuss the implications of this in a moment. For now, we'll select a collection of BMPs and one WAV file.

5. If you are ready to add a URL at this point, click *File | Add URL*. This is the location on the Web server from which your finished ASF movie will ultimately be streamed.

6. All of the file names of the media in your project should now be visible in the Content window at the bottom of the Editor UI. To begin assembling your media in the Edit Window, you can either use the *Tap and Snap* method or drag the media files directly from the Content window to the Edit window.

   While the Tap and Snap method is interesting (and explained in the Help system), experienced Premiere users will probably want to use the more efficient drag-and-drop approach. This is where you'll begin to appreciate the pre-release nature of the software.

7. Now it gets interesting. If you have added an audio track, it will appear as a blue-lined rectangle at the bottom of the Edit window. Depending on their richness and file type (and how you added them), the picture files you added will probably appear as green-lined rectangles scattered around the Edit window. You may even see some of them overlapped and producing error conditions.

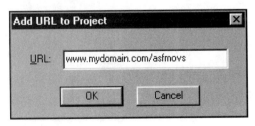

Figure 12.10

Adding a URL to an ASF project.

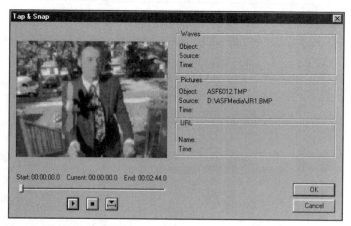

Figure 12.11

The Tap & Snap dialog box.

If you really want dramatic results, check the DIB (Uncompressed) radio button and pick 16 in the Colors combo box— assuming the original image was richer than that (like 256 colors).

Premiere users may get frustrated here, but you can't drag on the edge of a rectangle representing a media file to shrink it (or expand it). Simply put, the width of a media rectangle—even a single bitmap— reflects the time it takes to stream it. You can, however, drag the rectangles around from left to right.

8. If you want to condense a rectangle's width, you have to select it (the line pattern will change), then click *Edit | Convert* from the main menu. In the resulting *Image Conversion* dialog box, there are various options for altering the visual quality of your pictures.

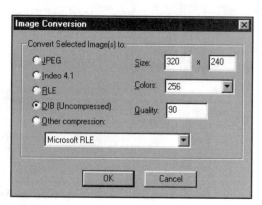

Figure 12.12

Converting an ASF image.

Expect to experiment heavily with the different settings in the *Image Conversion* dialog box if you are serious about understanding how the ASF editor works. There are some additional features available as well, which are detailed in the program's Help system.

9. Once you've got the size and position of your media elements under control, you can build your project by clicking *Stream | Build* All from the main menu. Following a successful build, you can play the new ASF movie if you click *Stream | Play*. Considering what the source media were, don't expect anything that looks like a real desktop movie.

What's going on here is pretty ambitious when you think about it, even if it's not yet ready for prime time. The editor is, in effect, enforcing bandwidth limitations. No wonder it doesn't let you import AVI or QuickTime movies yet—although such media types *are* part of the plan according to published documentation.

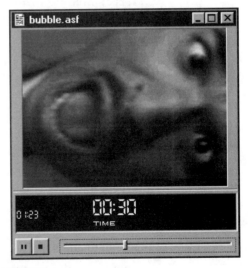

Figure 12.13
Playing an ASF movie locally.

VBScript

So how do you put an ActiveMovie Stream movie on a Web page, even if you know in advance that the performance is still at an unacceptable stage? The answer lies in another part of the overall ActiveX environment: Visual Basic Scripting Edition, also called VBScript, which is based on Microsoft's powerful and mature Visual Basic software development product.

In fact, the Add-On kit you can download with the ActiveMovie Stream Editor includes a sample HTML document with some ActiveMovie objects referenced in a Visual Basic Script. Listing 12.3 contains a fragment of it.

Microsoft's Web pages are full of VBScript examples. A great place to start is http://www.microsoft.com/vbscript.

Listing 12.3   Referencing an ASF Movie

```
<SCRIPT LANGUAGE="VBS">

'----------------------------------------------------
' Load the specified file
'----------------------------------------------------
SUB SelNewFile_Click
  ActiveMovie.Filename = NewFile.value
  Status.value = "Loading..."
  Content.value = ActiveMovie.FileName
END SUB
'----------------------------------------------------
' Start the ActiveX Movie Control
'----------------------------------------------------
SUB CONTROLstart_Click
  Status.value = "ActiveMovie Stream Playing"
  Content.value = ActiveMovie.FileName
  result = ActiveMovie.Run
END SUB
```

JavaScript

JavaScript resources at Netscape's site.

Like VBScript, JavaScript can be embedded in an HTML document to add sophisticated interactivity and multimedia control to otherwise normal Web pages. The advantage of JavaScript over Java is that you don't need C++ programming experience to come up to speed quickly.

Unfortunately, the price you have to pay is in execution speed.

JavaScript is actually a Netscape product, and it is supported by Navigator in both its Windows and Mac versions. To quote from Netscape's Web page, JavaScript is: "...a programmable API that allows cross-platform scripting of events, objects, and actions. It allows the page designer to access events such as startups, exits, and user mouse clicks."

"Based on the Java language, JavaScript extends the programmatic capabilities of Netscape Navigator to a wide range of authors and is easy enough for anyone who can compose HTML. Use JavaScript to glue HTML, inline plug-ins, and Java applets to each other.

"Using JavaScript, even less-experienced developers will be able to direct responses from a variety of events, objects, and actions. It provides anyone who can compose HTML with the ability to change images, play different sounds, and more in response to specified events such as user mouse clicks or screen exit and entry."

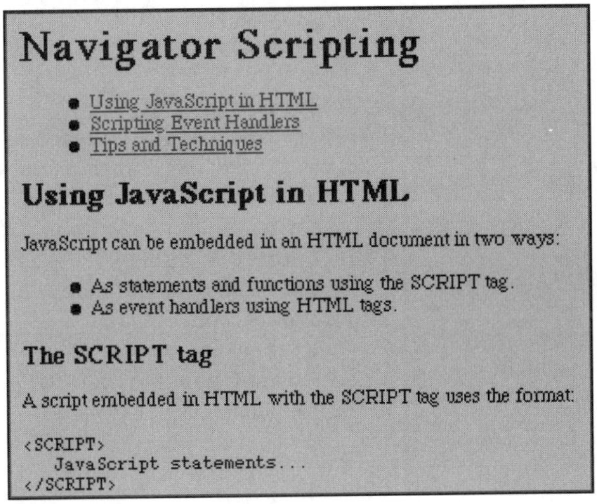

Figure 12.14
More help at Netscape.

Clearly, Web site producers who want to add multimedia to their pages should take a good look at both VBScript and JavaScript. Neither one has a particularly good streaming facility, and you can offer download-only desktop video clips with just some simple HTML code.

In effect, what VBScript and JavaScript are best at now is providing user interactivity. Listing 12.4 contains a partial listing of an HTML script that includes JavaScript code.

Doing a Yahoo or Alta Vista search on JavaScript will turn up all kinds of good examples.

JavaScript Index

Listing 12.4   The HTML Source behind the JavaScript Index (http://www.c2.org/~andreww/javascript)

```
<HTML>
<HEAD>
<TITLE>JavaScript Index</TITLE>
<script Language="JavaScript">
<!-- Helpers for JSI page...
// Navigation - Start
function goback(){
alert("Good Bye!");
history.go(-1);
}
function gettheDate() {
Todays = new Date();
TheDate = "" + (Todays.getMonth()+ 1) +" / "+
  Todays.getDate() + " / " + Todays.getYear()
document.clock.thedate.value = TheDate;
}
// Navigation - Stop
// Netscapes Clock - Start
// this code was taken from Netscapes JavaScript
// documentation at www.netscape.com on Jan.25.96

var timerID = null;
var timerRunning = false;
function stopclock (){
  if(timerRunning)
    clearTimeout(timerID);
  timerRunning = false
...
```

Key Topics:

- **HTML-based authoring tools**

- **Java-based authoring tools**

- **A close look at Microsoft's Internet Assistant**

Chapter **13**

Web Authoring Software

There is no shortage of authoring tools for creating professional-looking Web pages and Web sites. Most of the big players (Microsoft, Apple, Sun, Netscape, Adobe, and so on) already have products in both of these categories, and others are on the way.

More ambitious tools are currently in development. As Web sites get bigger and richer with multimedia assets, the tedium involved in keeping everything in synch grows geometrically. Think of all the HTML pages, still images, media clips, and server files that are inter-related—even in a medium-sized installation.

A strong market has developed for applications that can automate the overall Web site management process. This is especially true for validation and testing, which, paradoxically, often require some degree of aesthetic judgment.

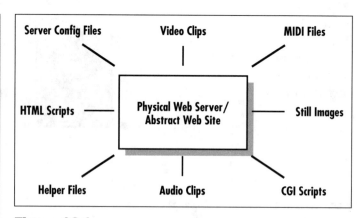

Figure 13.1

A media management nightmare?

The problem is that there are currently very few people who have the experience to design such Web site automation tools intelligently, especially when it comes to multimedia clips that are frequently updated or recycled (such as streaming video and audio clips). Again, plenty of development is underway, but the ultimate winners will not achieve victory overnight.

So what does it mean, exactly, to talk about authoring for the Web? One approach is to see HTML page creation as analogous to composing screens for a desktop game or educational product using a CD-ROM authoring tool— such as Director.

Another perspective is to view Web authoring as a lower-level, more comprehensive process. This is where authoring starts to blur into traditional software development, especially when VRML and Java coding are involved.

We'll discuss both approaches in this chapter, but concentrate on HTML-based authoring products. That's where most of the real multimedia action is—at least for now. After an overview of some of the currently prominent

Going to Yahoo and searching on "Web Authoring" will yield bountiful results.

It will be interesting to monitor how companies like Macromedia reshape their authoring systems. As noted earlier, a Shockwave movie is essentially a Director movie playing on a Web page.

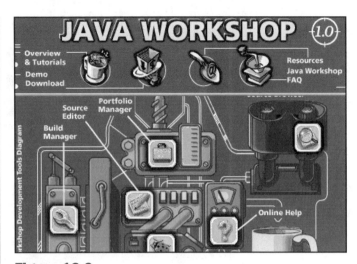

Figure 13.2
Part of Sun's impressive line.

contenders, we'll walk through a session using Microsoft's Internet Assistant (a free add-on to Microsoft Word).

If you decide to invest in one of the standalone brand name solutions, you should keep in mind that it might not be able to accommodate all the multimedia file types that you want to offer on your site. In other words, you may have to manually edit the HTML script generated by the product.

Generally speaking, most of the big-ticket solutions will handle still art, background audio, and *some* complex multimedia types just fine. But if you want to add (for instance) RealAudio, VDOLive, or Shockwave clips, you should be prepared to open the hood and get your hands dirty.

HTML-Based Tools
FrontPage

This is Microsoft's lead product for Web-based (and intranet) publishing. As of this writing, a free Beta version is available for download and it works pretty much

Apple's strategy in the authoring department seems to be packaging other people's products (similar to the way they are positioning the QuickTime Live suite). The authoring system they include with their server hardware is currently Adobe's PageMill.

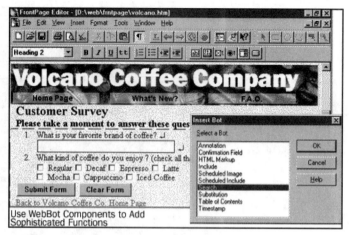

Figure 13.3

The main FrontPage user interface.

as advertised. Microsoft is pushing this product as both an authoring tool *and* a site management solution—specifically for non-programmers.

Just about everything in FrontPage is automated with templates and Microsoft-style wizards. You can also add sophisticated interactive features by dragging and dropping so-called *WebBot* components right onto your pages.

Finally, FrontPage seems to be largely designed for workgroups—teams of people who like creating and managing big Web sites together. Check out the rest of the story at *http://www.microsoft.com/frontpage*.

PageMill/SiteMill

Adobe took an early lead in the Web-based authoring game with two key products: PageMill (for drag-and-drop Web page creation) and SiteMill (for Web site management). Both were designed for industrial strength Web site chores, although PageMill is a much more mature product at this point. More information is available on both products at *http://www.adobe.com/prodindex*.

Figure 13.4
Check out PageMill and SiteMill.

Netscape Gold

In a certain sense, Netscape Gold is just a superset of the standard issue Netscape Navigator. All the Gold product really adds is an HTML editor, but it is considered a very good one. You can download Netscape Gold for free from the Netscape site (*http://www.netscape.com*). For some reason, many people seem to think the Gold version means it comes with a manual and you have to pay for it, which is untrue.

The editor itself is known for being very fast, and it integrates seamlessly with the Navigator browser. In other words, you can work on a Web page for a while, then

Two other products worth checking out:

- *DeltaPoint's QuickSite (http:// www.deltapoint .com)*
- *Spider from Incontext (http:// www.incontext .com)*

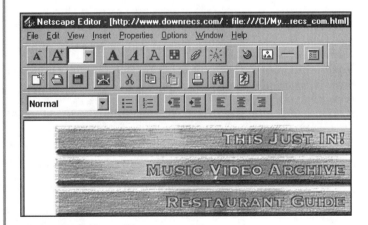

Figure 13.5
The Netscape Gold user interface.

switch to the Navigator to see how the page will look live with just one or two clicks. (Note that you have to start Navigator first to get into the editor).

The editor's UI is completely WYSIWYG, but unfortunately there is not as much support for multimedia file types as there is in other authoring products—even Internet Assistant. It's hard to know whether this is by design or not, since the rest of the editor works so well.

Some other drawbacks:

- No facility for form creation

- No drag-and-drop support for some of the proprietary Netscape extensions

- General lackluster feel until you appreciate its underlying power

WebAuthor

Like Microsoft's Internet Assistant, WebAuthor, from Quarterdeck, Inc., is an add-in module for WinWord 6.0. Also like IA, it provides a custom View in WinWord (just like Normal, Outline, and Page Layout) where you get access to proprietary HTML functions.

Because of its extensive use of Word macros, WebAuthor requires a relatively powerful machine. Consider at least a Pentium with 8 MB of memory if you want to work completely free of sluggishness.

Unlike Internet Assistant, WebAuthor is not free (the complete version is $49.95), although you can test drive it for 30 days. In fact, WebAuthor differs from Internet Assistant in many ways. For example, it actually manages *two* documents relative to your in-progress Web page (a separate HTML script *and* the underlying Word file).

If you go through Word's menus after WebAuthor is installed, you'll see a lot of new items. This is indicative of the level of power that WebAuthor gives you for authoring HTML pages. Unfortunately, it seems to have no special love for handling multimedia files. Some of the program's significant features are:

- An intelligent conversion facility for large existing WinWord and RTF files

- Support for Imagemap graphics (to some extent)

- Good support for tables and forms

- Good support for hyperlinks

- Good support for formatting individual elements of a document

- For more information, point your browser to *http://www.qdeck.com*

Java-Based Tools
Java Workshop

Sun's entry in the Web authoring/site management sweepstakes is Java Workshop. As you might expect, the product is powerful and sophisticated, but it might lack the visibility to get Windows and Mac-based Web authors interested before they start using solutions like FrontPage or PageMill.

As of this writing, Java Workshop is only available for Windows 95 and Windows NT.

To be honest, I cannot even begin to do justice to Java Workshop in two paragraphs. The best way to get a complete picture is to visit the Sun Web site at *http://www.sun.com/sunsoft/Developer-products/java/literature/ProductGuide*.

A New IconAuthor?

A product named Jamba has recently been announced by the venerable Aimtech company. Jamba is worth mentioning here because of Aimtech's long-standing reputation in the field of multimedia authoring through sophisticated visual programming (as in its flagship IconAuthor application).

Jamba is designed to let nonprogrammers create Java-based Web pages (and sites) by manipulating Java objects in a visual programming environment. Threading is supported, as well as CGI and JDBC (Java Database Connectivity).

As with other Aimtech products, templates are provided for such operations as Web-based marketing and training. Script files generated by Jamba are also readable by the native Aimtech player for any platform. For more information, surf to *http://www.aimtech.com.*

Authoring with Microsoft Internet Assistant

Internet Assistant (IA) is a free but powerful add-on to Microsoft Word for Windows (version 6.0a and higher). If you are already a Word user, IA will let you create HTML pages almost as easily as standard Word documents. As you work, you can flip back and forth between Web Browse View and HTML View to see how your pages will look live.

For users who haven't switched to Windows 95, IA version 1.0z works just fine with WinWord 6.0a running on Win31 (but lacks the sophistication and additional features of v2.0z).

Two versions of the product are currently available: 1.0z and 2.0z. Both support the English version of WinWord, as well as several European versions, and are available at *http://www.microsoft.com/msword/Internet/ia/default.htm.* Other limitations are detailed at the Microsoft Web site.

Version 2.0z is much more powerful than 1.0z, but it only works with Word for Windows 95 and Word for NT (English, Italian, German, and French editions). Most common extensions are supported, as well as the ones for the Microsoft Internet Explorer (both proprietary and HTML Level 2 standard). We'll focus on 2.0z in this chapter.

Figure 13.6

Microsoft's Web site.

Assuming you have Word for Windows 95 on your system, download and run the self-extracting IA installation program, followed by the standard Microsoft setup routine (all plain vanilla). You might want to read the documentation on the Microsoft site just to give yourself some basic background information.

Internet Assistant Views

The Word View menu.

If you're familiar with WinWord, you'll know that one of its organizing principles is the idea of the Document View (Normal, Outline, Page Layout, etc.). IA provides two more views for the Word user: HTML View and Web Browse View. Depending on which view you're in, you have different options for working with a document.

In IA's HTML View you get access to some new menu items and a new toolbar—which gives you shortcuts to some common HTML-related operations. Two basic ideas to keep in mind are:

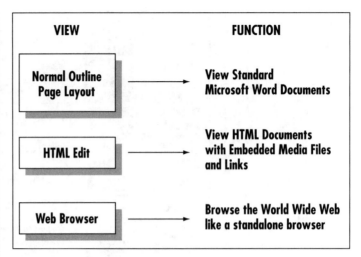

VIEW	FUNCTION
Normal Outline Page Layout	View Standard Microsoft Word Documents
HTML Edit	View HTML Documents with Embedded Media Files and Links
Web Browser	Browse the World Wide Web like a standalone browser

Figure 13.7

An abstract view of Word's View menu.

- You can only enter the HTML View by opening an HTML file from Word's File menu using the *File | Open* sequence. In other words, you can't switch to HTML View from within a normal Word document.

- Almost all the things you can do in HTML View can be done in Word's other views. Some important exceptions are working with hyperlinks and changing fonts and point sizes (you can't, at least not in the current version of IA).

Adding a Picture

That's the overview of Microsoft's Internet Assistant. Let's now move on to adding multimedia assets to Web pages using IA's HTML View user interface. We'll start with adding still images.

1. From the main Word file menu, select *Insert | Picture*. If you're not in HTML View, you'll just get Word's standard dialog box for inserting a graphic—which is fine at this point, as long as the picture file to be

If you depend on WinWord as an office productivity tool, remember that you have not affected its capacity in this regard by installing Internet Assistant. All you have done is add a Web browsing facility and the ability to work with and save documents as HTML files.

*Remember, JPEG
and GIF files are the
only still-image file
types supported,
which is still a
WWW convention
at this point.*

inserted is a GIF or a JPEG file. IA will incorporate the image into your HTML document when you select it.

2. If you're already in HTML View when you click *Insert | Picture*, IA will give you its own dialog box for inserting a graphic, as shown in Figure 13.8.

3. In the *Image Source* text field, key in the full path to the picture file you are inserting. You can expedite this process by clicking the *Browse* button, then navigating to the file you want via the file selection dialog box.

4. Use the *Alternative Text* field to supply any descriptive text you want for the picture.

5. Click the *Options* tab at the top right of the dialog box. In the *Alignment with Text* drop-down list, shown in Figure 13.9, choose how you want to align text relative to your picture.

6. Also in *Options*, fill in the image height and width attributes. If these numbers are not the actual height

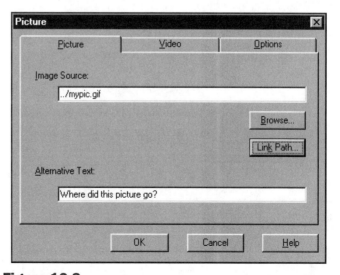

Figure 13.8
IA's Insert Picture dialog box.

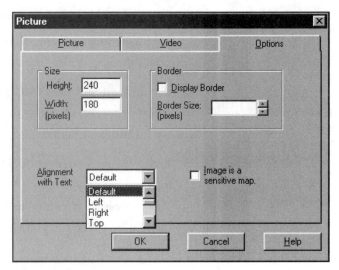

Figure 13.9

Aligning the text.

and width of the image, the user's browser will scale it. Don't assume all browsers will do a great job at this.

Adding a Background Sound

Note that other types of audio clips are supported besides WAV files. As shown in Chapter 7, MIDI files can also be used to provide background sound.

While Internet Assistant 2.0z makes it easy to add advanced HTML tags to your pages to support lists, forms, and tables, we'll stick with multimedia files as our main focus. Documentation for all IA features is readily available at the Microsoft Web site.

To add a background sound to a Web page using Internet Assistant, click the *Format | Background Sound* menu item. In the resulting *Background Sound* dialog box, shown in Figure 13.10, key in the complete path to the desired audio file or click the *Browse* button to navigate to it with the file selection dialog box.

If you want to play your background sound continuously, enter the number of times the clip should loop in the *Playback loop* field. To make the clip loop forever, press the down arrow as soon as the dialog box appears.

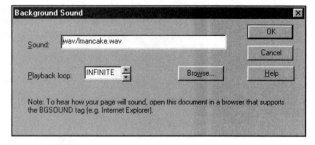

Figure 13.10

Adding a background sound.

Adding a Video File

Finally we get to high-end multimedia. The first thing to consider is that Internet Assistant currently supports only one species of desktop video clip: *non-streaming* Video for Windows AVI files (as opposed to VDOLive movies, which are technically AVI files).

If you use version 2.0z of IA to add video files to your Web pages, you will pretty much be working with the following model:

- Author uses IA to edit Web page to create a link to an AVI file.

- Author puts edited Web page and AVI file on Web server.

- User browses Web page and clicks on a movie reference. Movie download begins and movie is played by Windows Media Player when it is successfully downloaded (assuming user's browser is configured correctly).

To add a video clip to a Web page using Internet Assistant, click *Insert | Picture* while in HTML View mode. When the *Picture* dialog box appears, click the *Video* tab at the top. The dialog box should now look like the illustration shown in Figure 13.11.

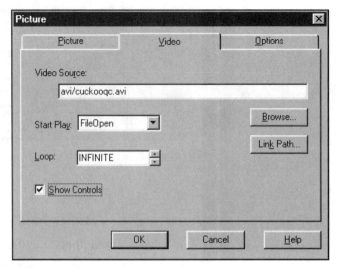

Figure 13.11

Adding an AVI file.

Next, adjust the video controls as follows:

1. Enter the complete path to the AVI file or click *Browse* and navigate to the clip with the file selection dialog box.

2. In the *Start play* drop-down list, select when you want the clip to start playing (from the user's perspective).

3. If you want to play the video clip continuously, enter the number of times that you want it to loop in the *Loop* field. To make the clip loop forever, press the down arrow as soon as the dialog box appears.

4. Checking the *Show Controls* checkbox permits the user to control playback of the video clip when it comes up in his or her browser. This is done with the standard AVI movie controller interface, as shown in Figure 13.12.

When you're finished adding video clips to your pages, check out the HTML script generated by Internet Assistant. As you can see in the code fragment in Listing 13.1, several

The implication of proprietary extensions, of course, is that browsers other than Microsoft's Internet Explorer might not be able to deal with the video and audio clips you put on your pages. As it turns out, however, many other browsers do implement a lot of Microsoft's HTML extensions.

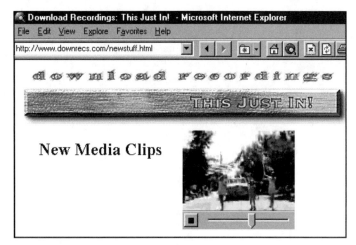

Figure 13.12

Letting the user control the movie.

proprietary Microsoft HTML extensions for multimedia have been enlisted.

Listing 13.1 An HTML Script with Multimedia

```
<HTML>

<HEAD>

<TITLE>Download Recordings: Restaurant Guide</TITLE>

<META NAME="GENERATOR" CONTENT="Internet Assistant
  for Microsoft Word 2.0z">

</HEAD>

<BODY bgcolor="#FFFFFF" text="#222222"
  link="#FF0E00" vlink="#3188D4" alink="#8F8FBD">

<P>

<CENTER><IMG SRC="art/foodhead.gif" BORDER=0>
  </CENTER>

<BGSOUND SRC="wav/vernon.wav" LOOP="INFINITE">

<H2><CENTER>Vernon's Virtual Victuals</CENTER></H2>

<P><P>

<IMG DYNSRC="avi/vernon.avi" START="FILEOPEN"
  LOOP="3" CONTROLS>

<TABLE>
```

```
<TR><TD VALIGN=TOP><B><IMG SRC="art/vernon.gif">
  </B></TD><TD VALIGN=TOP>Welcome to what could be
  a wide ranging but hopefully not too
  self-indulgent look at the many aspects of the
  world of food. I am heavily involved with food,
  but I am by no means a professional or expert.
  Hopefully we can use this opportunity to bring
  the world of food down to earth and share our
  good fortunes as well as some misfortunes,
  whether it be a great dinner or finding good
  tomatoes.</P>

<P>

Feedback is expected! Let me know you're out there.
  Share some of your food experiences from
  restaurants to cookbooks, recipes to farmers'
  markets, soup to nuts, good and bad. Let's bring
  this place to life! Reach me for now at
  <A href=mailto:wvmc3d@earthlink.net>wvmc3d@
  earthlink.net</A>.
```

Adding a Marquee

Taking the marquee feature to an extreme, it's not hard to imagine interesting visual effects with stacked marquees displaying scrolling block characters—in effect rendering composite moving images.

Another useful feature of Internet Assistant is the Marquee tag. This feature, based on Microsoft HTML extensions, lets a Web page author add scrolling text in a special window. The text can scroll either left or right, and you can set both the window size (in pixels) and the background color.

The nice thing about marquees is that no server pushes, CGI scripts, or multipart GIFs are necessary. All the animation effects are handled at the browser level, based solely on the HTML script (using Microsoft's HTML extensions).

To add a marquee to a Web page using Internet Assistant 2.0z, click the *Insert | Marquee* menu item—the dialog box shown in Figure 13.13 will appear. You don't necessarily have to be in HTML View mode to add a marquee.

Here's how to calibrate the controls in the marquee dialog box:

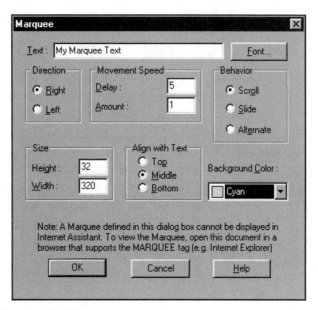

Figure 13.13

Adding a marquee.

1. In the *Text* field, enter the sentence or phrase that you want to scroll in the window.

2. Check either the *Right* or *Left* radio button (to set the side of the window from which scrolling will commence).

3. Under *Movement Speed*, enter a number in the *Delay* box to set the scrolling speed. The number you enter in the *Amount* box determines (in pixels) how far the text shifts each time it's redrawn. Smaller numbers here will increase scrolling smoothness.

4. The radio buttons in the *Behavior* group determine how the text moves. If no button is checked, the *Scroll* behavior is used by default. In this case, the text starts offscreen, moves across the scroll area and disappears offscreen. *Slide* does the same thing as *Scroll*, but all the text is visible from start to finish. *Alternate* does the same thing as *Slide*, but the text moves back and forth continuously.

Note that you can't see the results of adding a marquee from IA itself. Load the file locally with the Internet Explorer to test its behavior.

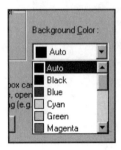

5. Set the size of the marquee in pixels using the *Height* and *Width* controls.

6. Align the text adjacent to the marquee by checking the *Top, Middle,* or *Bottom* button in the *Align with Text* group.

7. Choose the background color you want for the marquee from the *Background Color* drop-down list.

8. Click the *Font* control and choose a font (and font color) for the scrolled text.

As with adding a reference to a video file, it can be interesting to see the actual HTML code generated by adding a marquee. The script fragment in Listing 13.2 shows a generic example.

Listing 13.2   HTML Tags for a Marquee

```
<H5><CENTER>

<FONT COLOR="#ff0000" FACE="Arial" SIZE="3">

<MARQUEE BGCOLOR="#00ffff" ALIGN="TOP"
  DIRECTION="RIGHT" BEHAVIOR="SCROLL" HEIGHT="24"
  WIDTH="320" SCROLLDELAY="5" SCROLLAMOUNT="1">
  Marquee Test Text</MARQUEE>

</FONT> </CENTER></H5>
```

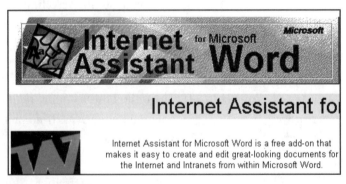

Figure 13.14
A marquee in action.

Actually, there are Internet Assistants already available for Excel and Access. More information on these products can be found at the Microsoft Web site.

Web Browse View

This facility offers the option of turning WinWord into a Web browser. In one sense, this is quite handy and demonstrates the power of the Internet Assistant technology. On the other hand, it can seem like a wasted miracle if you have your favorite browser already tweaked and ready for action.

Probably it's just another way that Microsoft is prepping us for its forthcoming Active Desktop ("Sweeper") environment, where all Windows apps are Internet-aware and any Web asset is always just a few mouse clicks away.

To switch to Web Browse View, click the Switch to Web Browse View icon (the one with the pair of glasses) in the upper left corner of the WinWord main window. Two new tool bars, shown in Figure 13.15, will appear to facilitate Web navigation.

Most of the icons in these new tool bars work in very familiar ways, especially the forward and back arrows, bookmark, and home. If you want to actually start surfing, don't forget to activate your dialer to get a Winsock session going first!

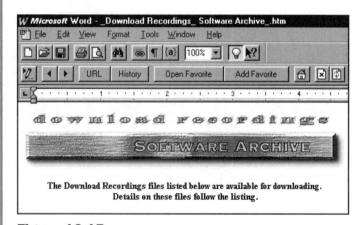

Figure 13.15

Online with Internet Assistant.

The advantages
of working with
remote Web
servers, and how
to configure
them.

Chapter 14

A detailed tutorial on installing and maintaining Microsoft's free, NT-based Internet Information Server is presented in Chapter 17.

Configuring a Remote Web Server

Managing a Web site is a different job than producing Web-based media, even though the processes are closely linked. For example, if you develop Web media (or the software that plays Web media), it helps to know how to configure a server to handle those assets. Conversely, if your job is server administration, you may feel uninformed if you don't know at least the basics of Web media production.

That being said, not every Web media creator needs a *local* Web server. Maintaining such machines almost always involves unexpected time and effort (despite good site management software), and the new hardware honeymoon rarely goes on forever. Oh, and don't forget all those long-distance tech support calls.

If you'd rather be making Web movies, audio clips, or VRML worlds, you'll find renting or sharing space on someone else's server a viable alternative. The catch is

Unix commands— not just for breakfast anymore.

that getting advanced media types to perform requires a convenient means of *configuring* that remote server, and an efficient way to upload files. This usually means a substantial number of Telnet and FTP operations, followed by lots of test browsing—but it all comes with the territory.

The rest of this chapter will cover the day-to-day mechanics of transporting HTML files and media assets to remote Web servers, testing those files, and configuring servers remotely—assuming you have permission to do so. Chances are you'll need to know some Unix commands, since most existing Web servers are still Unix-based.

Remember that while many Internet Service Providers (ISPs) now offer server space to their customers for setting up personal Web sites, not all those ISPs can handle requests for, say, RealAudio or VDOLive compatibility. Most ISPs should be able to offer configuration for free technology like Shockwave, but it helps to get this in writing.

It will be interesting to see how fast and how well big ISPs offer streaming media to their at-home customers. If they don't, or do it poorly, it may hasten the demise of many me-and-my-dog personal sites.

If you can find another Web developer to share a server in return for professional services (or as part of a joint development effort), you will have the best of both worlds. Since that other developer will likely want his or her server configured with all the latest software, you'll be spared

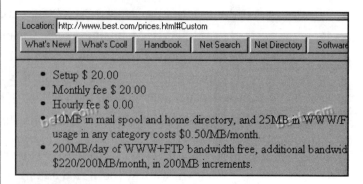

Figure 14.1

Server space for rent.

having to petition your normal ISP for these items—and you'll have the luxury of working with someone who probably wants new software up and running as fast as you do.

Of course, willing partners with good attitudes are always in extremely short supply, but you may have a lot more to offer a prospective collaborator than you realize. For one thing, you may legally be able to exploit single licenses for media streaming technology if both of your sites are resident on the same physical server. Or, if the other party specializes in programming while your expertise is media production, you might find unexpected synergy.

General Server Administration

On most Unix systems, security is an all or nothing proposition. In other words, there are basically just Users and Super Users. Other types of systems have more elaborate security levels.

Remote server administration chores fall into several distinct categories. We'll concentrate on the activities related to Web-based media, here, but feel free to look at other types of media to help you clarify the big picture. As noted, the main focus will be on remote Unix-based systems.

Before getting into detail, however, we need to touch on two high-level issues: privilege levels and permissions. To do any serious damage (like basic system configuration) on a secure server, a logged-in user needs a high level of clearance.

On some networks, people with a high security clearance are defined as network *Administrators*. On others (with Unix servers), such people are deemed to have *root* privileges. Under Unix, this is the same thing as being a so-called *Super User.*

How do you get root privileges? The short answer is, from another Super User. If this sounds somewhat cyclical,

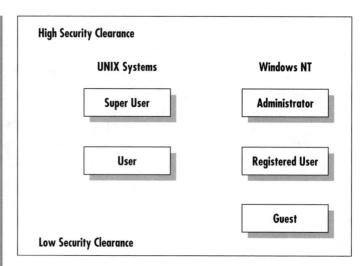

Figure 14.2
The Net security food chain.

don't worry—it's mainly about security issues, not skill level (although this is assumed). In reality, you probably won't be granted Super User privileges, since it can feel like a fairly risky proposition to the remote server owner.

Now the good news: You don't really need Super User status to perform most of the remote server configuration discussed in this chapter. What you *will* need is the help of an existing Super User or System Administrator to accomplish the following:

- Put entries for your site in the server's host table(s)—if you don't have such entries already. These are the places where your domain's name and IP address are associated with a base directory on the server hardware.

- Set the read, write, and execute flags for the base directory that constitutes your physical domain on the remote server, so that you can make changes to your subdirectories and files (or run them) when you log on with a given user name.

Flag viewing in a Telnet session.

- Configure processes like the Progressive Networks (RealAudio) virtual server to start up and run in the background each time the remote physical server is rebooted. These are easy things to forget until users start complaining. Non-Super Users generally will not have start-up privileges for virtual servers.

On some systems you may find that additional configuration tasks are required, but the list should be short, not seriously time-consuming, and essentially a one-shot deal. After the Super User sets you up properly, you'll be able to log in remotely and perform all the non-threatening configuration you wish. This overall scenario should work in most cases.

Once the Windows NT Internet servers catch up to Unix systems (and they are gaining fast), Web site management will undergo an enormous change.

With a base directory and read/write/execute permissions established, we can now consider three general remote administration tasks:

- Creating and modifying directory structures

- Setting file and directory permissions

- Checking access logs

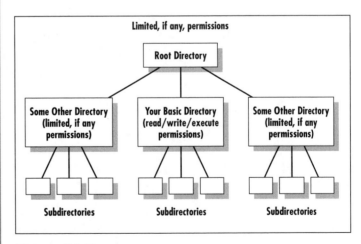

Figure 14.3

How limited permissions work.

A sensible strategy for creating a Web site directory tree on your remote server (including all your media files in categorical subdirectories) is to organize that tree in the same manner as the one on your local production machine—assuming your local machine is structured in this manner, which is highly recommended.

This strategy pays off when you make mission-critical archives of your site (for restoring to your server in the case of a meltdown), since working with mirror images of directory trees always saves time. Plus, it keeps things clear to other people who might need to work with your files down the line.

We'll assume in this example that your remote system is a Unix computer. To go in from scratch and establish a directory hierarchy on that server for the HTML and media files that will constitute your Web site, you'll need to execute the following steps in pretty much the following order:

1. Establish an FTP session with the remote server. As noted in other chapters, a good program for doing this under Windows is WS_FTP (shown in Figure 14.5). On the Mac there is the trusty Mac Fetch application.

The base directory for your HTML files will probably not be the same as the base directory for your physical site. At the site-base level there should be peer directories for your logs, CGI files, and configuration files—as well as your HTML files. All your media directories can then go under your base HTML directory.

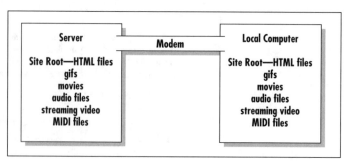

Figure 14.4
Matching directory trees.

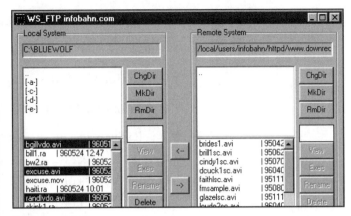

Figure 14.5

Moving files with WS_FTP.

2. Assuming you have navigated to your base HTML directory, use the *Create Directory* facility of your FTP tool to make subdirectories for all of your media files, as shown in Figure 14.6.

   Some typical media directories you might want to create are:

   • gif (for still image GIF files)

   • jpeg (for still image JPEG files)

   • mov (for flattened QuickTime movies)

   • avi (for Video for Windows movies)

   • wav (for WAV audio files)

   • mpg (for MPEG movies)

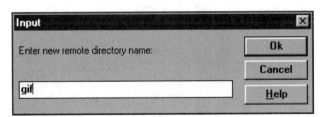

Figure 14.6

Creating a remote subdirectory.

- vdo (for streaming VDOLive movies)

- ra (for streaming RealAudio files)

- midi (for MIDI files)

- dcr (for Shockwave movies)

3. With all your media directories created (more can be added later, if necessary), you can now begin the laborious process of uploading the files themselves. Most people begin with their HTML scripts, then do the GIFs and JPEGs, effectively saving the larger and more exotic files till last (MIDI sequences would be an exception, since they are relatively small). If you have a lot of movie files, you can expect to spend a fair amount of time uploading them—just like your audience will when they download the same clips.

In most cases, you won't have to change the permissions for any subdirectories you create or for any files you upload—with the possible exception of Perl scripts and other CGI-related items. Asking the remote system administrator about the server's overall permissions strategy is a recommended way to begin this process.

As for access logs and error logs, you won't need to check them much in the beginning (other than to make sure

A good practice when using the Mac Fetch program is to transfer all your files as raw data, regardless of their file type.

CGI files probably won't conform to the mirror image directory tree strategy suggested earlier. We'll cover remote CGI directory issues shortly.

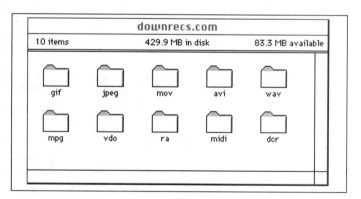

Figure 14.7

A list of sample directories.

they're working), but they'll become much more interesting and valuable as time goes on—and your site gets more popular.

Log file names and locations are often specified in a configuration file in or near the base directory for your site. Such configuration files are discussed below. More and better tools are being developed all the time to read log files and make sense out of the data they contain; but even in their raw form these files can be interesting. Figure 14.8 shows a sample log file.

Configuring MIME Content Types

A quick reminder: MIME is an acronym for Multipurpose Internet Mail Extension.

In Chapter 7, we discussed configuring a Web browser application to recognize various types of MIME content. This allows the browser to determine whether it needs a helper program to play an incoming data stream, or if it will try to read and display the contents of that data stream directly.

One the server side, MIME types are identified as well, but not in the same way as with, say, Netscape Navigator. According to the official HTTP spec, a Web server is

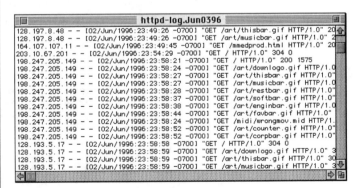

Figure 14.8

A native log file.

The Macromedia Web site (http:// www.macromedia .com) has much more detailed directions on how to configure a server to handle shocked movies.

supposed to include MIME type data at the start of all documents transmitted to a given browser.

The default behavior of a browser that does not recognize the MIME type of an incoming data stream—either because the MIME type is not defined at the browser level or the server has not identified it—is to prompt the user to save the stream as a file.

Let's say you want to add Macromedia Shockwave capability to your site. Assuming you have your *shocked* media file ready to go, the steps are:

1. With an FTP tool, transport the shocked movie to the appropriate location on your remote server—perhaps your dcr directory. (Production of shocked movies is covered in Chapter 5.)

2. Browse to the directory that contains the file that registers MIME types. On the Unix server used to test the procedures described in this chapter, the file is named mysite.conf and is in the same directory as the HTML base directory. In other words, it is one directory level up from where the HTML files are stored. Note that this may also be the file where logging is configured.

3. If possible, view this file in place. It should contain a section that has entries in the form of:

```
* [Some media name] enabling MIME type
AddType .aaa    bbbbbb/x-cccccccc    binary
```

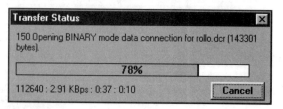

Figure 14.9

Transferring a shocked movie.

Again, going into this much detail for just one platform would be unnecessary if it weren't for the fact that so many servers are currently Unix-based and follow this model.

If the server was already configured for Shockwave, the section would contain these entries (subject to how the server interprets its configuration files):

```
* Shockwave for Director enabling MIME type
AddType .dcr    application/x-director    binary
AddType .dir    application/x-director    binary
AddType .dxr    application/x-director    binary
```

4. If the remote server configuration file does not contain such MIME type entries, you'll have to add them yourself (or ask your system administrator to do it). The most direct way is to Telnet in, invoke the Unix text editor, open the configuration file, and simply key in the new entries.

   Another way to add MIME type entries is to download the configuration file with your FTP tool, edit it locally with your own favorite text editor, then upload it back on top of the original configuration file. Even though it is a text file, you should FTP it back as raw data.

For Shockwave compatibility, this is the entire scope of the configuration task. The tricky parts are finding the right files to modify, dealing with their permission status, and getting the syntax right when you make the MIME type entries. If things still aren't working after three or four tries, contact the system administrator for help.

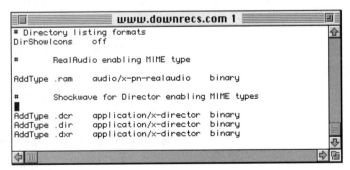

Figure 14.10

Editing the configuration file in place.

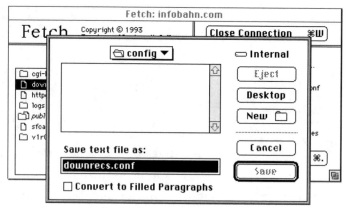

Figure 14.11

Downloading the configuration file.

If you were able to get things working without any help, you might feel ready for the next challenge: RealAudio. Of course, the full-on RA Server is not free (like Shockwave), but it does follow the standard MIME type configuration model.

Assuming you have made the investment, installed the RealAudio Server correctly (covered in Chapter 6), and are ready to proceed, here is the procedure:

The Progressive Networks Web site (http://www .realaudio.com) has much more detailed directions on how to configure a server to handle RealAudio files.

1. With an FTP tool, transport your files with a .RAM extension to the appropriate location on the remote server (perhaps your RA directory). Upload the RA files (the actual audio media) to the appropriate directory where they can be seen by the RealAudio virtual server. Production and placement of RealAudio assets is also covered in Chapter 6.

2. As with the Shockwave configuration, browse to the directory on the Unix server that contains the file that registers MIME types—in this case named mysite.conf—which is in the same directory as the HTML base directory. In other words, one directory level up from the HTML files.

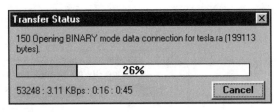

Figure 14.12

Transferring a RealAudio file.

3. If your FTP tool allows it, open this file in place. As we have seen, it should contain a section that has entries that look like this:

```
* Shockwave for Director enabling MIME type
AddType .dcr    application/x-director    binary
```

If the server was already configured to handle the RealAudio MIME type, the section would contain the following entries (subject to how the server interprets its configuration files):

```
* RealAudio enabling MIME type
AddType .ram    audio/x-pn-realaudio    binary
```

4. If the configuration file does not contain this MIME type entry, you'll have to add it yourself (or ask your system administrator for help). The options are:

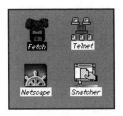

- Telnet in, invoke the Unix text editor, open the configuration file and simply make the changes.

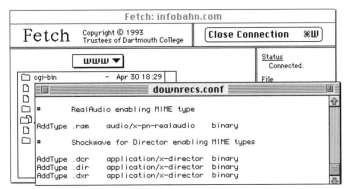

Figure 14.13

Using the Unix text editor.

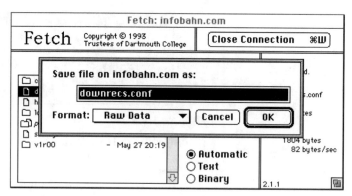

Figure 14.14

Uploading the changed configuration file.

- Download the file with your FTP tool, edit it locally with your own favorite text editor, then upload it back on top of the original.

Unlike when configuring Shockwave, this is not the whole story. Until you get the RealAudio virtual server up and running and put your RA files (as opposed to your RAM files) in the right place, your audience won't be able to hear your carefully crafted productions. Once again, these tasks were detailed in Chapter 6.

Remember that the developer of the software that plays a given type of asset usually provides the final word on how to best perform the server side configuration.

This is about as complex as it gets for configuring MIME content types on a remote server. For the record, setting up the VDOLive server and the configuration file for delivery of streaming video files follows the RealAudio model almost exactly.

For example, the specific entry setting the VDO MIME type is:

```
* VDOLive enabling MIME type
AddType .vdo    video/vdo    binary
```

Of course, there are other Web-based media types that need similar entries in a server's configuration file(s) if a Web site manager expects his or her assets to be handled efficiently when requested by logged-in browsers.

CGI Mapping

It is not uncommon to specify a CGI execution directory in the same server configuration file that contains MIME content type and logging file definitions. Standard Unix servers generally adhere to this practice, while Windows- and Mac-based servers are known to handle CGI mapping somewhat differently. The place where CGI scripts and Web media converge is often the animation of sequences of small images (as shown in Figure 14.15) in so-called *server pushes*.

It is fair to say that problems with CGI programs (such as Perl scripts) occur more out of misunderstanding how they work than out of misconfiguration. Essentially, the server needs to be told if a file is an executable CGI program, as opposed to something that should be downloaded to the user.

In reality, defining a CGI execution directory is an almost trivial type of server configuration. It can usually be accomplished by asking your system administrator which configuration file to change, then editing that file to include the path to the cgi-bin directory. A fragment from a generic Unix configuration file is shown below.

```
# Scripts; URLs starting with /cgi-bin/ will be
  understood
# as script calls in the directory /your/script/
  directory
Exec  /cgi-bin/*    /httpd/www.downrecs.com/www/
  cgi-bin/*
Map   /img/*   /cgi-bin/htimage/*
```

You'll notice that a directory for image maps is also defined in this fragment, which is another area handled differently by Unix than by other operating systems, specifically Windows. An image map is a clickable graphic in an HTML document that invokes different types of actions depending on which part of it is clicked.

Figure 14.15
A server push example.

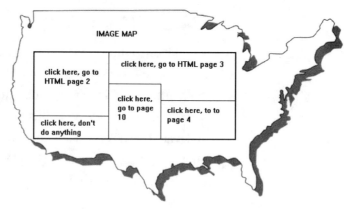

Figure 14.16

How an image map works.

This communication is accomplished by specifying the directory in which executable CGI programs are stored, which is done in the configuration file (at least under Unix). Once you have this part set up correctly, all that remains is referencing the CGI programs correctly in your HTML documents.

Testing and Troubleshooting on a Remote Server

Two of the ugly realities of multimedia Web site development are:

- Lots of testing is required.

- Sometimes things just stop working.

If your Web site is maintained on a remote server, the developmental testing process can take a little longer, but you'll have the advantage of working under field conditions. This actually brings up an important question: What is your philosophy for doing construction on the live version of your site?

Figure 14.17

Have you seen me?

If you perform server configuration while the public visits your pages, you risk distracting them with disabled functionality. Many developers (those that can afford it) work only on private remote copies of their sites, then transfer the whole directory tree to the live site during off-peak hours (whatever those are deemed to be).

It's a tricky business, but there is very little getting around it. Fortunately, seasoned Web surfers are generally a forgiving lot—if you don't waste too much of their time. One can only imagine the time wasted at big corporate sites sorting these issues out.

Because there are so many variables involved with any new or different Web media type, a time-consuming testing cycle is inevitable—and should be factored into any mission-critical development project. The hours spent on repetitive HTML tweaking and FTP transfers alone can be staggering when you add them all up.

As with traditional software development, planning and discipline are crucial if you want to meet deadlines. Lots of fooling-around time is, of course, required for anyone who wants to become an expert, but professionals know how to budget this in before a serious project gets started.

No wonder there is such a demand for powerful Web site management tools—and such different approaches to designing them.

Of course, you'll already know how long the testing cycle takes if you have spent non-business time simply exploring or creating a personal project on a remote server using technology like Shockwave, RealAudio, VDOLive, and multipart GIFs (just to name a few). Whole days simply vanish.

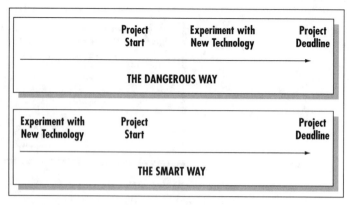

	Project Start	Experiment with New Technology		Project Deadline

THE DANGEROUS WAY

Experiment with New Technology	Project Start			Project Deadline

THE SMART WAY

Figure 14.18

The correct and incorrect ways to handle a project.

For example, assume you're not a world class Director programmer, but you do have enough experience to create a 160 × 120 Director animation that you want to put on a Web page as a Shockwave movie. How hard can that be?

You go through the Afterburner and HTML embedding processes (see Chapter 5), upload the movie and the modified HTML file to your remote server, fire up your WWW browser—but you can't see the movie playing. What's wrong?

After several hours of remaking the movie in Director, confirming the correct syntax in the HTML document that contains the movie, FTPing the movie to the server, and retesting, it's still not happening. Finally you prevail upon a Director specialist (or hire one) who tells you the reason you're not seeing the movie is because it was not built flush to the upper left corner of the Director stage.

Director Stage

In other words, the movie was running on the Web page all along, but was being cropped out of the Web page presentation rectangle. As an inexperienced Director programmer you built the animation in the *center* of the stage—not realizing how the two rectangles are related.

As noted earlier, another good place to waste time and get really frustrated is making CGI scripts work. Understanding the big picture first before coding anything is always rewarding in the long run—as any experienced software developer will testify.

Unfortunately, this kind of stuff happens all too often. One reason is that Web-based media is exciting enough to make developers want to jump right into it without reading the directions—much less doing any serious planning or design work.

The thing to remember is that even though your remote server may seem to be the source of problems when things go wrong, it is more often the case that the media themselves are to blame or that user configuration has been performed improperly.

Managing Web
media assets
regardless of
their creation
platform (Mac
or Windows).

Chapter **15**

Cross-Platform Issues

This chapter will be helpful to developers who create multimedia assets on either a Mac or a Windows machine, but need to offer *both* Mac and Windows versions of those assets on their Web servers. Working with multiple versions of desktop media assets (and doing conversions back and forth between them) is generally referred to as cross-platform development.

While most cross-platform developers will have at least one Mac and one Windows computer in their production suites, they are not likely to do *platform-specific* digitizations for each multimedia asset on their Web sites (although this would be arguably better for optimum quality and performance).

In other words, if you have a movie you want to offer as both AVI and QuickTime (separate clips), that movie would generally look better to its audience if the AVI

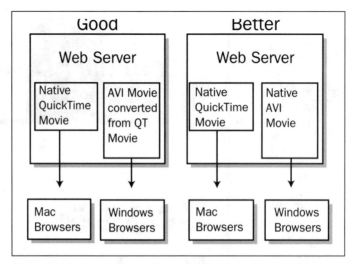

Figure 15.1

The benefits of multiple versions.

version were captured on a Windows machine and the QuickTime version was digitized on a Mac. Unfortunately, real-life budgets and schedules don't normally permit this level of luxury.

When you think about it, we're actually talking less about cross-platform compatibility than about media *continuity*. Since any desktop video clip produced for the Mac probably has a Windows version in its future (and vice versa), finding a reliable way to convert such a clip instead of re-digitizing and postproducing it would be a major advantage.

Moreover, assuming this conversion was easy and reliable, you would then have, in effect, a single video asset available in all three formats: QuickTime Mac, QuickTime for Windows, and AVI (provided the tool in question could convert with no data loss in both directions).

Unfortunately, no robust commercial tool currently exists. There are some 90 percent solutions and workarounds, but each has its own particular problems. For instance, Microsoft provides utilities that can convert from QT to

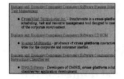

Note that serious cross-platform issues really only concern video. Audio files (like Windows WAVs) can be platform-specific, but you can convert them without worrying that they'll sound different. However, due to factors like gamma, Mac QuickTime files can look different when converted and played on Windows machines.

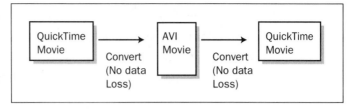

Figure 15.2
The beauty of media continuity.

AVI, and vice-versa, on the Mac. On the Windows side, Intel (*http://www.intel.com*) offers a program named SMARTCAP.EXE for converting Indeo files, and Download Recordings has posted a popular utility named TRMOOV.EXE on its Web site (*http://www.downrecs. com*).

Finally, while Adobe Premiere for Windows is capable of outputting in both QuickTime and AVI formats (with some limitations), its price may not justify it being purchased simply as a file format conversion tool—although most professional developers probably have invested in Premiere by now.

With these limitations in mind, the balance of this chapter will present strategies for converting from one desktop video format to the other, regardless of whether you're working on the Mac or the PC. We'll also cover conversion to MPEG and some relevant cross-platform compatibility issues for servers.

Converting on the Mac

QuickTime to AVI— Uncompressed Source

The first rule of thumb is to always perform conversions on files that are as uncompressed as possible. Since this

example begins on the Mac, the appropriate uncompressed format is the QuickTime *None* codec. Starting with movies that are already compressed (with the Cinepak codec, for example) requires a different strategy, which is detailed later in this chapter.

If you grab video on the Mac with a board that saves raw captures in MJPEG, you can convert those clips to None in Premiere with no loss of quality (although you could need up to eight or ten times as much hard disk storage space as the MJPEG files require). None essentially means straight RGB encoding with no effective data loss. Premiere for Windows 4.2 now uses this term as well.

One good technique is to install software on your Mac that can read DOS-formatted external hard drives (or Windows software than can read Mac drives). Formatter Five from Software Architects (206-487-0122) does this very reliably on the Mac. Thus equipped, you can move your uncompressed movies around easily and enjoy cross-platform portability at its finest.

Speaking of hard drives, you're going to need a way to transport the converted movie file to your Windows environment. If you're not using a LAN, plugging and playing mass storage devices (1 GB and larger hard drives, Jazz drives, etc.) can be quite acceptable in this context—as long as you manage them carefully and intelligently.

Assuming you have a None-encoded QuickTime file ready to go on your Mac, the next task is to convert it to an AVI file. The Microsoft Macintosh program VfW Converter is custom made for this purpose. You can download this program (as part of a Stuffit archive named QTAVI.SIT) from CompuServe's Windows Multimedia forum (GO WINMM).

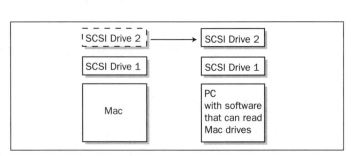

Figure 15.3

Transporting movie files on big hard drives.

While QTAVI.SIT was rumored to be on Microsoft's Web site at one time, recent searches there have not produced results. It is worth trying once in a while to see if this situation changes.

Here's how to use the VfW Converter:

1. Double click VfW Converter on your Mac desktop. The main User Interface will appear, as shown in Figure 15.4.

2. Click the *Open Source* button to invoke the file selection dialog box, shown in Figure 15.5, then navigate to the directory that contains your source QuickTime movie(s).

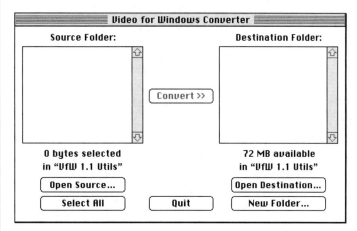

Figure 15.4

The VfW Converter main user interface.

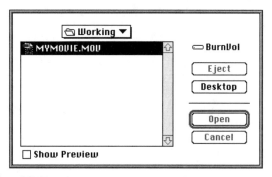

Figure 15.5

Selecting a source movie.

3. Back in the main UI, click *Open Destination* to navigate to the target drive and directory. Then click the *Convert* button; the dialog box shown in Figure 15.6 will appear.

4. Enter the target file name in the *Destination File Name* field (if you want it to be different from the default).

5. Choose the top combo box in the *Video* group and select *Uncompressed*, as shown in Figure 15.7. This step is very important!

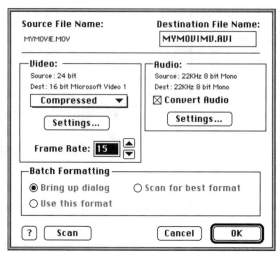

Figure 15.6
The conversion window.

Figure 15.7
Selecting the Uncompressed option.

6. Choose the bottom combo box in the *Video* group and select *24 bit*, as shown in Figure 15.8.

7. Set the *Frame Rate* control to match the frame rate in the source QuickTime movie (for instance, 15 frames per second). Note that VfW Converter preserves the key frame frequency from the source to the target. In this case, however, it doesn't matter since all the target movie's frames are key frames (since the clip is uncompressed).

AVI to QuickTime— Uncompressed Source

Since we've established that working with uncompressed source movies is always preferable, let's take a look at VfW Converter's masterfully-named companion program: AVI to QT Utility (another Microsoft product).

This application is included in the same Mac StuffIt archive (QTAVI.SIT) that contains VfW Converter (when you download the archive from CompuServe). Also included is a file for your Mac's system folder named Windows Compressors, which needs to be installed when using AVI to QT Utility.

Our goal is to derive an uncompressed (again, the None codec) QuickTime movie which we can then process and compress just like any other raw QuickTime clip. To be

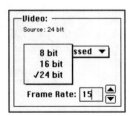

Figure 15.8
Selecting the target bit depth.

Surprisingly enough, many desktop producers expect Apple and Microsoft to spend development money on converters that could possibly benefit their competition. Don't forget that these two desktop video superpowers are still engaged in a winner-take-all standards conflict. Company reps may claim that giving users solutions to their multimedia problems is the new corporate mission, but there is simply too much at stake to take such positions completely seriously.

honest, the AVI to QT Utility seems to be slightly less reliable than the VfW Converter, but it is still regularly used for professional multimedia production.

Here's the blow by blow:

1. Get the uncompressed AVI file onto your Mac, either via a LAN or by connecting an external hard drive that has the file on it. The codec type of the file will appear to VidEdit as *Full Frames (Uncompressed)*, and to Premiere for Windows 4.2 as *None*.

2. Launch the AVI to QT Utility by clicking its icon on your Mac desktop. Its main user interface will appear, as shown in Figure 15.9.

3. Navigate to the directory containing your source file using the drop-down combo box in the upper left of the UI. Double click the source file (or highlight it and click the *Add* button) to move it into the *Files to Convert* list box.

4. When all the clips you want to process are added to the *Files to Convert* list, click the *Convert* button.

5. In the resulting dialog box navigate to the destination folder for the converted clip(s). Check the radio button labeled *Save Self-Contained Movie*. Checking the other radio button, *Save Normally (dependency*

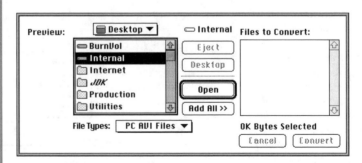

Figure 15.9
The AVI to QT Utility main user interface.

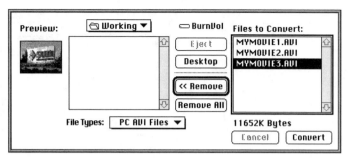

Figure 15.10

Selecting the source file.

to AVI file), does just what it says: It creates a pilot QuickTime clip that refers to the source AVI file for the movie data at playback time. When you're done, click the *Open* button.

6. As the conversion proceeds, a progress bar will follow the action in a separate dialog box.

If you really want to make sure the movie is in good shape structurally, you should check it using Premiere's movie analysis tools.

7. When the conversion is complete, open the file in the QuickTime Movie Player. Check to see that the converted clip is well formed by simply playing it and also checking its attributes in Movie Player's various movie information menus.

8. As a final precaution, do a *Save As* on the file from Movie Player. This will ensure that audio chunks are interleaved correctly and generally enforces

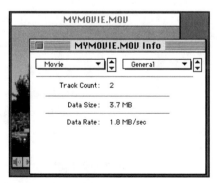

Figure 15.11

Confirming proper conversion.

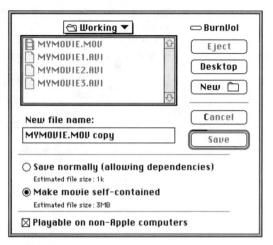

Figure 15.12

Flattening the movie while saving.

healthy movie data organization. Remember to flatten the movie when you do the Save As.

QuickTime to AVI— Compressed Source

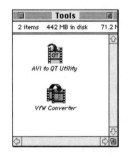

If you must convert starting with a compressed movie, VfW Converter can still do the job, but you need to watch out for a few things along the way. We'll point those out as we go through the following steps. This example assumes the source QuickTime movie is encoded with the Cinepak compressor.

1. Double-click VfW Converter on your Mac desktop. The main UI will appear, as shown back in Figure 15.4.

2. Click the *Open Source* button to invoke the file selection dialog box, then navigate to the directory that contains your source QuickTime movie(s).

3. Back in the main UI, click *Open Destination* to navigate to the target drive and directory; then click

To switch to another codec, you must have the Windows Compressors System Extension installed. This file is included in the QTAVI.SIT archive, along with the VfW Converter and AVI to QT Utility.

the *Convert* button—the dialog box shown back in Figure 15.5 will appear.

4. Enter the target file name in the *Destination File Name* field (if you want it to be different from the default).

5. Choose the top combo box in the *Video* group and select *Direct Transfer*. This means the target movie will be encoded with Cinepak, just like the source. If you select the *Compressed* option, you can convert your source movie to a QuickTime file encoded with a non-Cinepak compressor—such as Video 1. However, this would take longer than a direct transfer since the clip would be physically recompressed.

6. Set the *Frame Rate* control to match the frame rate in the source QuickTime movie (for instance, 15 frames per second). Again, note that VfW Converter preserves the key frame frequency from the source to the target.

As previously noted, VfW Converter does not adjust the audio/video interleave in the target AVI movie. This is significant because AVI movies generally perform best when the AV interleave ratio is 1 to 1. The standard QuickTime interleave factor is a half second of audio to a half second of video. This means that if a QuickTime movie's frame rate is ten

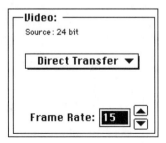

Figure 15.13

Selecting the Direct Transfer option.

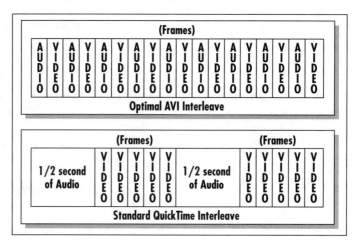

Figure 15.14

QuickTime vs. AVI audio interleaving.

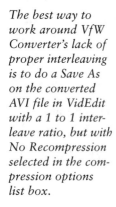

Re-interleaving a
converted
AVI file.

*The best way to
work around VfW
Converter's lack of
proper interleaving
is to do a Save As
on the converted
AVI file in VidEdit
with a 1 to 1 inter-
leave ratio, but with
No Recompression
selected in the com-
pression options
list box.*

frames per second, there will be five video frames
together before there is any audio data.

7. Check the *Convert Audio* check box. If you need to
resample the audio track, click the *Settings* button in
the *Audio* group and choose a new sample size and
rate from the controls in the resultant *Audio Settings*
dialog box.

8. When you have everything calibrated, click the *OK*
button. A dialog box with a progress bar will appear,
showing you the relative time remaining in the conversion process. Since our target codec is the same
as the source, this process should move along pretty
quickly.

9. The converted file can now be read by a Windows
machine (at least Windows 95 or Windows 3.1 with
Video for Windows installed) as long as the appropriate decompressor is present—in this case
Cinepak. Assuming the converted file is on a DOS-
formatted external drive that you can plug into your
DOS SCSI chain, plug it in now. (Don't forget to
turn off your machine first!)

10. From your Windows desktop, launch the Media Player and test the converted clip. As noted above, you may want to open it in VidEdit and resave it to ensure 1 to 1 AV interleaving.

AVI to QuickTime— Compressed Source

While both the AVI to QT Utility and the VfW Converter do well with Cinepak and uncompressed movies, Intel's Indeo can be another story. As noted earlier, Intel has a free Windows-based converter for Indeo files, as well as a white paper on cross-platform development with Indeo. Both of these items are available on their Web site (http://www. intel.com).

Of the four main methods for employing the VfW Converter/AVI to QT Utility combination, the one that follows is likely the one you'll use least. Still, it does merit some attention if you don't want to capture on the Macintosh.

Our goal is simpler than when working an *uncompressed* AVI source file. All we want is a compressed QuickTime movie that will play well on the Mac desktop. Again, the AVI to QT Utility sometimes seems a little less stable than the VfW Converter application, but it is definitely worth getting to know.

The steps for using the AVI to QT Utility when the source movie is already compressed are as follows:

1. Get the compressed AVI file onto your Mac using a LAN or external hard drive.

2. Launch the AVI to QT Utility. Its main user interface will appear, as shown in Figure 15.15.

3. Navigate to the directory containing your source file using the drop-down combo box in the upper left of the UI. Double click on the file you want converted in the current source directory to move it into the *Files to Convert* list box. If you want to see the first frame of a potential source movie, you can simply highlight it in the source directory list.

4. When all the clips you want to process are added to the *Files to Convert* list, click the *Convert* button.

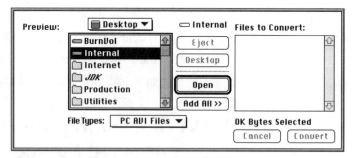

Figure 15.15

The AVI to QT Utility's main user interface.

5. In the next dialog box, navigate to the destination folder for the converted clip(s). Check the radio button labeled *Save Self-Contained Movie* and then click the *Open* button.

   As noted earlier, checking the radio button labeled *Save Normally (dependency to AVI file)* creates a pilot QuickTime clip that refers to the source AVI file for the actual movie data at playback time—a very Mac-centric idea.

   While elegant in design, this facility is mainly used to view the contents of an AVI file if there is no other way to play it. Few, if any, commercial Macintosh products have been released that use this approach to playing movies.

6. As the conversion proceeds, a progress bar will follow the action in a separate dialog box.

7. When the conversion is complete, open the file in the QuickTime Movie Player. Check to see that the converted clip is well formed by simply playing it, and also by checking its attributes in Movie Player's various movie information menus.

8. As a final precaution, do a *Save As* on the file from Movie Player. This will ensure that audio chunks are interleaved correctly and generally enforces

If it hasn't already occurred to you, just doing a Yahoo or Alta Vista search on the phrase "cross-platform" can be very illuminating. When this book was written, such a search on Yahoo yielded 66 references.

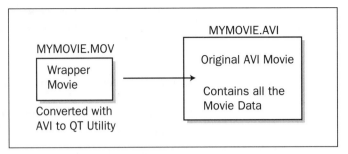

Figure 15.16
A non-standalone QuickTime movie depends on an AVI file.

Neither Video for Windows nor QuickTime for Windows needs to be installed for TRMOOV to perform a conversion. Playback of the converted movie, however, does require installation of the appropriate software—either VfW or QTW.

healthy movie data organization. Remember to flatten the movie when you do the *Save As*.

TRMOOV

TRMOOV.EXE is a Windows application for converting back and forth between the QuickTime for Windows file format and the Video for Windows (AVI) file format without recompression. A copy of TRMOOV is included on the CD-ROM that comes with this book.

TRMOOV is specifically designed to convert movie files that have the same source and target codec. For instance, if the source file is a QuickTime Cinepak movie, the target movie will be a Video for Windows Cinepak movie.

Two other features of TRMOOV are:

- Conversion back and forth between QTW sound-only movies and Microsoft WAV files (the target file must have the .WAV extension).

- Batch mode conversions. Since TRMOOV takes command line arguments, a Test Basic-style script can be constructed using multiple RUN statements. For example:

```
RUN "TRMOOV.EXE MOVIE1.MOV MOVIE1.AVI"
RUN "TRMOOV.EXE MOVIE2.MOV MOVIE2.AVI"
```

```
RUN "TRMOOV.EXE MOVIE3.MOV MOVIE3.AVI"
RUN "TRMOOV.EXE MOVIE4.MOV MOVIE4.AVI"
(more lines in script)
```

The steps involved in running TRMOOV are:

1. Start the program from your Windows 3.1 or Windows 95 desktop. Its main user interface will appear as show in Figure 15.17.

2. Click the *Browse* button opposite the *Source Movie* text field, then navigate (via the file selection dialog box) to the movie you want to convert. The first frame of the movie should appear in the window in the middle of the UI.

3. Click the *Browse* button opposite the *Target Movie* text field, then navigate to the directory for the converted movie and name the clip in the text field.

4. Click the *Start* Button. A progress bar will track the relative time left until the conversion is complete.

Figure 15.17

TRMOOV's main user interface.

TRMOOV is also available on the Web site http://www.downrecs.com, along with some additional information concerning its redistribution policy.

Figure 15.18

Selecting a source movie.

Known Restrictions of TRMOOV:

- When going from QTW to VfW, make sure your source movie's audio sampling rate is MPC (11.025 kHz, 22.05 kHz, 44.1 kHz, etc.). The current version of TRMOOV preserves the source movie's sampling rate, and some Windows sound cards do not handle Mac audio rates (such as 22.254) very well.

- If your source movie has a palette attached, it may not be present in the target movie.

- Longer movies output by TRMOOV may lose their audio/video synch after several minutes.

Cross-Platforming with Premiere

While working with a bunch of tried and true utilities can be satisfying and at least fairly efficient, some people still like to use big tools that do it all. In the case of Premiere 4.2, this impulse is *almost* completely justified.

The problem is, you can't make AVI movies with the Mac version of Premiere 4.2. If you could, you would be able to convert in one pass from the QuickTime MJPEG format of a fresh Mac capture to a VDOLive-encoded AVI movie.

What makes this seem *close* to possible is finding compressors like Microsoft RLE and Video 1 available in the *Make Movie* dialog boxes. Unfortunately, when Premiere for the Mac makes movies with these codecs, you get QuickTime files—not AVI files.

For added quality assurance, remember to open and resave (with MoviePlayer) any QuickTime movie encoded on the Windows side—even clips output by Premiere for Windows.

Which brings us to Premiere 4.2 for Windows. You can indeed make Mac-playable QuickTime movies with this product, and can go in one pass from the MJPEG format of a Windows capture card to a Cinepak-compressed QuickTime clip. Producers with Premiere experience generally have this side of the cross-platform equation down to a fine art.

If Mac capture card makers provided QuickTime for Windows versions of their MJPEG codecs, you could at

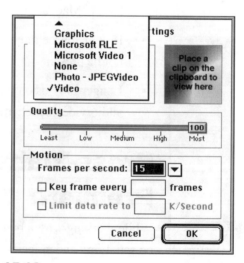

Figure 15.19

Windows compressors in Mac Premiere.

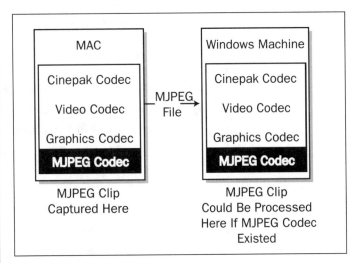

Figure 15.20
A more perfect world.

least take a freshly captured Mac file directly over to a Windows machine—without having to export to None as an interim step. Perhaps this will happen in the not-too-distant future.

Converting to and from MPEG

Note that we are talking specifically about downloadable MPEG files here—not the streaming MPEG files that Xing's Streamworks uses. Xing's technology is covered in other chapters.

Technically speaking, converting a movie to or from the MPEG format is not a cross-platform operation—mainly because MPEG has no native *platform* per se. Contrast this with QuickTime, which is core technology on the Mac, and Video for Windows (AVI), whose name says it all.

On the other hand, since MPEG constitutes a different file format than either QuickTime or AVI, some cross-platform issues do often come up. The important ones for Web media developers are:

- How do I produce MPEG clips for downloading from my Web site?

- What software does the user need to play them?

- What are the advantages of offering MPEG clips?

The short answer to the first question is: Capture MPEG clips with dedicated MPEG capture boards. These cards used to cost upwards of $20,000 but are now starting to break the $5,000 barrier. Forget about converting from existing AVI or QuickTime files, at least for the near future.

Question two also has a quick answer: Go to the Web sites of the browser makers (like Netscape) and see what they offer or recommend in the way of MPEG-specific helper apps or plug-ins. Software-only MPEG playback used to be a joke (as opposed to doing it in hardware, like with the ReelMagic card), but this is changing quickly with better technology and Pentium-class machines proliferating. While you're at it, search for MPEG-related topics in general to see how fast things are changing.

Finally, the general advantages of offering downloadable MPEG clips seem slight—judging by how many sites are actually doing it. If you client wants it, great, but there are few compelling reasons to do it—at least for now.

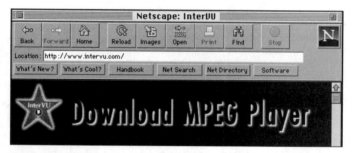

Figure 15.21

Netscape's MPEG helper application.

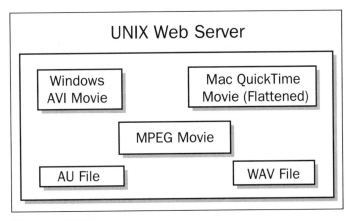

Figure 15.22

Cross-platform assets on a Web server.

Cross-Platform Assets and Web Servers

To a server, a file is a file—at least from a hardware/data processing point of view. Mac Web servers deliver Windows files, Windows machines serve Mac assets (if the files obey certain naming conventions) and Unix servers have been doing it longer than either Mac or Windows computers.

In general, the cross-platform issues that confront Web media asset developers rarely come up for server administrators. Being unfamiliar with the basic user interface of a Mac, a Windows machine, or a Unix box could be classified as a cross-platform-*like* problem, but this is stretching the definition.

Not that these problems are trivial—as you'll quickly learn the first time you Telnet to a Unix server and you only know Mac or Windows commands. The bottom line is, if you represent yourself as a cross-platform Web developer, be sure to specify what basic areas you work in.

Chapter 16

Assembling a Web Media Production Facility

Setting up a facility for Web media production is a lot like building a traditional multimedia studio (if there is such a thing). The main difference is that you'll need extra computers for maintaining the physical Web site. Even if your site runs on a remote server (covered in Chapter 14), it's a good idea to have at least one machine dedicated to uploads, downloads, and general browsing.

The decision to use Mac gear or PC equipment will likely be a function of the environment in which you are most comfortable, as opposed to the relative merits of either. If you've had positive experiences working on both platforms, you will probably incorporate elements of each, particularly if your media is cross-platform (see Chapter 15). These days, not being a cross-platform shop can put you at a disadvantage.

Because of market pressures, Mac developers are more likely to venture into the Windows world than vice versa. The fact remains, however, that experienced Windows-based media makers will still be lured by the top-notch digitization they can achieve with high-end Mac capture devices.

In Chapter 8 we proposed an abstract media capture station composed of abstract components. The idea was to visualize how those components worked together (or limited each other) based on understanding the potential bottlenecks. When building your own Web media studio, you should consider using that abstract model, as shown in Figure 16.1, as an overlay for the actual components you plan to integrate.

Getting Set Up

Regardless of your production platform (Mac or PC), there are some basic habits you should consider for the day-to-day operation of your computer systems and analog media hardware. These practices fall into two categories: technical and practical.

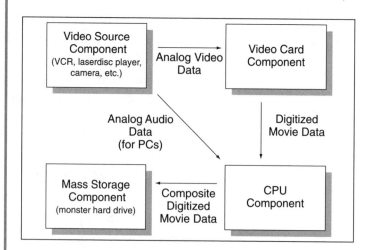

Figure 16.1

An abstract capture station.

Technical Setup Recommendations

- Number your SCSI devices in the order they are connected on your physical SCSI chain, as shown in Figure 16.2. For instance, make your external hard drive SCSI ID 1, the CD-ROM drive SCSI ID 2, your SyQuest unit SCSI ID 3, the ZIP drive SCSI ID 6, and so on, assuming they are connected in that order.

- Think of your mega hard drives as rapid deployment gear, ready for space-hungry raw captures at any given time. If you have both Mac and PC capture stations, keeping a big hard drive wiped clean between capture sessions will let you switch it between the two platforms with a minimum of overhead.

- For real-time editing with possibly hundreds of MB worth of raw clips, burning those files to CD (to free

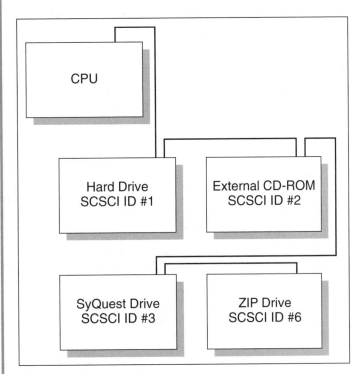

Figure 16.2

Numbering your SCSI devices in order.

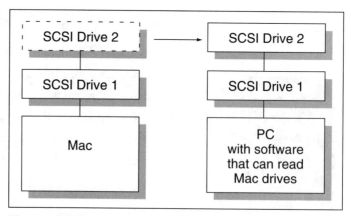

Figure 16.3

Efficient hard drive management.

up hard drive space) can backfire if your CD-ROM drive is too slow (under 4X). If you want fast previews and updates in your Premiere Construction window, plan on keeping your working clips on a hard disk—unless you have a speed demon CD-ROM drive.

- Think carefully about whether you really want to install a local area network (if you don't have one

While products like DeskLink and LapLink are fine for moving small files between computers without the overhead of a LAN, don't consider them for day-to-day transfers of movie files—especially raw movies. Serial port products just aren't fast enough compared to LANs and hard drive swaps.

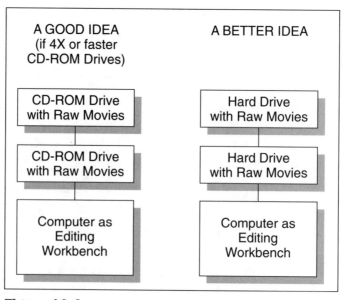

Figure 16.4

Raw asset management.

already). Granted, LANs are essential for business offices. But if your production studio is all in one room and the only files you're moving among machines are big media clips, you might find it more efficient to do it all with 1 GB (or larger) hard drives.

Practical Setup Recommendations

- Draw some stick diagrams of your work area on a yellow legal pad before shelling out for any new furniture. Include power and data cable paths in the sketches. Check with building authorities to make sure the existing circuitry can handle the increased electrical load.

- Use reinforced metal racks for all your equipment. Why torture expensive wood-grain tables and shelves with the inevitable wear and tear? Anthro carts (*http://www.anthro.com*) are worth looking into if you expect to move pieces of your studio around a lot.

- Give all your gear lots of space to breathe. In other words, only keep one or two components on each shelf, and ensure that there is air space between

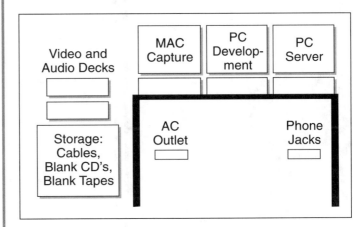

Figure 16.5
Planning your studio.

Figure 16.6

Keeping things functional.

Do you need a CD-ROM burner in your Web media studio? The short answer is probably yes, if only for making archives and keeping clients happy. Burners are relatively cheap now, and the software that runs them has matured greatly.

them. Temperature issues notwithstanding, you'll want continuous and convenient access to all cable connections.

- Even if your work area is relatively small, leave adequate room behind your racks for you to re-cable and track down bad connections. You'll be glad you did.

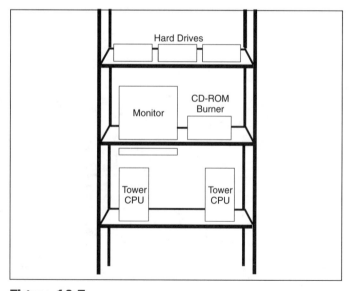

Figure 16.7

Give your equipment room to breathe.

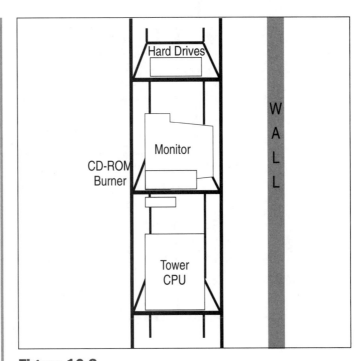

Figure 16.8

Allow for easy access.

- If your computers are of the desktop variety—as opposed to the tower models—don't pile peripheral gear on top of them (such as big hard drives or even monitors). If you do lots of production, you'll find yourself opening up your machines frequently to swap adapter cards, add RAM, and even upgrade Pentium chips. Few things are more grim than clearing heavily-wired components off your CPU when you need to reterminate your SCSI adapter card— or watching the whole lot crash to the floor if the equipment was stacked carelessly.

- Color code your cables to keep them organized (don't laugh). Yellow is good for video, white for the left audio channel, and red for the right. If you can stand it, label each end of your serial, telephone, and SCSI cables with a strip of tape. Okay, laugh a

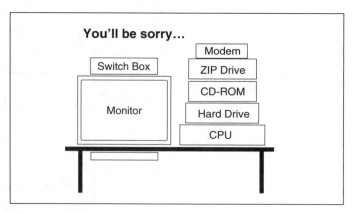

Figure 16.9

Avoid stacking your gear.

little—but someone else might be laughing at you later when you're lost in a sea of cables in the midst of a deadline.

- Use switch boxes as necessary (for at least audio and serial cables) but be careful how you arrange the wires. To prevent buzzing and general electrical interference, avoid coiling of data cables and having them in close proximity to power cables. Check out *http://www.vir.com/cablek* for some ideas on this subject (at press time the site was available intermittently).

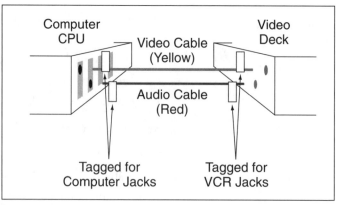

Figure 16.10

Color code and tag your cables.

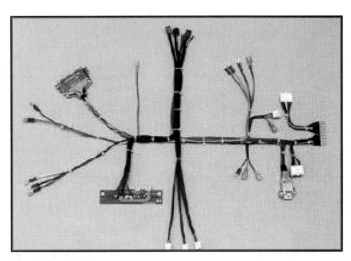

Figure 16.11

A cable harness.

Building a Mac-Based Web Media Studio

For information on generic Macintosh hardware, as well as media capture and editing software, please refer to Chapters 8 and 9. As of this writing, most professional Mac moviemakers have invested in Power Macs as their workhorse CPUs. The standard 8100 is a common choice (with lots of extra RAM), but many media producers are now turning to the 9500.

Don't forget to look at the Mac clones as candidates for your core production machines. Chip speeds rivaling the top Pentiums (180 MHz and greater) have been announced from the clone makers as of this writing.

If you have a Quadra 840AV, or even a Quadra 950 that continues to make movies reliably, there is no reason to give it up. Since Web clips are generally less than quarter screen, new life can be breathed into many older Macs, at least for the time being. You probably wanted to use that new 9500 to browse with anyway.

Figure 16.12 shows the basic components of a capture station, including standalone Web server/browser. Of course, a corporate publisher's HTTP server would probably be in a much more secure environment, but less ambitious sites can easily be run from less official environments.

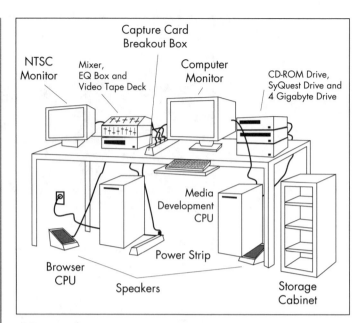

Figure 16.12

A Web media production station.

Building a PC-Based Media Studio

We need to give at least a nod here to the next generation of digital decks and cameras (digital Betacam decks already exist). Will this new gear make PC-based video capture obsolete? Probably in the long run, but not immediately.

Again, for information on generic hardware and media capture and editing software, please refer to Chapters 8 and 9. As of this writing, most professional Windows-based moviemakers have invested in Pentiums (with lots of extra RAM) as their workhorse CPUs and many are running Windows NT.

As with Quadra-era Macs, if you have a 486 that keeps on giving (as in making movies reliably), there is no reason to retire it from show business. Since Web clips are generally less than 320×240, new life can be breathed into many pre-Pentium machines, at least for the time being. As on the Mac side, you'll likely want to use your best machine(s) for Web duty.

Again, Figure 16.12 shows the basic components of a generic capture station, including a standalone Web server and browsing machine.

Equipment Issues

Miscellaneous Equipment

Without a few boxes of loose cables, connectors, and adapters, you have no right to hang out your media production shingle. Below is a short list of the types of spare parts you'll want to have handy. For brevity, it's expressed in techno-geek, but any Radio Shack salesperson will get some for you without a fuss.

And don't forget lots of blank videotapes, head cleaner tapes, extra batteries and a charger for you video camera, and a supply of blank CD-ROMs if you decide to get a burner.

- Loose audio and composite video cables

- Loose S-Video cables

- Loose SCSI cables with various SCSI connectors (SCSI 1, SCSI 2, etc.)

- Loose modem and other RS-232 cables

- Y connectors

- RCA to phone jack (and plug) adapters

- RCA to mini phone jack (and plug) adapters

- Phone jack to mini phone jack (and plug) adapters

- BNC to RCA and BNC to phone jack connectors

Figure 16.13

The Radio Shack cornucopia.

And the list goes on. Imagine you're on a deadline for the next morning with rented gear. Around midnight you determine that some re-cabling is necessary, but you've already used up your modest supply. Unfortunately, most Radio Shacks are not yet 24-hour stores. Who are you going to call? This stuff really happens, so be prepared.

Other miscellaneous items like microphones, headphones, and cheap analog audio components like mixers and EQ boxes will also come in handy sooner or later, as will rip-ties and other types of cable organizers. Don't forget a generous selection of tools either, such as a variety of different gauges of screwdrivers and a pair of needle nose pliers.

Video Equipment Issues

As for analog video equipment, the more work you do, the more you will handle content provided by unpredict-able clients. Despite the changing aesthetic and quality issues discussed in Chapter 8, such content will often be in Betacam SP format. This can mean renting a Betacam deck, the cost of which should be passed on to the client, if possible.

These are big issues for small desktop media production shops. Beta decks are expensive and do not decrease in price over time at the same rate as personal computers. Buying one outright can seem non-cost-efficient until, a year later, you look at how all those rentals added up. If you have the vision to know you're going to be in busi-ness a year from now, buying a Beta deck on credit may be an acceptable risk.

Since this chapter is about setting up a media production studio, you might want to get into a little more detail. The rest of this chapter, therefore, is devoted to understanding

http://asrt.cad.gatech.edu/Library/Materials/P/ProVideo.html

B&H Photo-Video

The Professional Video Sourcebook

It's worth mention-ing video device control here, but the subject has become less crucial for pro-ducers of multimedia assets. If you need to control the opera-tion of your video deck from your Mac or PC, you can get more information from Adobe Tech support or by searching on MCI device control at the Microsoft Web site.

The Deck: Sony UVW 1600
The Price: Approximately $6,000 New

Plan A: Inefficient but safe

$$\frac{\text{Rent one day per month at \$250 per day} = \$6,000}{\text{Two years (24 months)}} \longrightarrow$$

Plan B: Much more efficient, but some risk

$$\frac{\text{Buy for \$6,000, pay \$250 per month (not including interest),}}{\text{but have it on-site all the time}} \longrightarrow$$
$$\text{Two years (24 months)}$$

Figure 16.14

Buying vs. renting a Beta deck.

less common (but potentially threatening) analog video problems, and the technical standards for analog video equipment.

Time Base Correction

If you don't have a background in analog video, you may not recognize time base correction (TBC) problems when you first see them. Often they appear as a particularly jagged form of distortion, but sometimes there are related symptoms as well.

TBC troubles stem from a number of factors:

- Videotape performance is a function of the tape *transport* mechanism inside the deck (or camera). The precision-tooled components comprising the transport can malfunction and skew the timing processes involved in the generation of video signals. This results in so-called *synchronization* problems, which are common in Hi8 and 8mm gear. One visible result, a wavering picture, is known as *flag-waving*.

Note: Most Betacam decks have some type of TBC already built in. Some top drawer Hi8 units also have TBC built in, but you'll need to consult the manual to be sure.

Flagging

A TBC condition.

- Sometimes analog color and brightness values don't translate efficiently to digital values. This happens frequently with NTSC signals (Never The Same Color, as video pros like to joke) and produces *level* and *chroma noise* problems. The visual effect is colors that are too hot and blurry.

Because consumer video gear is more tolerant of TBC problems than Mac and PC digitization equipment, distortion in your captured clips might not be evident on your NTSC monitor. This can drive you seriously over the edge when you run into TBC conditions for the first time.

The only good way to solve TBC problems is with a time base corrector. Most of the pro TBC products are standalone boxes, ranging in price from roughly $1,000 to $1,500, although TBC add-in cards are also available.

Key features to look for are:

- Infinite window memory. This is very important for Hi8 and 8mm VTRs.

- Composite and S-Video ins and outs.

- Processing amplifier controls (for adjusting color, intensity, and saturation).

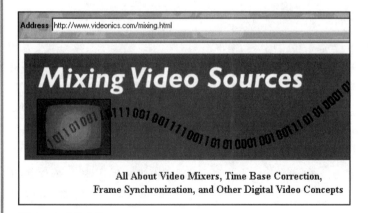

Figure 16.15

Alta Vista found this and more.

- Frame synchronization, phase controls, drop out compensation, freeze frame, and remote control.

Dropout Problems

Dropout happens when particles of metal oxide are detached from the surface of a videotape. Since those particles contain video information, the resultant video image will contain speckles when you play the tape. Hi8 tape is notorious for dropouts.

Two big causes of dropouts are:

- Tape cartridges are not conditioned properly and thus contain uneven and loose particles. Normal recording dislodges those bogus elements, resulting in lost video data (a.k.a. dropout).

- Moisture seeps into recorded tapes and then evaporates. This produces rocky areas on the tape surface. When you play the tape, the tape heads do further damage to the craggy surface.

There is not much you can do once the damage is done. Some analog gear contains dropout compensation circuitry, but no device can restore actual lost data. The best medicine is prevention: treat all your analog media with great care.

In terms of everyday video problems, TBC and dropout are arguably the most common. If you work exclusively with Beta-quality tape, you may never have to deal with these problems, since Beta decks and cameras normally prevent them from being introduced in the first place.

Transferring Film to Video

A whole separate industry exists for transferring Super 8 home movies to VHS cassettes (check out *Video* in the

A good way to condition your tapes is to record onto them all the way through in one pass (without an incoming video signal), then rewind to the beginning. This also helps pack your tape by relieving tight winding patches introduced at the factory.

Serious video synch problems.

Yellow Pages). Expensive, dedicated machines do the transfers. Quality can vary greatly, depending on the experience of the technician.

If you have film you want to transfer to video, let a service bureau do it. Aiming a video camera at a film projected on a screen might work in a pinch, but the resultant video will flicker—just like computer screens or television monitors you see in TV programs.

A final process worth noting is *3/2 pull-down*. You will likely hear this mentioned in technical deliberations concerning film-to-video transfer. 3/2 pull-down is basically a process in which 24 frames per second of film are converted to 30 frames per second of video. See Figure 16.16 for a graphical display of 3/2 pull-down.

More on Video Decks

Of all the video gear connected to your workstation, the VTR is the most crucial for real production chores. For

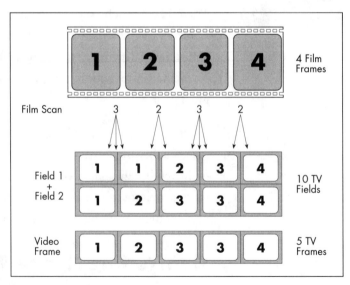

Figure 16.16
3/2 pull-down.

professional video work of any type, an industrial quality deck (at least S-Video or Hi8) is usually essential. If you haven't worked with such equipment before, it can be somewhat intimidating at first.

The rest of this chapter provides a list of issues to consider when looking for a workhorse VTR. You might not want to walk into Circuit City and try to impress the salesperson with technical minutiae, but it can be useful to know the right questions when someone tries to sell you a deck you don't know much about.

Tape Transport

For more information about this subject, try Alta Vista. A recent search on Tape Transport yielded 80,000 entries.

The value of any video deck is a direct function of the quality of its tape transport mechanism. These mechanisms are extremely delicate and subject to malfunction if not treated right, especially in Hi8, 8mm, and other compact gear. In general, the more expensive the deck, the more sophisticated the tape transport.

The apparatus that impels the transport system is the *servo motor*. The servo drives the fragile appliances which guide the tape through the transport mechanism. As the tape snakes through the system, it drags across the VTR's play and record heads, transferring analog video data (in either play or record mode).

Servos differ greatly in terms of precision. A common way to rate a servo motor is to determine the number of steps it performs in one rotation cycle. Because the servo drives the capstan, which indirectly drives the big cylinder that pulls the tape, more discrete steps means more control over positioning the tape.

In principle, the tape moves through the transport mechanism at a uniform velocity. This guarantees that the video signal stays synchronized. As noted earlier, all hell breaks loose when the tape speed is inconsistent. If you want accuracy to the frame in a VTR, you should get a deck with capstan override (ask the salesperson).

Tape Heads

No, not the John Cusack movie. An important difference between consumer and industrial VTRs is that most industrial decks have heads that record video and audio simultaneously. They also usually have a *flying erase head* which erases the tape just prior to recording onto it.

It's similar to explosives technology: the more surface area exploited, the bigger the payoff!

Heads are usually grouped in twos or threes in industrial equipment. In Hi8 and 8mm machines, however, tape head quantity is generally not as important as tape head *width*. In other words, the more your tape heads come into contact with the tape surface, the better the quality of the video (and audio).

If you've ever wondered what all the noise was when you started to play a tape in the VCR in your living room, it was the tape being extracted from the cassette.

In most decks, when the machine is not playing or recording, the tape remains in the cartridge (not in the transport system). Pushing the play or record button causes the transport assembly to go to work, pulling the tape out of the cartridge, laying it around the big tape cylinder, and then either playing or recording.

With a so-called *full-load* deck, the tape is kept in the transport mechanism between transport events (like play and record). The obvious benefits of this feature are faster response time when you push the play or record button, as well as increased stability of the image from when you push play until the tape is up to speed.

Other Video Issues

Some other VTR capabilities to research or ask about when shopping for a deck for your digitization station are:

- Signal to Noise (S/N) ratio—The S/N ratio gets more favorable as it increases. The official S/N ratios for most VTRs are posted in their manuals. Decent ratings for industrial decks start at about 40dB. For broadcast equipment, S/N ratios shouldn't dip below 55dB.

- Chroma noise reduction (CNR)—Simply stated, chroma noise degrades a video signal. Most industrial decks have built-in CNR, but it is worth asking about to be sure. Some chroma noise is inevitable. Certain manufacturers reduce it effectively, while others do not.

- Time base correction—Time base correction is covered earlier in this chapter. Worth noting here is that few Hi8 or 8mm decks have built-in TBC (unlike most Betacam decks, which do). Perhaps TBC high-quality circuitry will be added to video capture cards (or personal computers themselves) at some point.

Audio Features (in Video Decks)

As noted elsewhere in this book, audio issues don't get dealt with nearly as well as video issues, based on audio's importance in the final production. We're not downplaying their significance here, just working around equipment vagaries.

Design differences abound among prosumer (high-end consumer) and industrial VTRs when it comes to recording audio. Linear decks allow audio tracks to be recorded without disrupting existing audio (and video) tracks. Nonlinear VTRs permit existing tracks to be overwritten. Also understand that decks without a dedicated time code channel will use an audio track for recording time code (such as SMPTE).

Since most desktop producers capture and compress clips with monaural sound, this is probably not a bottleneck. If you want to add additional audio tracks to your AVI or QuickTime movies, you will likely do it in a movie editing program such as Adobe Premiere.

Consumer Decks

There are far fewer technical decisions to make when shopping for a consumer-level VCR than when comparing industrial-grade VTR decks. If you need to postpone purchasing professional equipment, here are some things to think about regarding off-the-rack VCRs:

- Picture quality—This is often a function of the number of heads in the tape transport mechanism. Four-head machines give significantly better performance than two-head VCRs.

- Stereo vs. monaural sound—As noted above, not many of your Web clips will need stereo sound—at least not yet. Don't pay extra for it unless you plan to repurpose the VCR later (like in your home theater).

- A/V in and out—Some bargain basement VCRs don't have the capability of having these connectors—just the straight coaxial cable jack. Remember to check for color-coded Video In/Video Out and Audio In/Audio Out RCA jacks (usually red and white or yellow and white) on the back of the VCR.

If you find it hard to choose among manufacturers offering similar features for the same price, you can always look in *Consumer Reports*. Another way to get third party evaluations is to log on to one of the special interest forums at CompuServe or America Online.

Setting up Microsoft's Internet Information Server (IIS) as your local Web server.

Key Topics:

- **Downloading and Installing IIS**

- **Configuring NT Server 3.51 to work with IIS**

- **Building up your site under IIS**

Building a Local Multimedia Web Site

This chapter is devoted to procuring, installing, and (initially) maintaining a Web server using Microsoft's Internet Information Server (IIS) software. This product is currently free and available for downloading from the Microsoft Web site. As of this writing, you need to boot NT Server 3.51 or greater (with Service Pack 3) to run IIS.

By the time this book is published, NT 4.0 (Server and Workstation) may well be in general release. The current Beta of the 4.0 product supports IIS and the overall feel is quite smooth. Of course, with NT 4.0 you get the Windows 95 user interface, which will likely cement NT into place as the OS of choice for any Windows user with a Pentium and 16 MB of RAM.

The version of IIS described here is 1.0. However, since Microsoft is spending a lot of time developing it, the software may be several versions down the road by the time you read this. But it will probably still be free at the Microsoft site, and the basic setup should remain the same. The machine used to host the examples used in this chapter is a Pentium 133 with 32 MB of RAM, connected to the Web with a BitSurfer Pro ISDN modem.

Getting Started with NT

Downloading the Internet Information Server

If you've got NT Server 3.51 (or greater) with Service Pack 3 (or greater) installed and are ready to go get IIS, point your browser at the address *http://www.microsoft.com/ Infoserv/IISInfo.htm*. Follow the instructions for downloading the product. There's a fair amount of bureaucracy to plow through prior to the actual download, but it is worth reading to get the flavor of Internet Information Server.

You might want to look ahead to the next page of this chapter and make sure you can config- ure NT adequately to work with IIS before you down- load it. The file size of the self-extracting IIS software is about 13 MB (for the full version).

Figure 17.1

The Internet Information Server home page.

Reference is made to a Planning Guide in the IIS product information pages. The document is certainly worth reading for completeness at this point, but not absolutely necessary if you just want to get the IIS installed and see what it feels like—which is the point of this chapter.

If you decide you want to use IIS as your mission-critical Web server after the first date, you should review the Planning Guide in detail. After you read this chapter, you may even want to erase the installation and follow the directions given here to be assured that you're starting with a clean slate.

Assuming you have NT Server properly configured to begin with, installation and quick testing of the Internet Information Server should take no more than a couple of hours. If you have problems, the best way to get answers is by joining the Microsoft Developer Network (MSDN).

MSDN is expensive for the highest level of support (which includes the NT Server products), but worth it if you need to save time. You also get access to Beta software and pretty much 24-hour service. For more information call 800-759-5474 or go to the Microsoft home page (*http://www.microsoft.com*).

Configuring NT Server

Have you obtained a domain name and an IP address from your ISP or the InterNIC directly? If not, you'll be unable to get the IIS up and running properly.

Configuring NT can easily fill a book or two—as opposed to a couple of pages. This is especially true for NT Server. What we'll do instead is follow the shortest path from sitting down at a generic machine running NT Server 3.51 to getting that machine visible on the Web once IIS is successfully installed.

There are several places to start working. Let's begin with the Network applet in the Control Panel. Since we're running NT 3.51 in this chapter, you might feel like you're back in Windows 3.1 if you've gotten used to Windows 95. Here are the steps to configuring the Network applet:

1. Double click the Network applet icon to invoke the *Network Settings* dialog box, shown in Figure 17.2.

2. Check that the following items are present in the Installed Network Software list box: Workstation, Server, Computer Browser, NetBEUI Protocol, NetBIOS Interface, NWLink IPX/SPX Compatible Transport, NWLink NetBIOS, Remote Access Service, RPC Configuration, TCP/IP Protocol, and MS Loopback Adapter Drive. If any are missing, you can install them from your NT installation media by clicking the *Add Software* button.

3. Double click the *TCP/IP Protocol* item (or highlight it and click the *Configure* button) to bring up the *TCP/IP Configuration* dialog box (see Figure 17.3). (TCP/IP is an acronym for Transmission Control Protocol/Internet Protocol.)

4. Fill in the *IP Address* field with the permanent number supplied by your ISP or the InterNIC. The *Subnet*

Strictly speaking, not all of the services listed in Step 2 are directly related to running IIS. But some of them depend on others, and including the whole list seems to be the most effective formula.

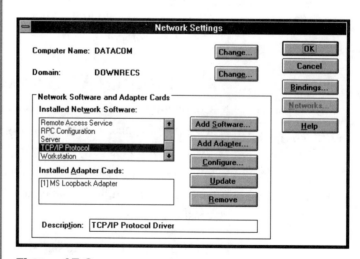

Figure 17.2

The Network Settings dialog box.

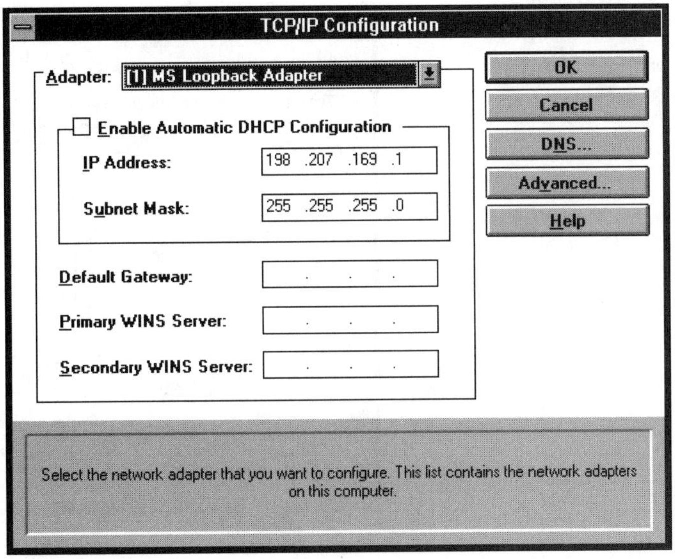

Figure 17.3

The TCP/IP Configuration dialog box.

*If you haven't in-
stalled a modem yet,
double click the
Remote Access
Service item in the
Installed Network
Software listbox. In
the Remote Access
Setup dialog box,
click the Add but-
ton. NT may try to
auto-detect your
modem hardware;
otherwise, select the
model you are using
from the choices in
the list box. When
this is done, return
to the Network
Settings dialog box.*

Mask will usually be 255.255.255.0. Do not check the box labeled *Enable Automatic DCHP Configuration.*

5. Click the *DNS* button. The DNS Configuration dialog box depicted in Figure 17.4 will appear.

6. In the *Host Name* field, fill in the name of the machine hosting the server software. Enter your registered domain name in the *Domain Name* field.

7. In the *Domain Name Service (DNS) Search Order* group, key in the primary and secondary DNS addresses provided by the ISP who registered your domain on their name server(s). If you have dial-up Internet service from that ISP, you'll likely have used these numbers already in configuring your Web browser. Click *OK*.

8. Click the *Advanced* button in the *TCP/IP Configuration* dialog box. This invokes the *Advanced Microsoft TCP/IP Configuration* dialog box shown in Figure 17.5.

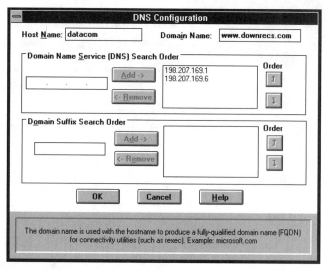

Figure 17.4

The DNS Configuration dialog box.

9. Check the box for *Enable DNS for Windows Name Resolution*. Click *OK* to return to the TCP/IP Configuration dialog box.

10. Click *OK* to return to Network Settings, then click *OK* to return to the Control Panel.

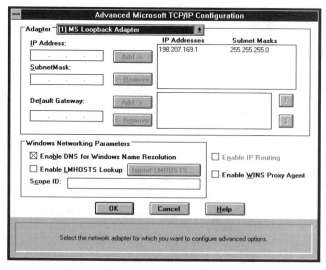

Figure 17.5

The Advanced Microsoft TCP/IP Configuration dialog box.

While ISDN should be considered the minimum bandwidth if you make your IIS site available to the public, you can perform all the tasks in this chapter with a 28.8 kbps connection.

Next, we need to set up the Remote Access Service:

1. Click on the RAS Icon to get to the *Remote Access* dialog box shown in Figure 17.6.

2. If you haven't defined a remote service, click the *Add* button to invoke the *Add Phone Book Entry* dialog box shown in Figure 17.7.

3. Fill in the text fields with the entry name, phone number, and (optional) description data, then select the port to which your modem is attached from the drop-down *Port* combo box. Check the box for *Authenticate using current user name and password* if

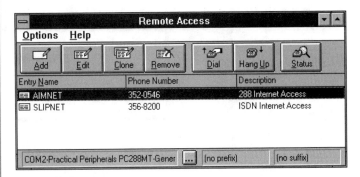

Figure 17.6
The Remote Access dialog box.

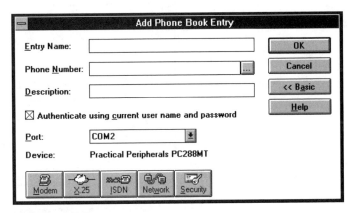

Figure 17.7
The Add Phone Book Entry dialog box.

the name and password you use to log on to NT are the same ones you use for logging on to your ISP.

4. Click the *Modem* button at the bottom of the dialog box and select the appropriate initial speed for your modem.

5. If you have an ISDN modem, click the *ISDN* button and select the appropriate *Line type* (either 64K digital or 56K digital) in the *ISDN Settings* dialog box, shown in Figure 17.8.

6. Click the *Network* button to bring up the *Network Protocol Settings* dialog box.

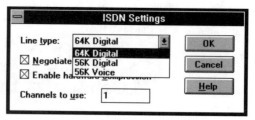

Figure 17.8

Selecting the ISDN line type.

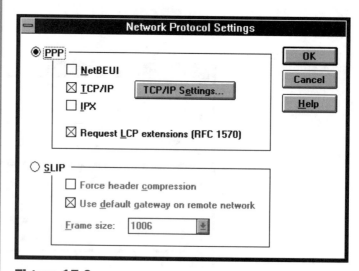

Figure 17.9

The Network Protocol Settings dialog box.

7. Assuming you have a PPP account, check the *PPP* radio button, then check the *TCP/IP* check box.

8. Click the *TCP/IP Settings* button. The *PPP TCP/IP Settings* dialog box will appear, as shown in Figure 17.10.

9. Check the *Require specific IP address* radio button, then fill in the IP address for your domain, as well as the IP addresses for your ISP's Domain Name servers. Exit out to the *Add Phone Book Entry* dialog box using the *OK* buttons.

10. Click the *Security* button to see the *Security Settings* dialog box (see Figure 17.11). Check the radio button for *Accept any authentication including clear text.*

11. If the log-in procedure for connecting to your ISP requires more information than user name and

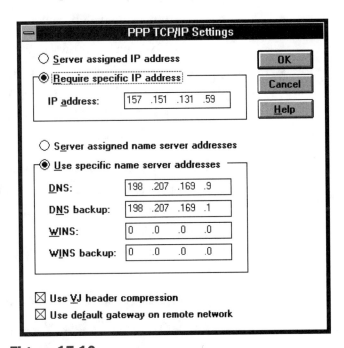

Figure 17.10

The PPP TCP/IP Settings dialog box.

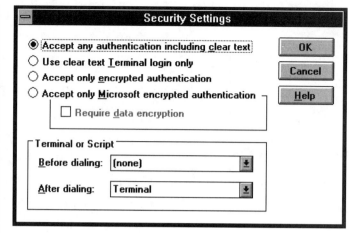

Figure 17.11

The Security Settings dialog box.

password, select *Terminal* from the *After dialing* combo box. This will give you a prompt screen which you can use to get connected at dial-in time.

12. Exit all the way out to the *Remote Access* dialog box using the *OK* buttons.

13. If you have a browser installed on your system (like the Microsoft Internet Explorer for NT), click the *Dial* button. Assuming you make a proper connection to your ISP, fire up your browser to make sure you can see the Web.

As you may know already, Web surfing (and remote access operations in general) under NT feels a lot different than under Windows 95 and Windows 3.1. There are reasons why people like NT—such as its reliability and stability—and with version 4.0 it's going to be even better.

Installing the Internet Information Server

Once you have successfully configured your RAS (the razz) and Control Panel TCP/IP settings, you should be

Download

Microsoft®
Internet
Information
Server

free

*Following a success-
ful installation, the
install directory
(built when the
downloaded archive
extracted itself) will
likely still be present
on your system.
There's no reason to
keep these files
around forever, but
you might want to
wait until IIS is up
and running before
killing them. At
least keep the origi-
nal download
archive in a safe
place for a while.*

ready to download and install IIS software. Assuming
you have completed the download procedure described
earlier in this chapter, we can now proceed to the actual
installation.

On the Microsoft page where you download the IIS software, there should be some basic instructions on how to
manage the setup. The main thing to look for are instructions
on how to run the self-extracting installation archive so
that the files it contains go into the right subdirectories.
This will probably be accomplished by adding a switch
(such as -D) after the file name, but read the directions
carefully.

Running the installation archive should produce an installation directory tree with a file named SETUP.EXE somewhere near its root (again, check the documentation).
Executing SETUP.EXE will commence the formal installation process.

The default root directory for IIS is C:\INETSRV. Unless
you have a compelling reason not to use this, it's a good
place to start when you first install the product. As you'll
see when the installation is complete, a number of logical
subdirectories are created under C:\INETSRV. As with any
Windows installation, it's always a good idea to reboot
your system when the process is complete.

The first visible sign that something has been installed is
a new Program Group on your NT desktop: IIS Server
(Common). There should be four items in it (as of this
writing): Internet Service Manager, The Microsoft Internet Explorer browser, a Microsoft Help file providing the
documentation, and a setup program for reinstalling IIS
(see Figure 17.12).

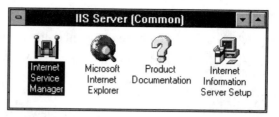

Figure 17.12

The IIS program group.

Double clicking the *Internet Service Manager* icon will bring up its associated dialog box, as shown in Figure 17.13. If NT is properly configured, the WWW, Gopher, and FTP services should be running normally. Take a minute to click around on the UI and its dialog boxes to get a feeling for the scope of your Internet services.

Exit the Internet Service Manager and double click the *Internet Explorer* icon. When it comes up it, it should find the default local home page for IIS. You might want to enter the NT Server name for your machine in Explorer's address box to see if the same local home page comes up. If both these things happen, you're on the right track.

Note: Theoretically, you can browse your IIS installation with the NT version of Microsoft Internet Explorer on the same machine, as if you were actually online. While this seems to work most of the time, it is not a completely reliable substitute for connecting over the Web from another machine.

Putting Your Server Online

Now the fun part. If you're ready to try going live without adding any of your own HTML pages or Web media

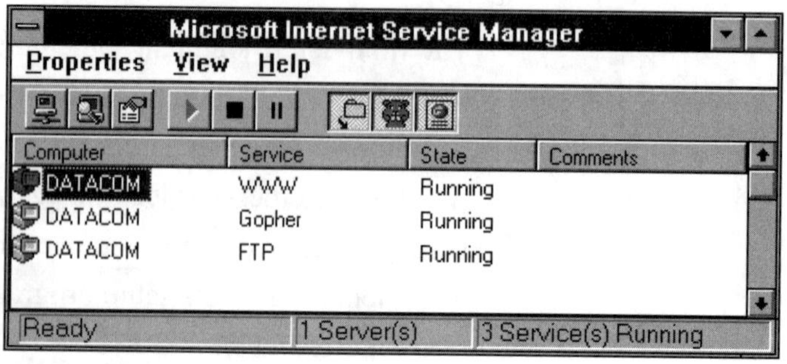

Figure 17.13

The Microsoft Internet Service Manager dialog box.

assets, you can do so now—and why not? It's only a few steps:

1. Go to the RAS program group and double click the *Remote Access* icon.

2. In the *Remote Access* dialog box, double click the ISP that you defined earlier in this chapter. Supply whatever name and password details are necessary to complete the connection.

3. Assuming you have another phone line and another computer to browse the Web, get that machine connected and its browser fired up.

4. Let's say your new domain name is *www.mydomain .com*. Plug that address into the address line of your browsing machine and see what happens.

Don't be alarmed if you don't make a connection right away the first time you try to connect. Domain names often take a while to propagate on the Web, and not all ISPs give the same level of service.

If you get an address-not-found message, try it again a few times. Are you sure your ISP has configured you correctly in the ISP's name servers? Double-check all the settings we covered earlier in this chapter. Check NT's *Event Viewer* in the *Admin Tools* program group (shown

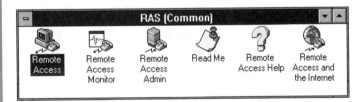

Figure 17.14
The RAS program group.

Figure 17.15
Hoping for the best...

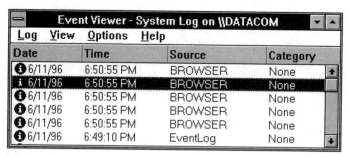

Figure 17.16

The event log.

in Figure 17.16) to see if any network services aren't starting.

If the *Event Log* shows problems, you'll need to read the documentation or, better yet, hound tech support until you get it fixed. Microsoft will usually take care of such problems quickly once you get them on the line. Don't frustrate yourself needlessly by shooting in the dark with endless trials and errors.

The information provided in the *Product Documentation* help file in the IIS Server program group can get you partially set up, but if you haven't been using NT you can feel lost very easily. Again, you'll get the best return on your time by calling Microsoft tech support. Presumably you have not made successful installation of IIS a mission-critical task.

If your browsing machine *does* find your new server, Kool and the Gang. On the other hand, think of all the headaches that lie ahead trying to get your media assets to perform as planned. Before beginning construction of your site on your new IIS server, you might want to try out some of the other features while things are still fresh (like the FTP and Gopher services).

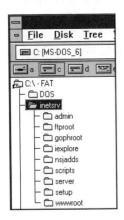

If you do decide to move an existing site over to your IIS installation as one massive copy operation, be prepared to spend some time tweaking it on the IIS side. It won't be as simple as it may seem at first, although it is a viable approach.

Building a Site with IIS

We'll assume that you don't want to re-install IIS and are ready to start building a permanent Web site (or at least as permanent as possible for the time being). If you come from a Windows background but have been running your site on a remote non-Windows platform, you should enjoy the heady feeling of knowing exactly what you're doing.

Since we are considering this permanent, a day or so of planning is reasonable—unless you just want to jump in and take the consequences. If this is the case, and you already have a sizable existing site, you might even want to make an image of that existing site on a CD-ROM or big external hard drive and dump that image on the machine that hosts your new IIS site.

The place to start is the WWWROOT directory under C:\INETSRV (the default target of the IIS installation). As noted earlier, the installer puts a default HTML page there, but you can substitute your own right away if you want to get personal. Keep it named DEFAULT.HTM for now. Before adding subdirectories, more HTML files, and media assets, however, you should complete the following steps:

1. Bring up the *Internet Service Manager* app in the IIS group.

2. Double click the *WWW Service* item to bring up the *WWW Service Properties* dialog box. There are a lot of controls to master in here (and in the other services), but the one we need to look at now can be found under the *Directories* tab.

3. Check the box for *Enable Default Document* and specify the name of that document in the text field. If your current base home page is INDEX.HTM, you can specify this filename here.

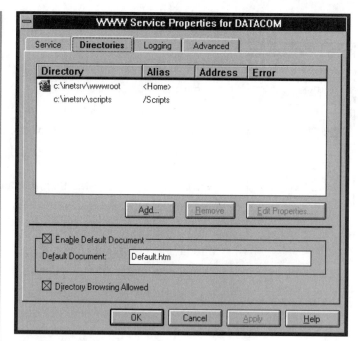

Figure 17.17

The WWW Service Properties dialog box.

4. Check the *Directory Browsing Allowed* box if it is not already checked.

5. We'll get to some of the other areas of this dialog box later in this chapter, but for now click *OK* to exit.

Finally we can begin the real construction process. For lack of a better place to start (unless you've got your own ideas), let's create some media directories similar to the

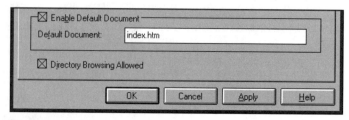

Figure 17.18

Specifying an alternate base page.

ones suggested in Chapter 14 *Configuring a Remote Web Server*. A few of those media directories were:

ones suggested in Chapter 14

- gif (for still image GIF files)

- jpeg (for still image JPEG files)

- mov (for flattened QuickTime movies)

- avi (for Video for Windows movies)

- wav (for WAV audio files)

- mpg (for MPEG movies)

- midi (for MIDI files)

We'll address Shockwave, CGI Scripts, and streaming media shortly. For now, it's worth making sure that you can embed and download (if appropriate) media files from the above categories. Assuming correct configuration, you should be able to hear MIDI files if you use Microsoft Internet Explorer version 2.0 or higher.

Starting Construction

Shockwave

Ready for the next level of difficulty? Let's talk about MIME mapping. According to the IIS documentation, over 100 MIME types are registered by default at installation time. If you've spent much time developing NT-based applications, you'd probably suspect that MIME mapping takes place in the NT Registry and you'd be right.

Our goal here is to add support for Shockwave. As it turns out, IIS already has Registry entries for Shockwave. To give you a feeling for NT Server's sophistication in this area, let's go take a look at them. The steps are:

1. Run the program Regedt32.

If you plan to copy the contents of a large existing site over to your IIS server, you might not want to spend too much time creating media directories here. For testing purposes you may only need to create a few.

As of this writing, NT does not support Shockwave at the browser level. In other words, if you are using Netscape on a machine running NT Workstation, don't expect it to work—even though Netscape with Windows 95 can handle shocked movies delivered by an NT Server running IIS.

2. Scroll your way down to the item:

```
HKEY_LOCAL_MACHINE\
    SYSTEM\
        CurrentControlSet\
            InetInfo\
                Parameters\
                    MimeMap
```

3. You'll see how the Registry entries look in Figure 17.19. This is where you'll be configuring the Internet Information Server to handle new MIME types in the future (assuming the ones you need aren't in this list already). Insert a shocked Web page and a DCR movie into your IIS WWWROOT directory tree and try it out.

CGI Scripts

Remember the section in Chapter 7 about so-called *Server Push*, a technique for animating a series of bitmaps? As noted, one reason server push is attractive to Web page developers is that it doesn't require investment in third-party software. The animation is instead driven by a Perl (CGI) script executing on the server. What you do need for server push animations is someone who knows how to write CGI code.

As of this writing, IIS does not come with a Perl interpreter. A third-party freeware solution that Microsoft

Of course, while server pushes executed by Perl scripts are interesting to Web media producers, Perl scripts are also useful for many other things, like forms processing.

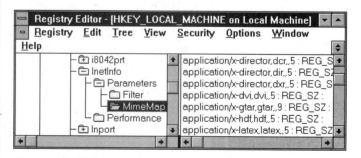

Figure 17.19

Pre-registered entries for Shockwave.

often recommends is available at *http://www.perl.hip.com* (double-check the freeware status when you visit there). Assuming you want to use this product, go ahead and download it, then follow the installation directions in the readme file after unpacking the downloaded Zip file.

Just as with Shockwave files, you've got to make some Registry entries to configure your new Perl script processor:

1. Run Regedt32 and go to the registry item shown below:

```
HKEY_LOCAL_MACHINE\
   SYSTEM\
      CurrentControlSet\
         Services\
            W3SVC\
               Parameters
                  ScriptMap
```

For the ultimate lowdown on Perl, you can always do a search on it (and CGI) in Yahoo or Alta Vista (or your favorite search utility). You'll find plenty to read, and maybe some newer solutions to processing scripts in IIS.

2. Select *Add Value* from Regedt32's *Edit* menu to invoke the *Add Value* dialog box. Enter .pl in the *Value Name* text box, then click *OK*.

3. In the *String Editor* dialog box, enter the complete path for the Perl program, followed by a space and %S, then click *OK*.

4. Repeat steps 2 and 3, but enter the file extension .cgi in the *Value Name* text box (instead of .pl).

The script map section of your NT registry will now look similar to Figure 17.22, and IIS should consequently be ready to handle Perl scripts. To make sure things are working correctly, try the following test:

1. With Notepad, create the following text file:

```
print "Content-Type: text/html\n\n";
print "<HTML>\n";
print "<HEAD>\n";
print "<TITLE>Perl Test</TITLE>\n";
print "</HEAD>\n";
print "<BODY>\n";
```

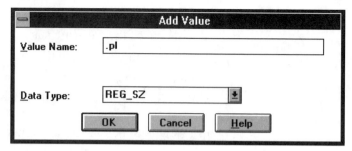

Figure 17.20

Adding a script file extension.

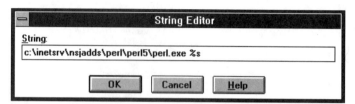

Figure 17.21

Adding the Perl path.

According to Microsoft, most existing CGI and Perl scripts should work fine under IIS with a Perl program like the one used in this chapter. Of course, Microsoft recommends its own methods for executing server side applications, which are detailed in the IIS documentation.

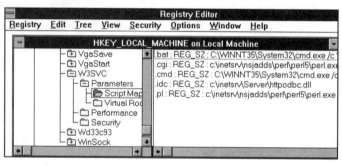

Figure 17.22

The revised Script Map registration.

```
print "<H4>Perl Test</H4>\n";
print "<P>\n";
print "Your IP Address is $ENV{REMOTE_ADDR}.\n";
print "<P>";
print "<H5>This concludes the Perl test</H5>\n";
print "</BODY>\n";
print "</HTML>\n";
```

2. Save the file in the scripts directory of your IIS installation as PERLTEST.PL.

3. Get your IIS server on line, and fire up a browser on another machine.

4. Surf to the address *http://<servername>/scripts/ perltest.pl?*.

5. If the browser finds your IIS server, you should see a screen similar to the one shown in Figure 17.23.

RealAudio and VDOLive

Before installing the heavyweight versions of either of these streaming products, you should try out the personal versions (RealAudio Personal Server and VDOLive Personal Server). As you may have seen in the Registry, entries already exist for RealAudio.

As of this writing, the installation process for each of these Personal Servers is very straightforward, but the products may have changed by the time you read this. Both Progressive Networks and VDOnet are aggressively marketing their server side products, and any problems you have getting them to work with IIS will likely be cleared up quickly with a call to tech support.

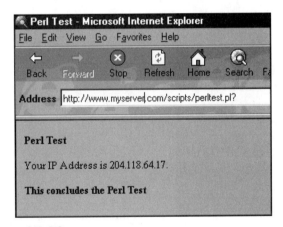

Figure 17.23
The executed Perl script.

Appendix

Hanging with the Blue Wolf

At various points in this book the Blue Wolf Network has been mentioned as a pioneering Web presence. When it comes to offering advanced Web technology in the name of pure entertainment, the Blue Wolf *Browseteria* site (*http://www.bluewolfnet.com*) has few, if any, equals on the World Wide Web today.

So where did the Blue Wolf and his network come from, and who's behind this excellent "Variety Show on the Web?"
John Barrows, owner and CEO of TBWN, was kind enough to answer some questions and present his philosophy of what it took to turn TBWN into a true destination site.

How would you describe the focus of the Blue Wolf Network?
The specific focus of the Browseteria is to provide entertainment using the Web as the delivery vehicle, and the

Figure A.1

Arriving at the Browseteria.

best Web technology available at the time as the communications medium. Most of this technology is not available to traditional radio, television, and print media.

Do you have a stated mission?
Our mission is to create a number of innovative sites, each focused on a different market segment.

What don't you focus on?
Specifically outside the Blue Wolf focus are chat rooms, discussion groups, and other such activities.

This seems consistent with your emphasis on media as opposed to text.

We keep text to an absolute minimum, since I believe people don't really want to read text on their computer screens. Instead, we try to maximize the use of animation, streaming audio, streaming video, and other types of advanced Web media.

Recording artist and actor John Doe, subject of a VDOLive interview at the Browseteria.

Figure A.2
Entering Blue's Joint.

What specific software are you using?
From an authoring perspective, the most important software we use is VRML, which provides the basic user interface for navigating the Browseteria.

Any limitations here?
There are some limitations in the current version, but we hope to get around them by using Netscape frames and VRML Moving Worlds—especially in our upcoming project called Bot Squad, which will be a site for kids.

What's next in the hierarchy?
After VRML, I would say streaming audio is the next most important type of software we're using, specifically RealAudio from Progressive Networks, who seem to own the market at this point. After that is VDOnet's streaming video product, VDOLive.

What's the best thing about VDOLive?
Using VDOLive, we can conduct interactive interviews with artists and celebrities that give a full flavor of the subject's personality. We're using some Shockwave movies as well, but haven't yet tapped its full potential. The same goes for Java at this point.

Poet Allen Ginsberg performed Howl at the Browseteria via RealAudio.

Did you set out to use multimedia and video on your site to the extent that you are using it now?

When I first conceived of the Blue Wolf Network—and the Browseteria in particular—practically none of the technology we use now existed. VRML was out there, but not widespread. RealAudio was just coming into commercial existence. Java wasn't public yet, nor was streaming video.

So you assumed things would fall into place?

My vision was to develop a full-on multimedia 3D site. I assumed by the time I launched the Browseteria that most ,if not all, of this technology would exist, even though I didn't know where it was going to come from. But I gambled on the fact that cool software for the Net was evolving so fast that it would be there when I needed it.

A frame of a live animation clip featured at the Browseteria.

What Are the Risks?

How much risk do you think there is in alienating your audience if you engage these new streaming technologies but they don't turn out to work very well?

Figure A.3
Politics As Usual at the Browseteria.

Of course, the risk in adopting new technology goes with the site's vision, which was to stay ahead of the curve and try to be a pioneer. When you do that, you don't risk alienating people, but you do risk losing their understanding. Most people operate in the present, and we try to operate in the future.

And if you don't take that risk?
The way I look at it, not taking such risks is the biggest risk, since you otherwise stand a good chance of falling behind in this fast-paced industry.

When you look at how television started out in the 40s and 50s, it was this huge box with a small screen, black and white, that didn't work very well—and good programming was in short supply. Also, very few people could afford it.

It was gratifying that *Timecast* [the online magazine] called us pioneers, because that's what we want to be, just like in the early days of television, when it was trying to deliver entertainment via a new medium.

If you believed these technologies weren't going to be available, would you have done the site anyway?

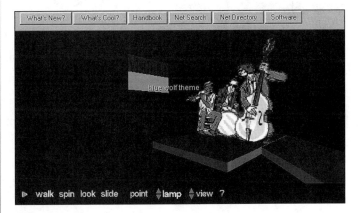

Figure A.4
The Browsetrio.

Attend a virtual poetry reading courtesy of RealAudio.

I knew I wanted to be a producer on the Web. I don't come from a technical background, so I might not have started my own site without the belief that they would be ready, but I would have been involved in the Web in some way until the technologies were there.

Are you personally satisfied with the quality of streaming video and audio on the Web, or do you find yourself just putting up with it sometimes?
Obviously it's nowhere near the quality of television. But the difference between having it and not having it is very significant. I don't think there's any question that it's good enough to be useable right now. That's the real issue. Plus, just the fact that it is still essentially experimental gives the site the kind of feel I want.

Everybody's heard these rumors about the coming Web meltdown late in 1996. Do you ever whistle past the graveyard or feel like you're part of the problem?
Sure I'm part of the problem, but you can't have a real solution until there's a big enough problem. I think ultimately that the Web will be our main means of communication and entertainment. It takes organizations like the Blue Wolf Network to create the problems that produce the larger solutions.

The Bad Joke Guy. Go ahead, ask him.

But what about the reported coming collapse?
I don't think there's going to be a major brownout because there are too many large corporations spending many millions of dollars to figure out these bandwidth problems. I've worked at big companies long enough to know they don't spend money foolishly, at least not in the long run.

So should we stop worrying about it?
I'm not worried. There's a lot of big money flowing into the solution right now, and I'm completely confident there will be a payoff in terms of opening up the bandwidth.

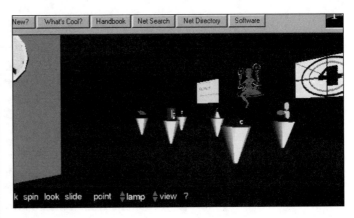

Figure A.5
The Gadgeteria.

Day-to-Day Management

You're the owner of Blue Wolf and have people working for you that keep the site operational. From where you sit, what's the hardest part about running it on a day-to-day basis?

The hardest part about running a site of this nature is getting enough sleep. I don't say this just because of the amount of work involved, but because of the faster pace you accept—thinking about what you should be doing next.

In other words, figuring out how to stay ahead of the curve and how to know where to go next can be almost as difficult as doing the day-to-day stuff, at least from a management point of view.

What about finding people to work for you?
Since I'm trying to do things that most Web sites aren't doing yet, it's hard to find good people that want to operate in this realm with me. There are a lot of talented people who are qualified enough, but often they just look at you like you're crazy for trying to make it all work.

The Zen Guy. Wonder what's on his mind this time?

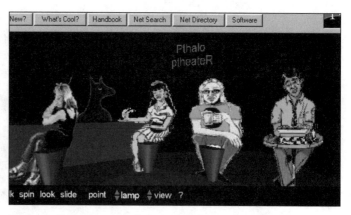

Figure A.6

The Pthalo ptheateR.

So does it take fast-trackers to make this work?
Can it be just a regular job or do you have to be driven
and dedicated?
Speaking for myself, you certainly have to be driven and
dedicated. The dedication has to come from the intense
desire to be different, and from trying to be a pioneer. I'd
like to be able to achieve something recognizable, which
takes enormous drive and dedication, in my opinion.
Anybody who's doing innovative work in this industry
understands what's required personally.

Does the distinction between video on demand and tun-
ing in to a stream in progress have meaning for you?
It's a huge distinction. I think the concept of *anything* on
demand is important to understand in this business. Media on demand is the name of the game in terms of making the Web the force that it is becoming.

Just tuning in to some site at 9:00 P.M. on Thursday
because that's when the show starts is too much like TV.
Time spent on the Web world-wide is rising sharply, and
this comes directly out of TV viewing time.

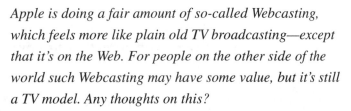

Figure A.7

The Browseteria's Comic Belief section.

The Karaoke Guy wants to hold your hand.

Apple is doing a fair amount of so-called Webcasting, which feels more like plain old TV broadcasting—except that it's on the Web. For people on the other side of the world such Webcasting may have some value, but it's still a TV model. Any thoughts on this?

Live events are important—people like to see things as they happen. I believe that eventually the Net will replace television as we now know it, so that viewing live events on the Web will be part of its function. What Apple is doing in this regard therefore has merit, but it is sort of a niche at this point.

Using Beta Software

Do you have any particular policies about using beta software, as opposed to released commercial products?
I would say that to be a pioneer, you usually have no choice but to use beta software. That's all there is to it. If you waited around for it to be officially released, you wouldn't be a pioneer any more.

Plus, now there's Web distribution.
That's the other thing. With the advent of Internet software distribution, new products and upgrades to existing

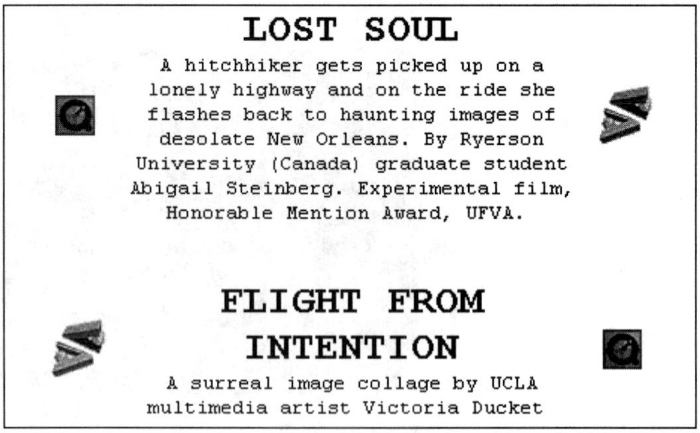

LOST SOUL

A hitchhiker gets picked up on a lonely highway and on the ride she flashes back to haunting images of desolate New Orleans. By Ryerson University (Canada) graduate student Abigail Steinberg. Experimental film, Honorable Mention Award, UFVA.

FLIGHT FROM INTENTION

A surreal image collage by UCLA multimedia artist Victoria Ducket

Figure A.8
Check out the Film No R Theatre.

products are much easier to get your hands on, as opposed to waiting for them to arrive in the mail like in the old days.

How stable is the beta software you're currently using?
The beta versions of the products I've been using have turned out to be very stable, and functionally the same as the full-release versions. Sure you're operating in a realm of imperfection, but so what? That's how it is now, and it's workable.

User Feedback

What's been the response to the site so far?
I'm happy to say that the response has been great. What we wanted this site to be was leading edge and innovative. Companies like clnet and Progressive Networks (makers of RealAudio) have officially recognized it for what it is. And not just, "gee, this is a leading edge site," but rather that it is downright entertaining.

A VDO interview with choreographer Gary Palmer.

Do they sense you're pushing the limits of the technology?

Yes, they do appear to recognize the Browseteria as one of the *kinds* of sites that is pushing the envelope in terms of creation and delivery of new types of content.

What kind of mail are you getting?

In terms of viewer feedback mail, I got one the other day that said, basically, "I just spent three hours at your site and it was a total waste of my time. Please make more."

I consider this high praise, since all I'm really trying to do with this site is deliver high quality entertainment in a form you can't find anywhere else. If viewers like this are losing track of time, I'm succeeding.

Is this better than good notices?

When we get unsolicited mail like this, I feel sure that our vision is solid. Of course it's good to get positive reviews from the press, but audience response is much more meaningful. As long as we keep getting such mail, I'll know we're on the right track.

Package from Ted. Can somebody sign for this?

Figure A.9
The Phone Guy and The Sensuous Woman.

What do your hit rates look like?
We've only been operational for three months after starting cold, but we're getting about a thousand visitors per day, and around ten to fifteen file hits per day. Of course, that doesn't begin to compare with heavy hitters like Netscape and Yahoo, but we're a completely different kind of site.

As I mentioned, we've had significant, to-the-point press. I think, however, that there will be a greater volume of reviews coming soon, which should translate into more hits.

Do the technology requirements limit your hit counts?
To some extent. Visitors do need to have most of the latest plug-ins and so forth, as well as fast computers and modems to really get the full experience.

To be honest, people who haven't upgraded their systems appropriately won't see everything we have to offer in the way it was designed to perform. But, again, I choose to operate in this realm.

Looking into the Studio

No introductions necessary.

How would you describe your media production studio?
It's uncomplicated, but we use good quality gear to get good quality results, so we don't waste time doing things over.

Do you use off-the-rack equipment?
If it does the job. Again, my goal is to streamline the process without sacrificing quality. We feel that we have strong enough content so that we're unlikely to get into academic arguments with anyone over desktop video and audio production values.

Do you use outside production services at all?

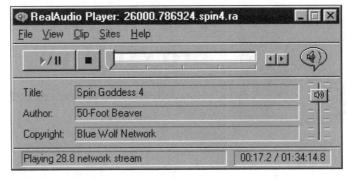

Figure A.10

Listen to the Spin Goddess's Web-based Radio Show.

Some, if necessary. If we have a deadline and our regular gear is booked, we have a network of contractors we can rely on. Our biggest challenge is presenting our media as effectively as possible—we assume that it will be prepared by people who know what they're doing.

Is your server located at your business office?
Not at the moment. We need to have it located where the Webmaster can get to it quickly if there's a problem. That may change in the future.

How do you archive the Blue Wolf's digital assets?
Everything is backed up on CD-ROM.

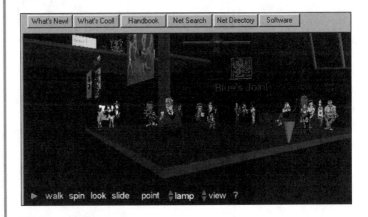

Figure A.11

Leaving the Browseteria.

Looking for a fight? Ask the Hostile Guy what's bugging him.

Past Highlights from the Browseteria

- A RealAudio performance of Allen Ginsberg reading *Howl*

- A visual tour of the work of rock artist Frank Kozik

- A VDOLive interview with author and celebrity Legs McNeil

- A VDOLive animation festival featuring works from the Ringling School of Art and Design

- A bar (Blue's Joint) full of colorful characters, each with something on his or her mind—via RealAudio

- Other cool sections, including *Film No R* (a virtual screening room and video store with VDOLive and QuickTime assets to consume), *Spin Goddess* (a RealAudio radio show), and a record review forum with RealAudio samples

Figure A.12
The Blue Wolf can dig it.

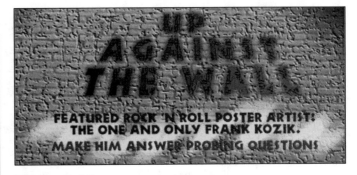

Figure A.13

Comic Belief.

Figure A.14

Legs McNeil at the Gershwin Hotel.

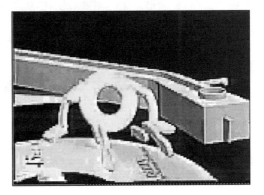

Figure A.15

Lots of mint animation.

Figure A.16
Meet Bonnie at the bar.

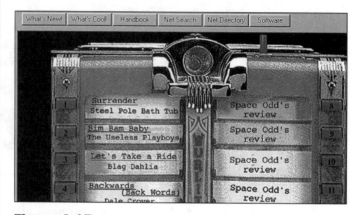

Figure A.17
Space Odd's Best Albums of All Time.

Upcoming Showcases and Performances

- A RealAudio poetry reading from Fielding Dawson

- A VDOLive modern dance performance from Choreographer Gary Palmer

- VDOLive interviews with rock performer, songwriter, and actor John Doe (X, The Knitters, The John Doe Thing), and artist Danielle Spellman

- More VDOLive animation from the Ringling School of Art and Design

- VDOLive clips of live rock club performances and stand-up comedy

- A room full of animated, nationally known political figures—each with something to say via RealAudio

- The *Bot Squad*—for kids (of all ages). A highly interactive game using artificial intelligence

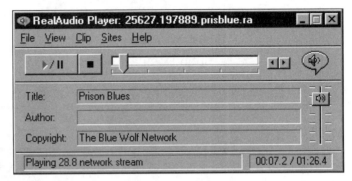

Figure A.18

Prison Blues being recited.

Figure A.19

Mad Jiggs and Broken Shadows.

Figure A.20

John Doe performing.

Figure A.21

Still more excellent animation.

Figure A.22

Guess who?

Note: If you try to
visit the Browseteria
with an indirect
service such as
America Online,
you may experience
problems. For best
performance, a
direct Internet con-
nection is highly
recommended.

Equipment Checklist

To fully appreciate your visit to the Browseteria, you my
need to upgrade your system with both hardware and
software. The most recent checklist may be consulted at
the site itself, but the following items should be considered essential:

- The latest possible version of the Netscape browser

- The RealAudio Player (*http://www.realaudio.com*)

- The VDOLive player (*http://www.vdolive.com*)

- The Shockwave plug-in (*http://
www.macromedia.com*)

- A 28.8 modem (ISDN is even cooler)

- Speakers, of course (for your Windows machine).

And be sure to leave some mail (in the Courier section)
for the Blue Wolf!

An interview with Tim Tully, Technical Editor of NewMedia magazine and digital media producer of Hyperstand, NewMedia's online forum for demonstrating solutions to the challenges posed by Web-based media.

Appendix **B**

A Visit to the Hyperstand

The prior interview with John Barrows concerned itself with the publishing perspective and management concerns of maintaining a Web presence, rich in multimedia. This interview focuses on the technical aspects of such a venture. Whoever said the devil is in the details obviously managed a Web site.

Our generous subject is Tim Tully, Technical Editor at *NewMedia* magazine and digital media producer of Hyperstand (*http://www.hyperstand.com*), in effect, the magazine's Web-based alter ego. Tim is the author, with Paul D. Lehrman, of the book *MIDI for the Professional*.

How did you get into all this?
My background is music, specifically the saxophone. At some point I got seriously into synthesizers, which led to a job at the magazine *Electronic Musician*. As time went on, I produced music for computer games, served in various editorial roles at *EM*, and eventually started working in multimedia.

Some internal links at Hyperstand.

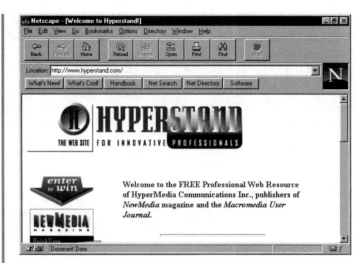

Figure B.1

Arriving at the Hyperstand.

For the last couple of years I've been Technical Editor at *NewMedia*. Most recently, I've been involved in developing several Web sites.

What are you working on right now?
Day to day, I'm doing digital media production for Hyperstand, although I'm also handling the multimedia assets for several private clients. My job at Hyperstand is to seek out new types of realtime media that we might be able to play over the Web, and see if it works.

The joy of working on the bleeding edge.
That's what it is.

In general, how are things going?
Well, lately I've been fairly frustrated, although there have been some particular successes.

Do you think there's a future in it?
Quite honestly, I sometimes think developers are getting so disillusioned with the reality of the hardware as it is now that we're all going to walk away from it for a while.

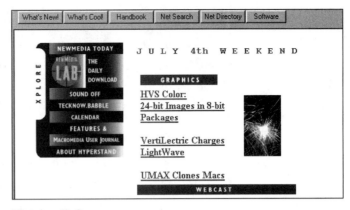

Figure B.2

Part of the Hyperstand menu.

Do you mean the computers?

No, the computers themselves, at least Pentiums and Power Macs, are fine. I mean the modems, the phone system, and the data networks.

What about the software?

Depends on what you're talking about. Multimedia software in general is pretty good for standalone PCs these days. When you start to use networks, you get into trouble.

With all types of multimedia?

Streaming audio, like RealAudio, can be made almost acceptable, depending on what you're using it for. MIDI's not a problem since the data rate is so low.

And streaming video?

Not great. Not even very good. It's way early in the game, and the software is brand new.

Regardless of all the cool Internet video the characters used in the movie Mission: Impossible?

Hell no. That was almost a cruel joke for people who are really doing this.

The funny thing was, all the crystal clear video seemed to be playing in big QuickTime movie windows, on laptops, but none of them appeared to have Apple logos or even looked like PowerBooks.

Exactly. Special hardware for special agents.

So is this stuff worth working with at all?

If you're into it. As I mentioned earlier, the frustration factor is very high. If someone wants to pay you to make streaming movies and they are satisfied with the results, I guess you'd be crazy not to.

When is the Web going to bog down completely?

Soon, maybe. Nobody knows for sure. You're the second person that has asked me that today.

Is this a real danger?

Yes and no. I heard an interesting story on the radio saying that the academic community was thinking about petitioning the government to build them a separate Web to function as the original Internet was designed.

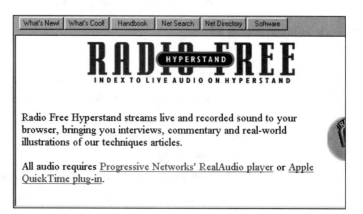

Figure B.3

Radio Free Hyperstand.

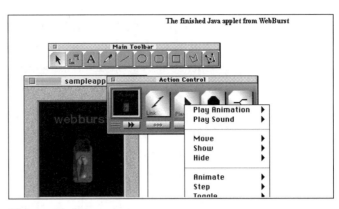
The finished Java applet from WebBurst

Figure B.4

A Java demo at Hyperstand.

Because the original Internet is filling up with garbage, as the academic people see it.

Right. Scientists at universities around the world used to be able to transmit important research files to each other with no delays, and now they're getting a busy signal.

And are you part of the problem?

Sure. I'm trying to play QuickTime movies on the Web, sucking up bandwidth like it's going out of style, while the cure for cancer is stuck in traffic.

Should they get their way?

In a perfect world, yes, since bandwidth improvements aren't happening just yet.

What about when there is more bandwidth? Won't the private sector just fill it up with even more garbage?

I don't know. Greed and human nature being what they are, it makes sense. Then again, audiences have tolerances.

But we're not just talking about entertainment. Don't you think that anything that can be digitized will be fair game for Web distribution?

If you say so. You're on your own there.

Do you believe that bandwidth problems are really caused by local switching? The so-called Internet backbone is supposed to be wide open at this point. Only the telecom companies know for sure. I've heard anecdotes to the effect that a Web page you load the first time may be routed through China when you hit the reload button. I'm overdramatizing this, but data flow decisions are made by computers based on conditions at the time.

Not to digress, but I remember in the 1970s there used to be those rumors that the auto companies could have made big cars that gave you 50 miles to the gallon, but they didn't, because they were in league with the oil companies. In other words, they let the technology out slowly because it served their purposes.
It's fun to think about, but there's nothing similar going on with the Internet. Sure, they are shifting pools of untapped bandwidth out there, but it's the result of switching systems that didn't anticipate the Web, not something out of [the movie] *The President's Analyst*.

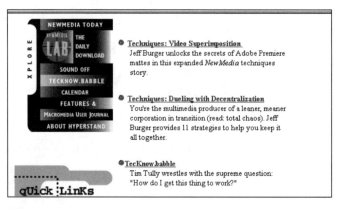

Figure B.5

Part of the TecKnow.babble menu.

In other words, the problem is economic, as opposed to political?

As much as you can separate those things, yeah. All the service providers I talk to are pedaling as fast as they can, regardless of their position in the food chain. There's big money to be made here if you take risks and don't sleep very much.

What kind of access do you have at NewMedia?

Right now, a T1 line.

How fast does it feel?

Sometimes like nobody's business. Other times it's ungodly, even when I'm hitting our own site with my office PC.

What do you attribute this to?

Hardware switching problems, as I mentioned earlier. It feels random.

Changing the subject here, if your job was making technical decisions that had big consequences, would you go with a product that was technically superior, orone that already had big market share—assuming the latter was technically adequate?

Well, I'm technically oriented, so better technology is always going to interest me and probably affect my decisions.

DVD

You're fresh from E3 and hyped up about DVD. You've read all the articles on the wonders of this new format. Now you're ready to start creating. You want some raw details, and we have them: I combed the Net to bring you the best DVD resources.

First, we have some excellent articles right here on Hyperstand:

"DVD Is Coming to Town," Becky Waring's First Look (first published in *NewMedia*, February 19, 1996)

"Digital Video Disc: A Single Standard Emerges" (September 1995)

Figure B.6
Mighty Mike's page.

Would you take the gamble?

It would always be a tough choice, but I would probably tend to gamble on the technically superior product—if I had a chance to test it to my own satisfaction.

How likely is that for most people?

These days, very. Most software companies, like Progressive Networks (RealAudio), VDOnet, and so forth, distribute so-called personal versions of their main products. Other companies put out test versions that are limited in some way. You can do a lot of test driving these days if you want to.

Any examples you can cite here?

Pretty much to the point is what I've been doing lately with QuickTime audio.

Using the new plug-ins?

That's right. We got hold of the new plug-ins early. And because our RealAudio server was down, I was looking for alternatives for delivering Web-based audio.

Streaming audio in particular?

Any way that might satisfy the user. So I put some sound-only QuickTime movies up there that had 16-bit, 11 K audio speech content.

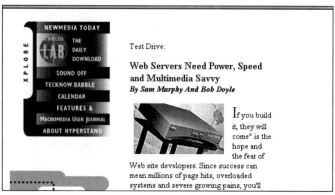

Figure B.7

The NewMedia Lab section.

Did you process them first for EQ, normalization, and so on?
Yeah, just like I do for RealAudio files, even though the 16-bit attribute put it ahead of the game to begin with. Anyway, with the new QuickStart feature in the QuickTime plug-in, the performance was quite good.

I'm noting here that these are audio-only QuickTime movies, with no video tracks.
Point taken, but all I'm concerned about here is QuickTime audio—especially as an alternative to RealAudio, which has license fees and required server components.

Which add overhead.
Right. Now, I've only done this using my shared T1 line, but as I said, that connection is subject to all kinds of slowdowns. I believe this will work just as well on a dedicated 28.8 line.

So from a user angle, if your files aren't terribly long, you can now get audio on demand from QuickTime, at a level of service approaching RealAudio.

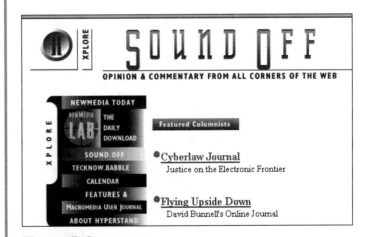

Figure B.8
The Hyperstand Sound Off section.

That's the point. Fortunately, QuickTime is both a market leader and technically more mature than RealAudio, at least in my opinion. In this case, given file length as a mitigating factor, I would choose QuickTime.

I can see why. What about the Windows side?
Good question. As it turns out, it seems to work well there also, even though I'm still testing it.

Will you still offer both RealAudio and QuickTime versions?
Probably, but that's because of our own goals at the magazine.

Which brings up a related question: Given that the magazine is a special case, how many versions of the same content should a given Web site offer to its visitors?
It's all special cases if you ask me. Really big operations should probably offer the lowest common denominator up front, but maybe offer alternative versions on special pages, if they can justify the expense.

Like Hollywood sites that normally offer QuickTime trailers, but might also offer VDOLive versions?
And like record labels that might start with WAVs, but also provide AIFFs and AUs.

Speaking of VDOLive, and this is pretty unqualified as a question, but do you think it should be a technical or a management decision to go with a technology like that?
I'm finding that management is making that decision regardless of what the technical people are saying.

How is this happening?
As a technologist, when I go to a management person who wants to do a site involving realtime media, I usually tell them what they're going to get and what it's going to cost.

Internet Commerce Expo (ICE) 9/9-9/12
Anaheim (800) 667-4423
http://www.idg.com/ice
This confernce is dedicated to the development of internet solutions for the enterprise; it will focus on Intranet enterprise solutions for increased corporate productivity and Intranet commerce for profitability.

COMDEX/Sucesu-SP South America 9/10-9/13
Sao Paulo, Brazil (617) 449-6600

HRMS/Expo 96 9/10-9/12
Dallas (800) 829-3976
This is the fourth annual human resources information technology conference.

Seybold San Francisco 9/10-9/13
San Francisco (800) 488-2883

MUJ on Paper

The Macromedia User Journal brings you the best information to improve your performance with Macromedia software, including Director, Authorware and Extreme 3D.

Monthly Features Include:

- Director and Lingo Tips, Techniques and Reusable Code

- Shockwave News and Techniques

MUJ on Electrons

MUJ Online is only available to pa subscribers of the MUJ.

800-546-6707

Trial subscribers must call to fulfill their subscription and receive their password.

Figure B.9

Gateway to the Macromedia User Journal.

Both up front and down the road?

Of course. Then I tell them about the time its going to take to do it right, designing it first, and so forth. At this point, they usually decline to do it, at least in my experience.

You mean put in the realtime media.

Right. They usually end up doing some type of site, but without the streaming technology.

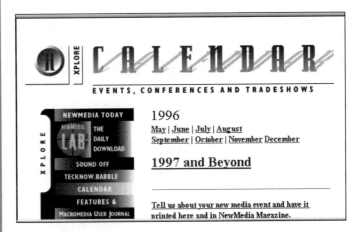

Figure B.10

The Hyperstand calendar.

Even if there are other technical people present at the meeting who endorse it?

Yup. Sometimes I can convince them of the value of using streaming audio, but it's much harder with video at this point. Lots of upper management people still don't surf all that often.

What about for Shockwave?

It depends. At least it's free, but it's basically animation with sound, and it doesn't really stream. You have to download the whole file before it starts to play.

Which is especially noticeable with Shockwave movies over 100 K or so—which in a way leads to the next question: What is your sense of how often the public is downloading non-streaming Web-based multimedia?

I believe not very many, and that what excitement there once was has pretty much worn off. People are using the Web to explore, satisfy base desires, and get information related to their job or ongoing educations.

You mean using the search engines?

Yes. You and I both know that downloading even a one or two MB QuickTime or AVI movie is usually not worth it, especially if there's no clear indication as to the content.

What about specialty items that still qualify as multimedia?

That can be a different story. I have a friend who has a big library of music samples online, and he gets lots of downloads.

These are samples for MIDI instruments?

Right. I forget if he charges directly, but he's on AOL, so I think there's some kind of kickback on each transaction.

Contents

- Online
- Authoring
- Audio
- Graphics
- Video
- Storage

Figure B.11

The Features section.

I understand there's a large built-in market for MIDI samples—good ones, at least, from reputable sound designers. By the way, now that Web browsers can play MIDI files, will this change how people like your friend do business?

Probably, although we are talking about samples here—not actual MIDI sequences.

Good point. So is there anything you can do to a plain old desktop video clip to make it valuable enough, or small enough, so that a user wouldn't need to think twice about downloading it from your Web site?

I guess so, but it's a lot of work on a clip-by-clip basis, which it might always have to be if the content is different in each clip.

Can you be more specific?

Well, to begin with, most of the standalone stuff that Joe Blow is putting on his personal Web site is ungodly stupid. Not to him, of course, but to the average browser. On the other hand, I've downloaded some stuff made by amateurs that is very cleverly down-sampled and decimated.

Quite talented amateurs, apparently.

That's just it. Just because it can be done doesn't mean everyone can do it, or even wants to.

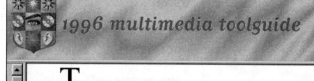

1996 multimedia toolguide

T his is as close to a complete directory of multime-
hardware and software suppliers as we can get in an indus
changes every few nanoseconds. Not only have we saved
trees by putting so much information online, it should be
convenient, too. In addition to the complete text, we h
provided downloadable tables (in Excel) that compare

Figure B.12

The Multimedia Toolguide.

*I remember back in the CD-ROM days, there were some
independent publishers who felt at last they had a way to
distribute DIY (do it yourself) musical performances and
others types of theatrical material outside the normal
channels.*

Yeah, there was a lot of that, wasn't there.

*What I'm wondering is, since that didn't work out as
planned, do you think the same people, or others like
them, will try to do the same thing via the Web?*

As I already said, some talented people are doing this
already: taking inspiration from the very limitations im-
posed by the medium. But how they collect the money is
still a big question.

Any idea when this is going to change?

Not in a year or so, probably longer. Entertainment is
sold to the mass market in ways that complete idiots can
consume it in their sleep. Only a small fraction of the
mass market has the equipment and connections necessary to do what we're talking about here, and only some
of *them* have the interest and the patience.

> **The Scene is Set for Multimedia On the Web**
>
> *by Dan Amdur*
>
> **Contents**
>
> ◉ Main Article
>
> ◉ Audio and Video over the Net
>
> ◉ From ISDN to Cable
>
> **W**ith a thousands a audience of millions, the Wide Web biggest stag

Figure B.13

Lots of to-the-point articles.

So it's the CD-ROM world all over again?
In many ways. Some problems have been solved, but new ones have replaced them—at least for would-be content publishers.

Which means starting a business to distribute multimedia assets via a Web site where you download them is a dicey proposition?
I'd say that's putting it kindly, especially if you believe you can jump right in. If you're an artist and you just want to promote yourself in some new way, then it's a great idea. If you want to make a living with a Web site, good luck. Aren't we getting away from the technical issues here?

You're right. So let me ask you this: How does someone get to the point, technically, where they can apply for your job?
If they've been making multimedia assets for a couple of years and are used to browsing the Web, they're a good part of the way there already. But if you want to do multimedia, you better know as much as possible about audio, video, and multimedia authoring—everything from recording sound and images to editing to integrating it all into a presentation.

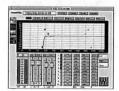

What's your opinion about cable modems, DSL, and so forth?

Anything that increases the bandwidth is going to make the Web better.

Does it feel like hype to you?

Again, more bandwidth is always better. But the convergence point is still out there over the near horizon.

What do you think about the future of QuickTime?

Actually, I've been very pleased with what Apple is doing with it. They've made some big new promises, but I think they're poised to deliver. The Netscape plug-in works, as does the QuickStart feature.

How about the MIDI issues?

Since MIDI is important to me, I like what they are finally doing with MIDI tracks in QuickTime movies.

What do you think about MPEG as a Web media data type?

Personally, I think MPEG has always been impressive, especially compared to AVI and QuickTime. For complicated reasons, it has not succeeded in the market, but I

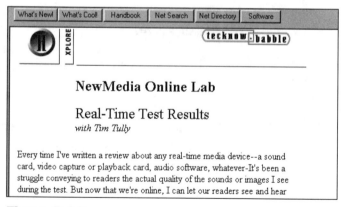

Figure B.14

From the NewMedia Online Lab.

Figure B.15
The Master at work.

think we're going to see this change in the near future if the rumors about Microsoft pan out.

Going back to the conspiracy theory, do you think the military still uses the Net? After all, that's where it started.

Last time I talked to the Joint Chiefs, they had no comment.

What's on the CD-ROM

The CD-ROM that comes with this book contains files that fall into two basic categories:

1. Tools for creating Web sites and Web media files. As with all software, be sure to check the requirements for use. If it's shareware, and you decide to use it on a regular basis, make sure you register and pay for it.

2. Sample media clips to help you understand what the finished product for different programs should look or sound like. There are also two pieces of code, to complement passages found in the book regarding Java and CGI scripting.

The Tools

VDOLive

If you wish to install the VDOLive software provided on the CD, please refer to the latest installation instructions available at the VDOnet Web site (*http://www.vdolive.com*). This software will enable you to:

- Compress your desktop movie clips into the VDOLive format for streaming video

- Set up your Web server (if you have one) to deliver those streaming movies

Note that this is not the full-on retail version of the VDOLive Server product. Instead, it is the VDOLive Personal Server, which lets you offer a smaller number of video streams simultaneously. Still, this is powerful software and worth test-driving if you plan to invest in the heavyweight version down the road.

Macromedia

The following Macromedia software is provided:

- *Director*—A special version of Macromedia's powerful and highly-regarded multimedia authoring program. Director has been used to produce many of today's top multimedia entertainment and educational titles. Note that not all the features in the full retail edition may be active in this version.

- *Shockwave*—This is the software you use to make a Director production playable on a Web page. Just run your Director movie through the Shockwave Afterburner program, and you can post it on your Web site. Be sure to refer to the latest instructions in the Shockwave section of the Macromedia Web site (*http://www.macromedia.com/shockwave/*) before putting up Shockwave movies on your own site.

- *Backstage Designer*—This is Macromedia's Web page creation tool. Backstage designer is worth looking at because it lets you create your Web pages by just pointing and clicking—no HTML coding required. This program is specially designed to handle multimedia files.

- *SoundEdit*—This is Macromedia's top of the line solution for working with digitized audio files.

All the professional effects and audio processing tools are included, although you may find some limitations in this special demo version of the retail product.

- *Deck 2*—A software-only multitrack recording studio that lets you record and edit up to 999 16-bit digital audio tracks. Again, some limitations may be present in this version.

Not all of the Macromedia programs provided on this CD-ROM are cross-platform, though both Director and Shockwave are available for both Macs and PCs. Backstage Designer, however, is Windows-specific, and Deck II and SoundEdit are Mac-specific. For more information on theses Macromedia products, check out the Macromedia Web site at *http://www.macromedia.com.*

TRMOOV

TRMOOV is a Windows application that converts between the QuickTime and Video for Windows file formats without recompression. It is designed to convert movie files that have the same source and target codec. It also converts between QuickTime sound-only movies and Microsoft WAV files, and is useful for batch mode conversions. TRMOOV is an extremely useful software tool for the Windows multimedia desktop.

PaintShop Pro

PaintShop Pro is a complete Windows graphics program for image creation, viewing, and manipulation. Features include: painting, photo retouching, image enhancement and editing, color enhamcement, image browser, batch conversion, and TWAIN scanner support. It also supports over 30 file formats, including JPEG and GIF.

Adobe Acrobat Reader

Adobe Acrobat lets you create electronic documents from a wide range of authoring tools for sharing across different computer platforms. Adobe is now pushing its PDF format as a replacement for HTML. Its advantages are unlimited options for layout, and what you design is what others see, which is not always the case with HTML. Of course, you need the Reader to see the files.

QuickTime Player from Apple

Although QuickTime has been a Mac standard for years, it's just starting to catch on with Windows users. It offers a few features that Video for Windows does not have yet and some of the new technologies being developed for it are amazing. Check out the QuickTime Web page (*http://quicktime.apple.com*) for the latest news and downloads.

The Sample Clips

The sample AVI and QuickTime files on the CD are representative (in size and duration) of those currently being posted around the Web. All the video formats that are discussed in depth in the book have representative clips included on the CD-ROM; there are also a number of sample RealAudio clips. Here's how all the clips are organized on the CD-ROM:

- The clips in the AVI and QT directories are standard Video for Windows and QuickTime movies, respectively. Taken from full-length music video clips, they tend to be 1 to 1.5 megabytes in size and have smaller frame sizes, which allow for longer running times given the size limitation.

- The clips in the DIR directory are Macromedia Director movies which you should be able to open with Director to see how they are put together. The DCR versions are the same movies which have been processed with Afterburner to turn them into Shockwave clips.

- The audio files in the RA directory are sample RealAudio clips that have been processed with the RealAudio encoder. You'll need to download the free RealAudio player from the Progressive Networks Web site (*http://www.realaudio.com*) to play them on your computer.

- The video files in the VDO directory are sample VDOLive clips which are compressed with the VDOLive encoder. You'll need to install the VDOLive software that is included on this CD-ROM, or download the free VDOLive player from the VDOnet Web site (*http://www.vdolive.com*) to play these clips on your local machine.

Suggested Reading List

Since all kinds of valuable information regarding multimedia production and Web delivery is now available online, any of the popular Web search engines is a good place to start when you need extra enlightenment. That being said, some additional books to consider are:

How to Digitize Video, Nels Johnson, John Wiley, 464 pp, $39.95

Inside Macintosh: QuickTime, Apple Computer, Addison Wesley, 600 pp, $29.95

Multimedia: Making It Work, Tay Vaughn, Osborne, 544 pp, $27.95

Multimedia Power Tools, Peter Jerran / Michael Gosney, Random House, 640 pp, $50.00

Multimedia Programming for Windows, Steve Rimmer, McGraw-Hill, 370 pp, $39.95

Web Developer's Guide to JavaScript & VBScript, Peter Aitken, The Coriolis Group, 500 pp, $39.99.

Web Developer's Guide to Sound and Music, Simpson and Helmstetter, The Coriolis Group, 450 pp, $39.99.

Index

Numbers

A

B

C

Q

QTC, 96
Quadra 650, 74
Quality, 37
QuarterDeck, Inc, 224
QuickStart, 97
QuickTime, 3, 4, 9, 65, 69, 71, 73, 74, 89,
    120, 127, 141, 159, 179, 215, 259, 299
    Cinepak movie, 273
    codecs, 6
    Conferencing, 96
    for the Mac 165
    for Windows 127, 158, 260, 273
    for Windows codecs, 11
    Live, 96, 97, 221
    Mac, 260
    movie, 48, 97, 165, 176, 199, 268
    Movie Player, 267
    movies to GIFs, 137
    None codec, 262
    plug-in for Netscape Navigator, 97
    TV, 37, 97
QuickTime to AVI
    Compressed Source, 268
    Uncompressed Source, 261

R

Radio Shack, 290
Radius VideoVision Studio, 143
RAS (the razz), 310
RasterOps/Truevision Targa 2000, 143
Raw, 5, 6
Real desktop video, 96
Real life footage, 106
Real-world delivery rates, 68
RealAudio, 16, 23, 43, 99, 106, 180, 192,
    193, 199, 210, 221, 240, 250, 255, 321
    Encoder, 185
    encoding, final, 106
    encoding tools, 101
    files, handling, 250
    Personal Server, 111, 321
    Player, 100, 111, 186
    Server, 116
    server software, 185
    streams, 16
RealMagic card, 15
Recording industry sites, 50
Regedt32, 317

Remote Access Service, 305, 307
Remote server
    administration, 241
    testing and troubleshooting, 254
Retail sequencer software, 123
RIFF (Resource Interchange File Format)
    file, 10
RLE, 11, 13
Run Length, 6
Rykodisc, 50

S

S-Video, 80
San Francisco Canyon Company, 10
Sawyer Brown, 194
Scalability, 69
Scientific-Atlanta, 28
SCSI (Small Computer Systems Interface),
    144
    manager for DOS/Win31 machines, 145
SCSI-3, 145
Security, 241
Server push, 121, 128, 131
Service bureau, 296
Setup program for reinstalling IIS, 311
shocked
    media file, 248
    movie, 88, 90, 95, 96, 317
Shockwave, 17, 33, 72, 89, 96, 121, 131,
    180, 184, 197, 199, 220, 221, 240, 248,
    250, 255, 317
    compatibility, 249
    movies, 45, 77
    movie, making, 90
    overview, 88
    plug-in, 95, 198
SHVS, 146
Signal to Noise (S/N) ratio, 299
Site Mill, 222
SmartDubbing, 137
SmartSound, 105
Software Architects, 262
Software development, 201
Software-only MPEG, 15
Sonic Foundry, 163
Sony Pictures, 45
Sound Blaster 16, 142
Sound Designer II, 148
Sound Forge 3.0, 108, 162